Lincoln's Sacred Effort

APPLICATIONS OF POLITICAL THEORY

Series Editors: Harvey Mansfield, Harvard University, and Daniel J. Mahoney, Assumption College

This series encourages analysis of the applications of political theory to various domains of thought and action. Such analysis will include works on political thought and literature, statesmanship, American political thought, and contemporary political theory. The editors also anticipate and welcome examinations of the place of religion in public life and commentary on classic works of political philosophy.

Lincoln's Sacred Effort

Defining Religion's Role in American Self-Government

Lucas E. Morel

LEXINGTON BOOKS

A division of
ROWMAN & LITTLEFIELD PUBLISHERS, INC.
Lanham • Boulder • New York • Toronto • Plymouth, UK

LEXINGTON BOOKS

A division of Rowman & Littlefield Publishers, Inc.
A wholly owned subsidary of The Rowman & Littlefield Publishing Group, Inc.
4501 Forbes Boulevard, Suite 200
Lanham, MD 20706

Estover Road
Plymouth PL6 7PY
United Kingdom

British Library Cataloguing in Publication Information Available

Library of Congress Cataloging-in-Publication Data

Morel, Lucas E., 1964-
     Lincoln's sacred effort : defining religion's role in American self-government /
Lucas E. Morel.
        p. cm.
     Originally presented as author's thesis (Ph. D.)—Claremont Graduate School.
     Includes bibliography references (p.) and indexes.
        ISBN 0-7391-0105-6 (cloth : alk. paper)—ISBN 0-7391-0106-4(paper : alk. paper)
        1. Lincoln, Abraham, 1809-1865—Views on religion and politics. 2. United
States—Politics and government—1861-1865. 3. Religion and politics—United
States—History—19th century. I Title. ISBN: 978-0-7391-0106-3

E457.2.M85 2000
973.7'092—dc21   99-053362

Printed in the United States of America

♾™ The paper used in this publication meets the minimum requirements of American
National Standard for Information Sciences—Permanence of Paper for Printed Library
Materials, ANSI/NISO Z39.48–1992.

To my wife, Cherie, our children, Luke and Hannah, my father, Carlos,

and the memory of my mother, Maria (1941-1995)

I am exceedingly anxious that this Union, the Constitution, and the liberties of the people shall be perpetuated in accordance with the original idea for which that struggle was made, and I shall be most happy indeed if I shall be an humble instrument in the hands of the Almighty, and of this, his almost chosen people, for perpetuating the object of that great struggle.

Lincoln's address to the New Jersey Senate at Trenton
February 21, 1861

Contents

Acknowledgments

This book bears the name of one author, but many helped along the way.

I am grateful to the Lynde and Harry Bradley Foundation, the Henry Salvatori Foundation, and the Heritage Foundation for their generous support of my education at the Claremont Graduate School, where the book first took shape as my doctoral dissertation. I thank my dissertation committee members, William B. Allen, Charles R. Kesler, and James H. Nichols Jr., for their teaching and friendship, and honorary member Harry V. Jaffa, for *Crisis of the House Divided*, the most important book written on American self-government in the last half-century.

Special thanks go to John Brown University and the Pew Charitable Trusts for a 1997 summer research grant to revise the book manuscript. JBU was my teaching home from 1994-1999, and I am especially appreciative of Professors Ed Ericson III and David Johnson and interlibrary loan librarian Simone Schroder for their encouragement and support of this project.

For cover art that debuts the best picture of Abraham Lincoln I have ever seen, I thank artist Matt Hall (and Jim Lewis for introducing us). I also thank Phillip Shaw Paludan, who helped me focus and clarify my argument. My thanks to Washington and Lee University; Jennifer Ashworth, who helped format the manuscript; and Serena Leigh and Stephen Driver at Lexington Books, who marshaled the book through its paces.

*　*　*　*　*

An earlier version of chapter 4 originally appeared as "Lincoln among the Reformers: Tempering the Temperance Movement," *Journal of the Abraham Lincoln Association* 20, no. 1 (Winter 1999): 1-34. Copyright 1999 by the Board of Trustees of the University of Illinois.

Introduction

The famed escaped slave and abolitionist orator Frederick Douglass once remarked, "We all know Abraham Lincoln by heart."[1] The sentiment is still true today. We feel somehow that we know him, that he's a part of us, and so much a part of what it means to be American that for us to know Abraham Lincoln is to know America at its core. One reason for Lincoln's continued resonance with the American people is the religious imagery with which he addressed the nation's most pressing concerns. Just imagine the Gettysburg Address or the Second Inaugural Address without their biblical allusions and cadences. To do so would be to strip those timeless documents of their most memorable phrases, if not their most telling reflections on American self-government.

This book examines what the public life of Abraham Lincoln teaches about the role of religion in a self-governing society. Because a statesman must consider not only the good of the citizenry but also their opinions, beliefs, and prejudices, we do well to assess Lincoln's statesmanship in light of his accommodation of the religious sentiments of his countrymen. While most people justly praise Lincoln for his commitment to human equality, few understand that his political acumen had as much to do with understanding where his countrymen then stood with regard to political right as with where Lincoln wished to take them. In this respect, his appreciation of their religious beliefs played a crucial role in his ability to elevate the American political horizon. "Father Abraham," in short, would not have achieved such status—ascribed to no other American statesman except the Founding Father *par excellence*, George Washington—had he ignored the religious sensibilities of the American people.

Lincoln's understanding of the requirements of republican government led him to direct religious sentiment toward responsible democracy or self-government. As a successful republic requires a moral or self-controlled people, he believed the moral and religious impulse of society should be nurtured. Both helped to moderate the excesses of passion and self-interest in the community. As a means of achieving this social order, Lincoln promoted "support of the Constitution" and "reverence for the laws" to become "the *political religion* of the nation."[2] Lincoln believed that the perpetuation of the free government established by the American Revolution depended on this patriotic law-abidingness and called on both politician and preacher to promote this "political religion."

If this sentiment constituted the only expression of Lincoln's understanding of the relationship between religion and republican government, one would be hard-pressed to understand him to be "the theologian of American anguish."[3] True, in his Gettysburg and Second Inaugural Addresses, he drew upon the religious sentiments of the American people to cultivate a civil religion in addition to his strictly "political" religion of reverent obedience to the laws.[4] But while the political uses of religion seem to predominate in Lincoln's politics, he never forgot that religion existed for a higher purpose. Lincoln's speeches and writings show that he not only saw the need for political and civil religion to control the passions of the people, but recognized that revealed religion had a claim on the souls of the citizenry wholly apart from its utility in preserving the government. Lincoln, in other words, did not confuse the political utility of religion with religion's true aim: to connect people to God, not to their government. These are not mutually exclusive purposes, but they remain distinct in Lincoln's mind and so one does well to preserve the distinction when analyzing his appeal to religion in a political context.

Lincoln developed a public approach to religion that would certainly draw upon its beneficent qualities for political ends, but that was also consistent with religion's own reason for being. In fact, Lincoln would argue—as did George Washington[5]—that government protection of religious liberty requires of the people a religious devotion to the principles and practices of self-government. Therefore, government stays within its sphere of authority and influence not merely by tolerating religious expression in the lives of the citizenry, but by protecting its very exercise as part of its duty to the people.

Lincoln noted, however, that religion was not all sweetness and light for the American republic. He concerned himself as well with the detrimental effect that religious extremists could have on free government, as exhibited by some moral reform movements that promoted temperance and abolition. Some of these reform societies tended to approach their causes with a self-righteousness that allowed little room for discussion and hence posed a threat to the deliberative processes of self-government.[6] In them he saw a religious character that could lead to excesses inimical to constitutional government: namely, theocratic absolutism, which would undermine a regime based on public deliberation as opposed to a theological litmus test. The dependence of self-government on public morality, influenced by the virtues and vices of revealed religion, presented Lincoln with a political burden intrinsic to free government. Lincoln addressed these issues with an eye toward preserving the respective domains of both government and religion.

Finally, an understanding of the place of religion in Lincoln's statesmanship must explain what Lincoln saw as the limits of pious as well as rational action in politics, best revealed in his Second Inaugural Address of 1865. This republican humility is consistent with the demeanor of religious folks as they seek, in the words of an Old Testament prophet, "to walk humbly with thy God."[7] What Lincoln offers is not so much a solution to what reason and religion failed to solve—what the nation as a whole was unable to solve—but rather our communal inability to discover a ready solution, and hence a call to moderate our expectations of public deliberation in resolving political disputes.

Lincoln saw both the utility and liability of religion in a republican regime. In addition, and perhaps most significantly for the purposes of contemporary discussion, Lincoln understood religion to have at least as good a claim to the adherence of individuals as that of their government. In other words, while religion may at times pose a problem for government, government as well may pose a problem for religion. To avoid stepping outside its legitimate sphere of influence and hence maintain its claim on the obedience of the people, government must respect and hence secure the free exercise of religious liberty. In securing the right of every citizen to "life, liberty, and the pursuit of happiness," government must remember that it serves only as a means to the individual's happiness. In other words, government was made for man, and not man for government. In this light, religion constitutes a means, an extra-constitutional or apolitical means, toward that happiness and hence is deserving of the government's protection. In the words of political scientist Harry V. Jaffa, "The American Founding limited the ends of government. It did not limit the ends of man."[8] In working to perpetuate a government devoted to the protection of both civil and religious liberty, Lincoln sought to protect religious freedom in a manner consistent with both the requirements of republican government and the purposes of God.

This book interprets Lincoln's political actions and statements using

Lincoln's own words as much as possible. This not only presents an extensive look at the speeches and writings of Abraham Lincoln, but also demonstrates the consistency of his interpretation of the operational principles of the American regime. His was not a simple view of religion's place in a free society. Lincoln's statesmanship of theological politics displayed an acute awareness of the reciprocal relationship between religion and politics: a discernment of their respective spheres of influence, at times conflicting in priority, and therewith an appreciation of the benefits and dangers of their dual obligation upon American citizens. This interpretation of Lincoln, therefore, aims to reveal his understanding of religion and politics with the utmost respect for his own words on the subject. "Father Abraham" and the nexus between religion and politics deserve no less.

Notes

1. "The United States Cannot Remain Half-Slave and Half-Free (16 April 1883)," in *The Life and Writings of Frederick Douglass*, Philip S. Foner, ed., 5 vols. (New York: International Publishers Co., Inc., 1955), 4: 368.

2. "Address Before the Young Men's Lyceum of Springfield, Illinois (27 January 1838)," in *The Collected Works of Abraham Lincoln*, Roy P. Basler, ed., 9 vols. (New Brunswick: Rutgers University Press, 1955), 1: 112. Hereinafter cited as *Collected Works*; all emphases in original except where otherwise noted.

3. Elton Trueblood, *Abraham Lincoln: Theologian of American Anguish* (New York: Harper & Row, Publishers, 1973), 121. See also Robert N. Bellah and Phillip E. Hammond, *Varieties of Civil Religion* (San Francisco: Harper & Row, Publishers, 1980), 12, wherein Bellah states that in America "there are no official interpreters of civil theology," and yet "we did produce at a critical juncture in our history at least one great civil theologian, Abraham Lincoln." See also Robert N. Bellah, *The Broken Covenant: American Civil Religion in Time of Trial* (New York: Seabury Press, 1975), 46. Sidney E. Mead described Lincoln as, "in a real sense, the spiritual center of American history." "Abraham Lincoln's 'Last, Best Hope of Earth': The American Dream of Destiny and Democracy," *Church History* 23 (March 1954): 3.

4. In a seminal article on civil religion, Robert N. Bellah defines American civil religion as the "set of beliefs, symbols, and rituals" that form our "public religious dimension." "Civil Religion in America," *Daedalus* 96 (Winter 1967): 4. N.b.: I will not focus on civil religion *per se* but rather on Lincoln's appeal to the religious sentiments of the American people as they influence both public and private life.

5. In a letter to Quakers, Washington wrote:

The liberty enjoyed by the people of these states of worshipping Almighty God agreeably to their consciences, is not only among the choicest of their *blessings*, but also of their *rights*. While men perform their social duties faithfully, they do all that society or the state can with propriety demand or expect; and remain responsible only to their Maker for their religion; or modes of faith, which they may prefer or profess. . . .

I assure you very explicitly, that in my opinion the conscientious scruples of all men should be treated with great delicacy and tenderness; and it is my wish and desire, that the laws may always be as extensively accommodated to them, as a due regard to the protection and essential interests of the nation may justify and permit.

"To the Annual Meeting of Quakers (September 1789)," in *George Washington: A Collection*, W. B. Allen, ed. (Indianapolis: Liberty Fund, Inc., 1988), 533-34.

6. Cf. John G. West, Jr., *The Politics of Revelation and Reason: Religion and Civic Life in the New Nation* (Lawrence: University Press of Kansas, 1996). West shows that some evangelical reform movements—in particular, those addressing the Sunday mails and the Cherokee removal controversies—made their social and political appeals not merely on religious grounds but on the basis of human reason:

Because government authority would be kept separate from ecclesiastical authority, churches now could be trusted to create—and defend—civic morality. Stripped of any pretensions that might have made them dangerous to republicanism, churches were free to reform society according to the moral law held in common by both revelation and reason.

The Politics of Revelation and Reason, 210. Robert N. Bellah observes that the more moderate wing of abolitionism, led by Theodore Dwight Weld, sought reform by calling for greater enforcement of the U.S. Constitution:

Weld and his associates developed a constitutional argument that even as early as 1835 described the treatment in the North of free Negroes and abolitionists as "denials of rights to the equal protection of the laws, the safeguards of due process, and the privileges and immunities of citizens," . . . Unlike Garrison the group around Weld believed that emancipation was implicit in the Constitution and that what that document needed was not burning [as Garrison did] but clarification and enforcement.

The Broken Covenant, 52.

7. Micah 6:8 reads: "He hath shewed thee, O man, what is good; and what doth the LORD require of thee, but to do justly, and to love mercy, and to walk humbly with thy God?" George Washington closed his Circular Address of 1783 with a gloss on this verse: "I now make it my earnest prayer, that God . . . would most graciously be pleased to dispose us all, to do Justice, to love mercy, and to demean ourselves with that Charity, humility and pacific temper of mind, which were the Characteristicks of the Divine Author of our blessed Religion, and without an humble imitation of whose example in these things, we can never hope to be a happy nation." "Circular to the States (14 June 1783)," in *George Washington: A Collection*, 249.

8. Harry V. Jaffa, "The American Founding as the Best Regime: The Bonding of Civil and Religious Liberty" (Claremont, Calif.: Claremont Institute for the Study of Statesmanship and Political Philosophy, 1990), 17.

Chapter 1

Religious Politics and Political Religion

The most significant contribution to the moral formation of a people has been religion. Put simply, a nation that governs itself under the auspices of God governs with an awareness that not all things are allowed. George Washington reflected on the importance of religion to the early American republic by noting the support it gave to public morality in his Farewell Address of 1796:

> Of all the dispositions and habits which lead to political prosperity, Religion and morality are indispensable supports. In vain would that man claim the tribute of Patriotism, who should labour to subvert these great Pillars of human happiness, these firmest props of the duties of Men and citizens. The mere Politician, equally with the pious man ought to respect and cherish them. A volume could not trace all their connections with private and public felicity. . . . And let us with caution indulge the supposition, that morality can be maintained without religion. Whatever may be conceded to the influence of refined education on minds of peculiar structure, reason and experience both forbid us to expect that National morality can prevail in exclusion of religious principle.
>
> 'Tis substantially true, that virtue or morality is a necessary spring of popular government. The rule indeed extends with more or less force to every species of free Government. Who that is a sincere friend to it, can look with indifference upon attempts to shake the foundation of the fabric[.][1]

Washington distinguishes the political contribution made by religion from that of morality simply. He then responds to a potential criticism that morality without a religious basis can support personal and civic responsibility. Supposing this to be true, he states that "National morality" will not produce good citizenship without the aid of religion. He implies that an abstract discussion of the relevance of religion to political prosperity, where morality is promoted in its absence, is folly: "reason and experience" conclude that religion plays an essential role in the maintenance of a prosperous regime.

Even Thomas Jefferson, a probable target for Washington's response to the alleged irrelevance of religion to national morality, gave public recognition to religion as promoting national morality and felicity. In his First Inaugural Address, he described the American people as

> enlightened by a benign religion, professed, indeed, and practised in various forms, yet all of them including honesty, truth, temperance, gratitude, and the love of man; acknowledging and adoring an overruling Providence, which by all its dispensations proves that it delights in the happiness of man here and his greater happiness hereafter.[2]

Jefferson added a reflection on God's concern for man's "greater happiness hereafter." Thus Providence manifests a concern for man's ultimate happiness through religion, and Jefferson credits religion for its highest calling—preparing men and women for the city of God—in addition to its more worldly calling—supporting the city and hence government of men and women on earth.

We see religion taking a prominent place in shaping the American character but also being shaped or interpreted itself by statesmen who seek to ensure its benefits to government. Jefferson, of course, carefully lauds only "benign" religion, as well as defines the laudable attributes of such a religion. Similarly, Washington speaks elsewhere of "the pure and benign light of Revelation," "Religion pure and undefiled," "genuine, vital religion," "true religion," "true piety," and "the pure spirit of Christianity."[3] Although Washington and Jefferson supported religious freedom, they reminded religious groups in particular that not all expressions of religion were socially or politically beneficial. Only "benign" or "pure" or "true" religion, though expressed in various ways, could produce a civil religion or public faith that all citizens could believe in and practice to the benefit of their common government.

Curiously enough, given Abraham Lincoln's penchant for employing a telling biblical metaphor or allusion, his speeches and writings never refer to "civil religion." He did use the phrase "political religion" once, but it has almost nothing to do with civil or revealed religion. In his Springfield Lyceum Address of 1838, wherein he discusses the problems that mobs pose for free government, he exhorts "every American" to "swear by the blood of the Revolution, never to violate in the least particular, the laws of the country; and never to tolerate their violation by others."[4] He hopes that this "reverence for the laws" will become the "political religion" of the nation. The only direct connection to religion that his political exhortation has is the religious commitment or fervor it requires of each citizen. One could as well call it "political zeal." And yet, this reverence for political things has much to do with a people's expression of their religion.

Some writers skew Lincoln's political theology toward the extremes of pragmatic politics or religious zeal. The fulcrum of this debate usually centers on speculations about his faith (or lack thereof). Lincoln becomes either "the mere Politician" or "the pious man" of Washington's Farewell Address.[5] But an examination of his speeches and writings shows that Lincoln transcends the mere politician and the pious man in a statecraft that is both politic and pious. In short, Lincoln the statesman strikes a mean between the "open enemy of, and scoffer at, religion"[6] and John Brown of Harpers Ferry infamy.

We begin by asking, where does Lincoln find political legitimacy in a community guided by truths both political and religious, truths assented to by one's reason and faith? Lincoln views the question of legitimacy in light of the theoretical basis and practical limitations of free government. The fundamental truths expressed in the Declaration of Independence embody the tension between the theory and the practice of self-government. The first truth about human nature, that "all men are created equal," means the natural right to govern oneself, the right each individual has to his "life, liberty, and the pursuit of happiness." This forms the basis of communal self-government, for the Declaration continues: "That to secure these rights, Governments are instituted among Men, deriving their just powers from the consent of the governed . . ." Lincoln restates it: "no man is good enough to govern another man, *without that other's consent*." The difficulty arises when those who wield the powers of government repudiate the equality that forms the basis of self-government. In the minds of slaveowners, they had a right to govern not only themselves, but other selves as well. This Lincoln calls "*more* than self-government—that is despotism." Lincoln recognized that the statesman must aim for the fullest measure of equality of rights to which the community would consent. He did this by constantly reminding the citizenry of the moral principle legitimating their own self-government, "the sheet anchor of our republican liberties," as a means to securing the self-government of all—both slave and free.[7]

In this context, Lincoln saw the threat that fanaticism—for example, certain abolition and temperance movements—posed to constitutional government. Abolitionists like William Lloyd Garrison declared they would have "NO UNION WITH SLAVEHOLDERS," calling the Constitution "a covenant with death and an agreement with hell."[8]

Though they pursued a just end, the abolition of slavery, their repudiation of constitutional means set them at odds against the very self-government for which they labored on behalf of enslaved blacks. As "human wisdom" could never bring "the governments of this world" into "conformity to the will of God," Garrison told Christians to withdraw from public office and forgo their civic responsibilities.[9] Denunciations by radical abolitionists, moreover, went so far as to malign not only the American government but also American churches.[10] These perfectionist ravings, needless to say, bode ill for a regime that depended upon "the cool and deliberate sense of the community" to perpetuate itself.[11] This explains why in his second term as an Illinois state representative, Lincoln co-sponsored a resolution that condemned slavery as "founded on both injustice and bad policy" but noted that "the promulgation of abolition doctrines tends rather to increase than to abate its evils."[12] Lincoln also saw in the early temperance movement a political counterpart to the "moral and peaceful revolution" waged by Garrisonian abolitionists. This zeal to impose one group's interpretation of the divine will on the rest of society left little room for the reasoned deliberation and compromise essential to democratic government.

This political absolutism stems from an imprudent devotion to a perfect society that does not accommodate the opinions, beliefs, and prejudices of the community. Lincoln addressed the problem of the rule of the self-righteous in his Temperance Speech of 1842, a speech aimed at moderating the growing influence of specious moral reform movements. Historian James G. Randall well described the disposition of the fanatical moral reformer toward his subject:

> One's own motives are pure; the opponent must therefore be a sinister person; there must be no compromise with him. You withdraw from him. You spurn his friendship. Your speeches and articles are presented not so much to your opponent; he is hopeless; they are presented to your own audience; your opponent is treated as a third person.[13]

Here one would not exaggerate if one equated rule of the so-called divinely inspired with that of the tyrant, for neither seeks political legitimacy on the only terms amenable to all men—that of human reason. Both effect their rule by strength, whether by mere superiority of votes or arms. One sees the arbitrariness of the rule of the supremely righteous, moreover, and hence its injustice, as it allows no questioning of authority: for example, you cannot second-guess someone who ends all his statements with "Thus saith the Lord!" Lincoln argued that Senator

Stephen A. Douglas attempted to do as much by affirming without qualification the *Dred Scott v. Sandford* (1857) decision:

> This man [Douglas] sticks to a decision which forbids the people of a Territory from excluding slavery, and he does so not because he says it is right in itself . . . but because it has been *decided by the court,* and being decided by the court, he is, and you are bound to take it in your political action as *law*—not that he judges at all of its merits, but because a decision of the court is to him a "Thus saith the Lord." He places it on that ground alone, and you will bear in mind that thus committing himself unreservedly to this decision, *commits him to the next one* just as firmly as to this.[14]

Here there exists no difference between theocracy and despotism. We will focus in part on Lincoln's awareness of this threat of religion to the body politic, and his actions to diffuse this threat.

Little has been written about Lincoln's view of revealed religion in light of his "political religion," though much has been written about his own religion or, as some claim, his lack thereof. Its importance remains, however, because Lincoln's appeal to and moderation of the religious sentiments of the American people illuminate much of his statesmanship. To understand Lincoln as the champion of equality, one must understand his approach toward religion in politics. This takes on special significance for the republican form of government, where public opinion manifests itself more clearly than in any other system of governance. Where the governed choose their rulers, their religious beliefs make their way into the halls of government just as well as their non-religious beliefs. Understanding Lincoln the politician, therefore, has as much to do with appreciating his handling of religion as a politician as it does with views regarding slavery, the Constitution, or the Union on strictly rational or non-religious grounds.

To accomplish this task, one must distinguish between Lincoln's own religious views and his actions in office with respect to religion. Although most of what has been written on Lincoln and religion focuses on his own religious beliefs, only a few books have explored his approach to the church-state question in the context of his "political religion." What is missing is an examination of "political religion" and revealed religion as reflected in Lincoln's political philosophy.

Lincoln and Religion among the Historians:
What's Left to Be Said?

When it comes to speculation about Lincoln's own religion, there are no agnostics: all conclude one way or another on his Christianity. Good examples include William E. Barton's classic, *The Soul of Lincoln* (1920); Richard N. Current, *The Lincoln Nobody Knows* (1958); William J. Wolf, *The Religion of Abraham Lincoln* (1963); Mark Noll, *One Nation under God? Christian Faith and Political Action in America* (1988); and Richard V. Pierard and Robert D. Linder, *Civil Religion and the Presidency* (1988). Barton examines the various claims of those who knew Lincoln as to his religious beliefs, while formulating his own summary of Lincoln's beliefs into a hypothetical creed. What he does not show is how Lincoln's piety and respect for religion both nurtured the public faith and contributed to the perpetuation of American self-government.[15] Current, in a chapter entitled "The Instrument of God," briefly reviews the various claims of Lincoln's piety or "infidelity" and provides a short bibliography on essential readings for those who wish to examine Lincoln's religion in greater detail.[16] Wolf traces the development of Lincoln's religious views through key social influences and political milestones in his life. He concludes, along with Barton, Noll, and Pierard and Linder,[17] that Lincoln was a Christian in practice if not in doctrine, satisfied that to such belong the kingdom of God.[18] Here we do well to remind ourselves, in the words of Glen E. Thurow, that "Lincoln's speeches were political speeches, not personal confessions. Religion is present Lincoln's speeches because of its relevance to political problems."[19] As such, Lincoln's personal beliefs and their relation to his public speeches and actions remain veiled. Speculation along these lines, therefore, has distracted scholars from a more rigorous examination of the ends for which he used religious imagery and appealed to religious sentiment as a statesman.

As for most books that discuss Lincoln's religion *and* politics, they either describe the effect that politics had on his religion[20] or the effect that faith had on his politics.[21] They examine the connection between his religious beliefs and his politics without addressing how his appeal to religion, God, and morality served the ends of the American regime.[22] This book addresses what few have asked within the vast corpus of writings on Abraham Lincoln: Exactly what role did Lincoln believe public piety should play in republican government?

Garry Wills's essay "Lincoln's Black Theology," in *Under God: Religion and American Politics* (1990), attempts to answer this question.

Robert Bellah, writing on American civil religion, comments that while "there are no official interpreters of civil theology . . . we did produce at a critical juncture in our history at least one great civil theologian, Abraham Lincoln."[23] But where Bellah sees the religious sentiments to which Lincoln appealed as abiding and necessary, Wills sees them as temperamental and unwieldy, and therefore harmful to republican government. He argues that Christianity, or religion in general, is important to the American people only in times of crisis, at which point its influence becomes too militant for any but the greatest of statesmen to control. Lincoln saved America during the Civil War, but not through facilitating religion's legitimate and rightful influence in the republic; rather, America benefited from his placation of a force that inevitably becomes destructive during a crisis.

Wills believes that Americans understand their country's mission in the world as millennial—"as God's pattern for the rest of the world"— but their expression of this belief becomes "less overtly theological" during times of relative calm.[24] "But when wartime calls for sacrifice," Wills continues, "American duty becomes again a divine imperative. The military note returns." For Wills, Lincoln's use of biblical language served to appease a citizenry excessively prone to religious zealotry at times of national crisis. Commenting on Julia Ward Howe's apocalyptic anthem "The Battle-Hymn of the Republic," he writes: "War fever encourages such absolutism, and Lincoln needed to use the enthusiasms of the North to support his war. But he had no stomach for the rhetoric of Mrs. Howe."[25]

To be sure, Lincoln did not blindly follow the religious impulses of American society; his Temperance Address of 1842 tells us as much. Wills, however, misreads Lincoln as a result of denigrating the religious impulse of America. Instead of acknowledging that religion can help as well as hinder republican government, he views it as an erratic phenomenon that necessitates appeasing statecraft. Wills sees the greatness of Lincoln following, in part, not from his nurture of religion as a boon to self-government but from his manipulation of it "to support his war." Wills concludes with an all too convenient identification of the faith of Lincoln with that of American slaves. Lincoln thus becomes not only the political savior of the enslaved blacks but their spiritual brother as well. As a result, his public theology is "black," and not what many understand as the longstanding "red, white, and blue" theology of our political ancestry.[26]

Moving from public piety to public moderation, there is little discussion of Lincoln's development of a "political religion." To his credit James G. Randall, in *Lincoln: The Liberal Statesman* (1947), notes Lincoln's concern for linking "moral self-control with governmental self-rule."[27] He even acknowledges that Lincoln's commitment to democracy, based on a universal premise of "government by the people," was "the pivotal factor in his political philosophy."[28] However, he does not explain how Lincoln sought to perpetuate the American republic by both relying on and shaping the nation's religious ethos. How did Lincoln's "political religion" as well as civil religion fit into his political philosophy?

Not until Harry V. Jaffa wrote *Crisis of the House Divided: An Interpretation of the Issues in the Lincoln-Douglas Debates* (1959) did the debate focus on an examination of this part of the question. Jaffa reaffirms Lincoln's right to bear the mantle of the Founding Fathers by his dedication to an American constitutional democracy maintained by the virtues of the citizenry as well as their elected leaders. In two noteworthy chapters, "The Teaching Concerning Political Salvation" and "The Teaching Concerning Political Moderation," Jaffa lays the groundwork for a discussion of Lincoln's understanding of the nation's religion and its role in his political philosophy and practice.[29] In the first, he examines Lincoln's 1838 speech to the Young Men's Lyceum of Springfield, which describes the threat of mob rule to "the perpetuation of our political institutions." Lincoln attempts to solve this problem with a "political religion" that preaches "a reverence for the constitution and laws." In the second, Jaffa explicates Lincoln's 1842 speech to the Washington Temperance Society of Springfield, which augments Lincoln's 1838 remarks by moderating the religious fervor of moral reformers. Jaffa focuses, as Lincoln did, on the religious excesses that would enfeeble constitutional government if not curbed by a citizenry vigilant not only for moral fortitude but for an appreciation of the imperfect nature of civil society this side of heaven.

With respect to religion and morality, Jaffa emphasizes morality or self-control as the key focus of Lincoln's political project: "For Lincoln, the question of the 'capability of a people to govern themselves' was always twofold: it referred both to the viability of popular political institutions and to their moral basis in the individual men who must make those institutions work." Gleaning from Aristotle's *Politics*, Jaffa concludes: "If the men who exercised the decisive influence in a popular government were not themselves 'self-governed,'—i.e., self-controlled—then it was vain to expect the institutions to be so."[30] Jaffa focuses on morality in general as Lincoln's aim for a self-controlled people, whose passion for justice and moral reform become moderated by a general

morality inculcated by respect for the Constitution and the laws—
"political religion." This book, in contrast, examines Lincoln's view of
religion and politics to see if he contented himself with developing a
"political religion" and civil religion to moderate the public passions, or
whether he saw the need for government to accommodate religion for its
own sake.

Glen E. Thurow's *Abraham Lincoln and American Political Religion*
(1976) explores the topic of political religion from an understanding
similar to Jaffa's. Thurow seeks to reconcile the apparently contradictory
conclusions of the Gettysburg Address and the Second Inaugural
Address: at Gettysburg Lincoln charges the American people to continue
the fight for the self-government of all, while at his second inauguration
he acknowledges the failure of human intentions and actions in light of
the transcendent purposes of Almighty God.[31] Lincoln as the priestly
politician—the statesman who enables the community to "see the limits
of political action as well as be aroused to the possibilities politics
provides"—reconciles the purposes of man and God.[32] Thurow calls this
solution "Lincoln's political religion." This requires some discussion, for
he argues that political religion in Lincoln's mind assumes a different
character depending on the state of the nation. Thurow states:

> In ordinary times, political religion preserves the superior spirit of the
> founding; in the fortunate circumstance of an extraordinary man in
> power, it becomes an instrument of his reforms. Political religion is a
> perfect valve, opening and closing as necessary under the direction of a
> man such as Lincoln.[33]

As a conservative principle, political religion "preserves" the founding
principles by preaching reverence for "the constitution and laws."
Lincoln explains this in his 1838 Lyceum Address. Lincoln also notes,
however, that the founding "had many props to support it . . . which now
are decayed, and crumbled away." The "temple of liberty" that is the
American regime will fall if the present generation does not "supply their
places [or props] with other pillars."[34] Political religion, according to
Thurow, thus becomes "an instrument of reform" in those circumstances
where the founding principles prove insufficient: namely, the era of
Lincoln.

Thurow admits that the Lyceum Address only hints at this latter
understanding of political religion. The full development comes in the
Gettysburg and Second Inaugural Addresses.[35] During the Civil War,
political religion no longer means mere law-abidingness and respect for
the Constitution and laws, because a substantial portion of the country

has ceased to practice the political religion of the Lyceum Address. Instead, political religion assumes its customary millennial definition—what Bellah calls the "national religious self-understanding."[36] Lincoln grafts religion onto a political religion that formerly concerned itself solely with politics: "a reverence for the constitution and laws." Thurow therefore explains that a "new political religion" derives from "the solid quarry of sober reason" described in the Lyceum Address. He follows Lincoln's wording in the conclusion of the Lyceum Address: "Hence reason (Lincoln) can furnish all the materials (the uniting of the Biblical tradition to the work of the Founders) for the country's future defense and support."[37] The reason or prudence of Lincoln molds the Christian sentiment of the American people into a civil religion that aims to reunite the fractured populace.

In keeping with the thesis that Lincoln meant to supply the deficiencies of the American Founding, Thurow posits a fundamental critique of the founding charter of the American regime by challenging the sufficiency of its guiding principle: "We hold these truths to be self-evident that all men are created equal." Thurow does not doubt that the Founding generation believed in the equality of man (albeit for some only in theory and not yet in practice), and based their governing principles and institutions upon this equality. The difficulty arose, according to Thurow, when the evidence of the truth of human equality to every American self waned as the antebellum period closed. The axiomatic "truth" for the body politic became a "proposition" to be proved—as opposed to apprehended or grasped on its own terms—under Lincoln's rule as president. Thurow invests great interpretive capital in Lincoln's use of the term *proposition* in his Gettysburg Address. He infers that although Lincoln did not doubt the truth of human equality, preservation of the regime required a "reinterpretation" that supplied the deficiency of the American Founding. Lincoln remedied the deficiency by transforming a political axiom or truth into a political proposition that required practical demonstration for its legitimacy.

Upon leaving Springfield, Illinois, for the White House, Lincoln remarked: "I now leave, not knowing when, or whether ever, I may return, with a task before me greater than that which rested upon Washington."[38] But though Lincoln saw himself taking on a role greater than the first president of the United States, he did not, as Thurow suggests, interpret the Declaration of Independence differently than they did. For example, in a short speech to a serenading crowd following the Battle of Gettysburg, Lincoln recalls the Founding declaration of human equality as a "self-evident *truth*." He then goes on to call the southern rebellion "an effort to overthrow the *principle* that all men are created equal."[39] (Emphases added.) He continues the homage he paid Jefferson, who introduced the principle of human equality as "an abstract *truth*, applicable to all men and all times," into the Declaration of Independence.[40] To be sure, as early as his Lyceum Address of 1838, "On the Perpetuation of Our Political Institutions," Lincoln refers to the equality principle as "a proposition." However, there he states that the American Founders "aspired to display before an admiring world, a practical demonstration of the truth of a proposition, . . . namely, *the capability of a people to govern themselves*."[41] He does not say that the demonstration proves the truth of the equal rights of humanity; rather, the demonstration puts into practice a truth understood, in the words of the Declaration of Independence, from "the laws of nature and of nature's God." Or as John Courtney Murray put it: "The American Proposition is at once doctrinal and practical, a theorem and a problem. It is an affirmation and also an intention. It presents itself as a coherent structure of thought that lays claim to intellectual assent; it also presents itself as an organized political project that aims at historical success."[42]

In keeping with the intentions of the American Founders, Lincoln did not reinterpret the equality principle but rather fulfilled its promise according to the circumstances of his time. As his repeated references to and praise of the Founding Fathers attest, Lincoln sought to perpetuate the "practical demonstration" of self-government in a manner consistent with the American Founding. As this project included a consistent and careful appeal to the religious sentiments of the nation, we turn in the next chapter to speeches of Lincoln that refer to both revealed religion and what he calls "political religion" as supporting pillars of the American republican.

Notes

1. "Farewell Address (19 September 1796)," in *George Washington: A Collection*, W. B. Allen, ed. (Indianapolis: Liberty Fund, Inc., 1988), 521-22. For a recent exposition of the Farewell Address that connects free government and religious sentiment *inter alia*, see Matthew Spalding and Patrick J. Garrity, *A Sacred Union of Citizens: George Washington's Farewell Address and the American Character* (Lanham, Md.: Rowman & Littlefield Publishers, Inc., 1996), esp. 76-80.

2. "First Inaugural Address," in *The Portable Thomas Jefferson*, Merrill D. Peterson, ed. (New York: The Viking Press, 1975), 292-93.

3. *In God We Trust: The Religious Beliefs and Ideas of the American Founding Fathers*, Norman Cousins, ed. (New York: Harper & Brothers, 1958), 55, 57, 59, 60, and 61, respectively, and 54-63 in general.

4. "Address before the Young Men's Lyceum of Springfield, Illinois (27 January 1838)," in *The Collected Works of Abraham Lincoln*, Roy P. Basler, ed., 9 vols. (New Brunswick: Rutgers University Press, 1955), 1: 112. Hereinafter cited as *Collected Works*; all emphases in original except where otherwise noted.

5. For Lincoln the politician, see Richard Hofstadter, "Abraham Lincoln and the Self-Made Myth," in *The American Political Tradition and the Men Who Made It* (New York: Alfred A. Knopf, Inc., 1948), 92-134; for Lincoln the saint, see William J. Johnson, *Abraham Lincoln: The Christian* (New York: Eaton & Mains, 1913).

6. "Handbill Replying to Charges of Infidelity (31 July 1846)," in *Collected Works*, 1: 382.

7. "Speech at Peoria, Illinois (16 October 1854)," in *Collected Works*, 2: 266.

8. William Lloyd Garrison cited in *William Lloyd Garrison, 1805-1879: The Story of His Life Told by His Children*, Wendell Phillips Garrison and Francis Jackson Garrison, eds., 4 vols., (Boston: Houghton, Mifflin and Company, 1889), vol. 3: *The Beginning of the End, 1841-1860*, 100.

9. William Lloyd Garrison cited in *Slavery Attacked: The Abolitionist Crusade*, John L. Thomas, ed. (Englewood Cliffs, N.J.: Prentice-Hall, Inc., 1965), 78.

10. "[T]he American church, which perpetrates all these enormous crimes [e.g., defending and exploiting slavery], is not the Church of Christ, but the synagogue of Satan." Thomas, *Slavery Attacked*, 87.

11. *The Federalist*, Jacob E. Cooke, ed. (Middletown, Conn.: Wesleyan University Press, 1961), no. 63, 425.

12. "Protest in Illinois Legislature on Slavery (3 March 1837)," in *Collected Works*, 1: 75.

13. J. G. Randall, *Lincoln: The Liberal Statesman* (New York: Dodd, Mead, & Company, Inc., 1947), 183. This calls to mind the definition of a fanatic as a person who won't change his mind and refuses to change the subject!

14. "First Debate with Stephen A. Douglas at Ottawa, Illinois (21 August 1858)," in *Collected Works*, 3: 27-28.

15. Barton does, however, relate a quotation from J. G. Holland (author of *The Life of Abraham Lincoln*, an 1865 biography) that explains why Lincoln may have kept certain of his religious beliefs from the public: "It was rare that he exhibited what was religious in him . . . A great deal of his best, deepest, largest life he kept almost constantly from view, because he would not expose it to the eyes and apprehension of the careless multitude." Cited in William E. Barton, *The Soul of Abraham Lincoln* (New York: George H. Doran Company, 1920), 102. Herein Holland supposes that amid the clamor of those who claim

Lincoln for their sect, Lincoln's acknowledged wisdom most likely would have led him to keep to himself religious beliefs *unrelated* to the public sphere.

16. Richard N. Current, *The Lincoln Nobody Knows* (New York: McGraw-Hill Book Company, Inc., 1958), chap. 3, "The Instrument of God," 51-75.

17. See Barton, *The Soul of Abraham Lincoln*, chap. 22, "The Constructive Argument," 260-90; Mark A. Noll, *One Nation under God? Christian Faith and Political Action in America* (New York: Harper & Row, 1988), chap. 6, "The Transcendent Faith of Abraham Lincoln," 90-104, "The Perplexing Faith of Abraham Lincoln," *Christianity Today* 29 (15 February 1985): 12-14, and "The Struggle for Lincoln's Soul," *Books & Culture: A Christian Review* 1 (September/October 1995): 3, 5-7; and Richard V. Pierard and Robert D. Linder, *Civil Religion and the Presidency* (Grand Rapids, Mich.: Academie Books-Zondervan Publishing House, 1988), chap. 4, "Abraham Lincoln and the Sacralization of American Civil Religion," 87-113.

18. "David Mearns has aptly called him a 'Christian without a Creed.' This may be the least inadequate phrase." William J. Wolf, *The Religion of Abraham Lincoln* (New York: Seabury Press, 1963), 197; originally published in 1959 under the title *The Almost Chosen People: A Study of the Religion of Abraham Lincoln* by Doubleday & Company, Inc.), 193.

19. Glen E. Thurow, "Abraham Lincoln and American Political Religion," in *The Historian's Lincoln: Pseudohistory, Psychohistory, and History*, Gabor S. Boritt with Norman O. Forness, eds. (Urbana: University of Illinois Press, 1988), 129. See also Ronald C. White, Jr., "Lincoln's Sermon on the Mount: The Second Inaugural Address," in *Religion and the American Civil War*, Randall M. Miller, Harry S. Stout, and Charles Reagan Wilson, eds. (New York: Oxford University Press, 1998), 208-23.

20. J. G. Randall and Richard N. Current, *Lincoln the President: Last Full Measure* (New York: Dodd, Mead & Company, Inc., 1955), the final volume of Randall's biography of Lincoln, is a good example. See especially chap. 16, "God's Man," 365-79.

21. Elton Trueblood's *Abraham Lincoln: Theologian of American Anguish* is typical, as is G. Frederick Owen's *Abraham Lincoln: The Man & His Faith* (Wheaton, Ill.: Tyndale House Publishers, Inc., 1976), originally published as *A Heart That Yearned for God* by Third Century Publishers, Inc.

22. This is true of an otherwise substantial and informative collection entitled, *Essays on Lincoln's Faith and Politics*, Hans J. Morgenthau and David Hein, Kenneth W. Thompson, ed. (Lanham, Md.: University Press of America, 1983). In Morgenthau's essay, "The Mind of Abraham Lincoln," he states the following about the political philosophy of Lincoln: "Yet the effectiveness of the Constitution to protect the rights of the people depends upon the strength of the government" (80). But what of the vigilance of the governed, as well as the political impulse of their religious inclinations? On this, Morgenthau is silent. He pictures Lincoln as confined in his prerogatives as president by the will of the people as expressed in the Constitution and periodic elections. He does not

explore Lincoln's appeal to religious sentiment in connection to his political aims, though his brief chapter on Lincoln's religion is incisive (6-16).

23. Robert N. Bellah and Phillip E. Hammond, *Varieties of Civil Religion*, 12. See also Robert N. Bellah, *The Broken Covenant: American Civil Religion in Time of Trial*, 46.

24. Garry Wills, *Under God: Religion and American Politics* (New York: Simon and Schuster, 1990), 208.

25. Wills, *Under God*, 211. Wills also asserts that Howe's "evangelical background had not mattered to her much until war renewed her childhood memories of biblical crises." Wills, *Under God*, 209.

26. Cf. Cousins, *In God We Trust*.

27. Randall, *Lincoln: The Liberal Statesman*, 200.

28. Randall, *Lincoln: The Liberal Statesman*, 201. George Anastaplo offers a similar observation, making even more explicit reference to Lincoln's appreciation that the nation's religious sentiments were "transcendent supports which the essentially temporal and temporary political enterprise seems to require." "American Constitutionalism and the Virtue of Prudence: Philadelphia, Paris, Washington, Gettysburg," in *Abraham Lincoln, the Gettysburg Address, and American Constitutionalism*, Leo Paul S. de Alvarez, ed. (Irving, Tex.: University of Dallas Press, 1976), esp. 123-25.

29. Harry V. Jaffa, *Crisis of the House Divided: An Interpretation of the Issues in the Lincoln-Douglas Debates* (Seattle: University of Washington Press, 1973; reprint ed., Chicago: University of Chicago Press, 1982, © 1959), chaps. 9 and 10, "The Teaching Concerning Political Salvation" and "The Teaching Concerning Political Moderation," 183-272.

30. Jaffa, *Crisis of the House Divided*, 185-86; Aristotle, *The Politics*, trans. Carnes Lord (Chicago: University of Chicago Press, 1984), bk. 5, chap. 9, 167 (1310a17-19): "If lack of self-control exists in the case of an individual, it exists also in the case of a city."

31. "While the Gettysburg Address endows actions with encompassing significance in history, the Second Inaugural seems to draw limits to their significance." Glen E. Thurow, *Abraham Lincoln and American Political Religion* (Albany: State University of New York Press, 1976), 110.

32. Thurow, *Abraham Lincoln and American Political Religion*, 117.

33. Thurow, *Abraham Lincoln and American Political Religion*, 35.

34. "Address before the Young Men's Lyceum of Springfield, Illinois (27 January 1838)," in *Collected Works*, 1: 113, 115.

35. "But the authority of the Founders is in need of support. This support can be found in a new political religion that unites Christianity to the work of the Fathers." Thurow, *Abraham Lincoln and American Political Religion*, 36.

36. Bellah, "Civil Religion in America," 8.

37. Thurow, *Abraham Lincoln and American Political Religion*, 37.

38. "Farewell Address at Springfield, Illinois (11 February 1861)," in *Collected Works*, 4: 190.

39. "Response to a Serenade (7 July 1863)," in *Collected Works*, 6: 319-20. See also his "Fragment on the Constitution and the Union [c. January, 1861]," in *Collected Works*, 4: 169, wherein he calls the equality of human liberty a "principle" four times, and similarly in his "Speech in Independence Hall, Philadelphia, Pennsylvania (22 February 1861)," in *Collected Works*, 4: 240.

40. "To Henry L. Pierce and Others (6 April 1859)," in *Collected Works*, 3: 376.

41. "Address before the Young Men's Lyceum of Springfield, Illinois (27 January 1838)," in *Collected Works*, 1: 113.

42. John Courtney Murray, *We Hold These Truths: Catholic Reflections on the American Proposition* (New York: Sheed and Ward, Inc., 1960), vii.

Chapter 2

The Political Utility of Religion

Following an American political tradition that stretches back to the colonial era, Lincoln drew upon the religious sentiments of the American people in a manner that has yet to be surpassed. Early in Lincoln's public life, he encouraged popular education so that (among other benefits) Americans could "read the scriptures and other works, both of a religious and moral nature, for themselves."[1] Here he follows the Northwest Ordinance of 1787: "Religion, morality, and knowledge, being necessary to good government and the happiness of mankind, schools and the means of education shall forever be encouraged."[2] During the Civil War Lincoln expressed gratitude for the support of churchmen and parishioners and proclaimed national days of thanksgiving, prayer, fasting, and even a Sabbath for military personnel. Most notably, he appealed directly and indirectly to religion in speeches and writings filled with biblical citations, allusions, and themes. But the question remains, exactly how did he understand religion to benefit a government based on the consent of the governed? Was there any particular way that religion could influence or support the American republic without bringing theological quarrels into the public arena?

Address before the Young Men's Lyceum of Springfield (1838)

If ever Abraham Lincoln addressed the requirements for a successful republic, and therewith any relevance of religion to self-government, he did so in a speech delivered on January 27, 1838, to the Young Men's Lyceum of Springfield, Illinois. Entitled "The Perpetuation of Our Political Institutions," the address focused on the preservation of American self-government in light of the increasing threat that vigilante justice carried out by mobs posed to constitutional government. Illinois state historian Thomas F. Schwartz notes that "local political orators had a longstanding fear of mobocracy and lawlessness" that came to light in their public addresses.[3] In one sense, then, Lincoln traverses territory familiar to his audience, which comprised fellow speakers and aspiring politicians. But a close examination of his Lyceum Address reveals a more serious appraisal of the threat that mobs posed to the nation's security than earlier orators had imagined.

Lincoln found a model both to emulate and improve in the Inaugural Address of Martin Van Buren, delivered just one year prior to his Lyceum Address.[4] Lincoln publicly supported Tennessee Senator Hugh L. White, one of three Whigs running for president in 1836 against Van Buren, the incumbent vice president under the retiring Andrew Jackson.[5] Given the stark partisan differences between Lincoln and Van Buren, one can only surmise that Lincoln used his appearance before the Young Men's Lyceum of Springfield to elucidate the flaws of Van Buren's presidential program and suggest an alternative governing philosophy for the nation.

Lincoln drew the title and central theme of his speech from Van Buren's observation "that the perpetuity of our ['political'] institutions depends upon ourselves."[6] Reflecting on the "success that has attended our great experiment," Van Buren rests hopeful that "if we maintain the principles on which they ['our institutions'] were established they are destined to confer their benefits on countless generations yet to come . . ." But where Van Buren finds in this "a ground for still deeper delight" in the prospects for future success, Lincoln is less sanguine. In his second of four consecutive terms in the Illinois House of Representatives, Lincoln examines the present threats to American self-government and the safeguards necessary for its perpetuation. He focuses on the then "increasing disregard for law which pervades the country." If religion was essential to perpetuating a republic, this speech provides a logical starting point for discussing its role in the eyes of Lincoln the legislator.

He begins by appreciating the land his listeners enjoy as Americans and describes their system of government as "conducing more essentially to the ends of civil and religious liberty, than any of which the history of former times tells us."[7] He then contrasts the seemingly lesser burden the current generation of Americans carries—that of transmitting the nation's "goodly land" and "political edifice of liberty and equal rights" to their posterity—with the founding generation's more arduous task of establishing it. We "found ourselves" in its possession, but we "toiled not" in its establishment. Our ancestors, "*once* hardy, brave, and patriotic, but *now* lamented and departed," did the difficult work while "'tis ours only" to make sure it passes on "to the latest generation that fate shall permit the world to know." Although the present generation's task may pale beside the original founding, it remains significant as Lincoln counts a "love for our species in general" among the motivations for fulfilling their duty. Philanthropy, therefore, becomes a beneficent motive for the continued success of American national life.

"How then shall we perform it?" Lincoln asks. After founding a self-governing regime, how can Americans preserve it? Lincoln gives short shrift to an external threat to America, like "some transatlantic military giant" overstepping the ocean and defeating her in battle. The more likely danger resides at home: "If destruction be our lot, we must ourselves be its author and finisher. As a nation of free men, we must live through all time, or die by suicide."[8] In speaking of the future of the American republic, Lincoln gives a providential or fateful spin with the words "our lot." In addition, Lincoln likens the civic duty of the American people with the sanctifying work of God with his statement that they are the "author and finisher" of any destruction that may befall them. The New Testament speaks of Jesus as the "author and finisher" of the Christian believer's faith (Heb. 12:2). Thus in Lincoln's allusion, Americans appear to assume full responsibility, one might say a god-like status, in completing their project or bringing about its demise.

They are not, however, fated to destroy themselves: as "freemen" they can either "live through all time" or "die by suicide." *Providence* may have blessed the current generation with "the peaceful possession, of the fairest portion of the earth" and a "political edifice of liberty and equal rights," but *the American people* have the choice and hence the responsibility to determine whether or not "these fundamental blessings" will prosper them and their posterity or lead to their ruin. Lincoln conveyed this notion of "luck" at the close of an 1859 speech at an agricultural fair: "Some of you will be successful, . . . others will be disappointed, and will be in a less happy mood. To such let it be said, 'Lay it not too much to heart.' Let them adopt the maxim, 'Better luck next time;' and then, by renewed exertion, make that better luck for themselves."[9] In the Lyceum Address, Lincoln's burden is to show how Americans can conquer fate and succeed in self-government, a task that apparently does not follow naturally from their present enjoyment of it.

The danger to the American republic, as Lincoln sees it, lies in "the increasing disregard for law which pervades the country." For several years mob violence, especially in response to incendiary abolitionist meetings, had spread throughout the country.[10] Just a few months prior to his address, a local meeting protested abolition efforts as "neither necessary nor useful."[11] A month later in Alton, Illinois, seventy miles

south of Springfield, a mob killed abolitionist editor Elijah P. Lovejoy as
he defended the installation of a third printing press—the other two
having been thrown in the Mississippi River by previous anti-abolition
mobs. Lincoln noted this tendency of abolitionism to stir up the passions
rather than the reason of a community in a protest resolution he co-
authored in the Illinois House of Representatives with fellow Whig
lawyer Daniel Stone. After declaring that "the institution of slavery is
founded upon both injustice and bad policy," they added, "the
promulgation of abolition doctrines tends rather to increase than to abate
its evils."[12] Given the Lyceum Address focus on the dangers of mobs as
opposed to their opposing provocateurs, Lincoln only makes passing
reference to Lovejoy's murder in his Lyceum Address.[13]

In January 1837 Lincoln highlighted the general menace of mob rule
in a speech before the Illinois Legislature. In it he stated his opposition to
encouraging "that lawless and mobocratic spirit, whether in relation to
the bank or any thing else, which is already abroad in the land; and is
spreading with rapid and fearful impetuosity, to the ultimate overthrow
of every institution, or even moral principle, in which persons and
property have hitherto found security." He also connected the lawless
spirit in society with the same passion exhibited by state representatives
who wished to investigate the State Bank at Springfield "without legal
authority." Lincoln declared, "To those who claim omnipotence for the
Legislature, and who in the plenitude of their assumed powers, are
disposed to disregard the Constitution, law, good faith, moral right, and
every thing else, I have nothing to say."[14] While the "lawless and
mobocratic spirit" in this earlier speech provides merely the context for
discussing the status of the state's bank, the Lyceum Address focuses
directly on the threat mob violence posed to the rule of law in the United
States.

Though Lincoln states that he hopes he is not too apprehensive about
this danger to America, he goes on to detail "the increasing disregard for
law which pervades the country." He contrasts "the wild and furious
passions" and "the worse than savage mobs" with "the sober judgement
of the Courts" and "the executive ministers of justice." The obvious
lesson is that *regard* for law holds the key to the successful maintenance
of the American regime. This is intuitive, as self-government implies
self-rule: namely, public moderation, and hence a people living
according to rules or laws they themselves choose as a limitation on their
freedom. But what strikes the listener as obvious Lincoln goes on to
expound, if only because the disregard for law is "increasing"—a not too
insignificant sign that not enough people see its dangerous connection to

the potential demise of the country.

Martin Van Buren's 1837 Inaugural Address also noted the presence of mobs in America:

> Occasionally, it is true, the ardor of public sentiment, outrunning the regular progress of the judicial tribunals or seeking to reach cases not denounced as criminal by the existing law, has displayed itself in a manner calculated to give pain to the friends of free government and to encourage the hopes of those who wish for its overthrow.

He downplays its threat to the American regime, though, when he adds: "These occurrences, however, have been far less frequent in our country than in any other of equal population on the globe, and with the diffusion of intelligence *it may well be hoped that they will constantly diminish* in frequency and violence." Van Buren concludes that "neither masses of the people nor sections of the country have been swerved from their devotion to the bond of union and the principles it has made sacred. *It will ever be thus.*"[15] (Emphases added.) Van Buren's optimism about the state of the American regime downplayed growing national concern over striking workers, mob violence, and sectional politics so as not to tarnish the Jacksonian legacy of "democratized" government he inherited upon becoming president.[16] In contrast Lincoln points out that the direct effects of vigilantes may be a "small evil," but the indirect or long-term consequences pose the great threat to perpetuating the American regime. Upon reading Van Buren's address, Lincoln would certainly count him as one American who does not see mob violence as a national concern.

Aristotle wrote that "when men [are] afraid, they get a better grip on the regime. Thus those who take thought for the regime should promote fears—so that they will defend and not overturn the regime, keeping watch on it like a nocturnal guard—and make the far away near."[17] George Washington made a related observation: "It is one of the evils of democratical governments, that the people, not always seeing and frequently misled, must often feel before they can act right."[18] Lincoln follows suit. He notes that "the proneness of our minds" had led the country to see the direct effects of mob violence as the only effects, thereby creating a false sense of security from the apparently limited scope of "mob law." In an attempt to "make the far away near," Lincoln presents the train of consequences that would follow mob rule if left to its own devices and not checked by the community at large.

The "full extent of the evil" of mobs comes to light as he explains how the "lawless in spirit, are encouraged to become lawless in practice" when they see mobs go unpunished.[19] In addition, "good men" become demoralized as they see "their property destroyed; their families insulted, and their lives endangered," and then become "not much averse to a change in which they imagine they have nothing to lose." Lincoln makes clear that the end result of "this mobocratic spirit" is the erosion of "the strongest bulwark of any Government, and particularly of those constituted like ours, . . . the *attachment* of the People." What follows from a disaffected citizenry is a government with too few friends "to make their friendship effectual." Accordingly, an opportunity presents itself for "men of sufficient talent and ambition" to assume the reins of government "and overturn that fair fabric" with little opposition.[20]

Now that Lincoln has pointed out the danger to the nation, he moves on to answer how they are to defend against it: "Let every American, every lover of liberty, every well wisher to his posterity, swear by the blood of the Revolution, never to violate in the least particular, the laws of the country; and never to tolerate their violation by others."[21] Van Buren remarked similarly: "How imperious, then, is the obligation imposed upon every citizen, in his own sphere of action, whether limited or extended, to exert himself in perpetuating a condition of things so singularly happy!" He continues: "We have learned by experience a fruitful lesson—that an implicit and undeviating adherence to the principles on which we set out can carry us prosperously onward . . ." Also, "the people . . . have the most direct and permanent interest in preserving the landmarks of social order and maintaining on all occasions the inviolability of those constitutional and legal provisions which they themselves have made." Following his own advice, and a commonplace of American statesmanship as far back as the nation's first president,[22] Van Buren states: "the principle that will govern me in the high duty to which my country calls me is a strict adherence to the letter and spirit of the Constitution as it was designed by those who framed it. . . . Looking back to it as a sacred instrument . . ."[23] In typical Jacksonian fashion, Van Buren is content merely to downplay the popular threat of mob violence and suggest without elaboration that Americans simply hold fast to the principles, laws, and constitution of the United States.

Lincoln's advocacy of law-abidingness, on the other hand, though similar in content requires further explanation to move his audience to acceptance and practice. He develops his answer by tying law-abidingness to the sacrifices of their forebears: "As the patriots of seventy-six did to the support of the Declaration of Independence, so to the support of the Constitution and Laws, let every American pledge his life, his property, and his sacred honor;—let every man remember that to violate the law, is to trample on the blood of his father, and to tear the character [charter?] of his own, and his children's liberty." He recognizes that simply telling people to forgo vigilante justice will not suffice. While Van Buren rests assured with an appeal to the Constitution as "a sacred instrument," Lincoln calls upon the patriotic and filial attachments of the nation to bolster the plain, uninspiring message of mere obedience to the laws. Lincoln sets the stage for mere obedience to the laws to become "reverence" for the laws, evoking an admiration of the accomplishments of their forebears bordering on piety.

No wonder, then, that Lincoln expresses hope that this law-abidingness will become "the *political religion* of the nation." Van Buren also noted this theme in his Inaugural Address: namely, that "the bounteous resources" of nature and "the diffused intelligence and elevated character" of the American people "will avail us nothing if we fail sacredly to uphold these political institutions . . ." He cautioned, "All the lessons of history and experience must be lost upon us if we are content to trust alone to the peculiar advantages we happen to possess."[24] But where Van Buren anticipates Lincoln's call for a sacred support of the government and laws, he does not explain how the danger will come if the nation relaxes its law-abidingness. "That predominating affection for our political system," Van Buren states, "which prevails throughout our territorial limits, that calm and enlightened judgment which ultimately governs our people as one vast body, *will always be at hand* to resist and control every effort, foreign or domestic, which aims or would lead to overthrow our institutions." (Emphasis added.) It is left for Lincoln to describe how "men of sufficient talent and ambition" will exploit the diminished respect for law to subvert the American republic.

Lincoln now adds religious devotion to a cause that so far he has only been implicitly connected to God:

> Let reverence for the laws, be breathed by every American mother, to the lisping babe, that prattles on her lap—let it be taught in schools, in seminaries, and in colleges;—let it be written in Primmers, spelling books, and in Almanacs;—let it be preached from the pulpit, proclaimed in legislative halls, and enforced in courts of justice. And, in short, let it become the *political religion* of the nation; and let the old and the young, the rich and the poor, the grave and the gay, of all sexes and tongues, and colors and conditions, sacrifice unceasingly upon its altars.[25]

His religious examples—"reverence," "seminaries," "preached from the pulpit," and "sacrifice unceasingly upon its altars"—and exhortative tone rouse the listener to the seriousness of his cause, a seriousness evoked earlier by calls to one's patriotism and ancestry and now complemented by the aura of religion. Religion, at this point, serves the republic as the handmaiden of government in the latter's effort to ensure obedience to its laws—an obedience conducive of not only civil but religious liberty.[26]

Lincoln's reference to "the pulpit" heads a list that calls for the gospel of law-abidingness also to be "proclaimed in legislative halls, and enforced in courts of justice." But why does he omit its proclamation from the seat of the executive, the one branch of government missing from his list? Lincoln appears to replace the executive seat with "the pulpit." Regarding "reverence for the laws," the sentence reads: "let it be preached from the pulpit, proclaimed in legislative halls, and enforced in courts of justice."[27] The conspicuous substitution of the preacher for the governor or president leads one to wonder about Lincoln's intention. Is he implying that a governor or president would overstep his authority by preaching the gospel of law-abidingness? This cannot be, because an implicit call for strict separation of church and state would as well exclude the legislature and judiciary Lincoln mentions. Conversely, an overly scrupulous adherence to a separation of church and state would exclude the preaching of Lincoln's "political" religion from "the pulpit." In fact, Lincoln the legislator preached this gospel of law-abidingness in the Baptist Church of Springfield![28]

Lincoln's political religion, moreover, is not inherently religious; only its conscientious observance gives it a religious semblance. A review of the immediate context of his listing of the preacher with the legislator and judge shows that Lincoln cites almost every significant influence on a citizen growing up in America:

> Let reverence for the laws, be breathed by every American mother, to the lisping babe, that prattles on her lap—let it be taught in schools, in seminaries, and in colleges;—let it be written in Primmers, spelling books, and in Almanacs;—let it be preached from the pulpit, proclaimed in legislative halls, and enforced in courts of justice.

Starting with the family, moving through the educational system, and concluding with the church and government (with the exception of the executive department), Lincoln shows his primary concern to enlist every possible influence on Americans to the cause of law-abidingness. Here he imitates Moses, who exhorted the Israelites to meditate continually on the commandments: "And these words, which I command thee this day, shall be in thine heart: And thou shalt teach them diligently unto thy children, and shalt talk of them when thou sittest in thine house, and when thou walkest by the way, and when thou liest down, and when thou risest up" (Deut. 6:6-7). Lincoln thus uses the pulpit to symbolize the influence of the church, while he includes the legislature and judiciary to represent the general influence of government.

But why include two of three branches of government and leave out the third? Why not leave the judiciary out, or better still, list the executive as well? A secondary consideration for Lincoln's omission of the executive comes from the concluding sentence of this paragraph, which immediately follows the sentence about preaching reverence for the laws from the pulpit: "And, in short, let it become the *political religion* of the nation; and let the old and the young, the rich and the poor, the grave and the gay, of all sexes and tongues, and colors and conditions, sacrifice unceasingly upon its altars." By calling strict obedience to the laws a political "religion," Lincoln emphasizes the seriousness of his advice and, therefore, the importance of spreading this message in the same manner that a preacher spreads the word of God. Perhaps the executive department is present under the guise of "the pulpit," implying that a religious aspect must be donned by the chief administrator of government—the executive, one uniquely situated among the branches of government to speak with one voice. As the political leader and chief law enforcer of the community, and thus one called to promote law-abidingness, the executive must adopt the mode of a preacher to enlist the community as fellow believers. In short, while explicitly referring to "the pulpit," and thereby invoking the aid of churches against mob violence, Lincoln's listing of the preacher at the head of his otherwise "governmental" list serves as an equivocal reference to the work of the executive in the cause of American salvation from the sin of mob violence. If a republic needs a "political" religion to survive, as Lincoln makes clear, its executive must become its "political" preacher—and as our citations of the Bible attest, Lincoln already acts the preacher in this address.

Lincoln's explicit call for the community's religious leaders and institutions to help promote the "political religion" of law-abidingness brings the first reference to the church's influence on the perpetuation of free government: preaching that strict obedience to the government and laws pleases God. Although the church is not a political institution, Lincoln enlists its support in a way consistent with its own teaching. For example, 1 Peter 2:13-14 states: "Submit yourselves to every ordinance of man for the Lord's sake: whether it be to the king, as supreme; Or unto governors, as unto them that are sent by him for the punishment of evil-doers, and for the praise of them that do well."

Lincoln's "political religion," ironically enough, has little if anything to do with religion proper. To be sure, he calls upon "seminaries" and "pulpits" to spread the message of political salvation through civil obedience. Lincoln even speaks of "altars" upon which the people are to "sacrifice unceasingly" as part of their obedience to all of the laws. His political religion, however, is more politics than religion.[29] The only direct connection to religion is the commitment it requires of each citizen. One could as well phrase it "political zeal" or "political faith," the former emphasizing the passion and the latter the trust of the public. The phrase chosen by Lincoln, "political religion," represents both the passion and trust necessary to ensure the perpetuation of the American regime.

With respect to political zeal, one might wonder why Lincoln would make such an appeal, for he has already shown the danger of community zeal when manifested in the form of vigilante pursuit of justice. Mobocracy, a zeal for the immediate gratification of a community's desire for justice, leads ultimately to the public's disregard for the laws and government. Lincoln appealed earlier, though, to the passions of his listeners by calling to mind the efforts of their forebears in establishing their present blessings, an appeal that vivifies an otherwise uninspiring call to mere civil obedience. One must involve the emotions of a community in order to move them to follow even the most rational advice: to wit, "let every man remember that to violate the law, is to trample on the blood of his father." Even though Lincoln counsels that the passionate excesses of a self-governing community will cause their downfall, he is careful not to exclude passion altogether, for it serves to support the regime when linked to the laws and the Constitution.[30] Furthermore, Lincoln follows the paragraph containing the phrase "political religion" with one describing it as "a state of feeling." To engender this "feeling" is his present project, albeit one argued meticulously on the ground of reason, as seen most clearly near the end of the address.

As for political faith being part of Lincoln's "political religion," he explains in the next paragraph that "a strict observance of all the laws" includes obeying bad laws as well as good ones: "although bad laws, if they exist, should be repealed as soon as possible, still while they continue in force, for the sake of example, they should be religiously observed." The best example of a "bad law" that Lincoln disagreed with, but explicitly counseled American citizens to obey until it could be changed, turned out to be a Supreme Court decision—the infamous *Dred Scott v. Sandford* (1857) opinion of Chief Justice Roger B. Taney.[31] In a speech responding to Senator Stephen A. Douglas's categorical endorsement of the *Dred Scott* decision, Lincoln explains that he offered "no *resistance*" to the controversial decision. "But when," he adds, "as it is true we find it wanting in all these claims to the public confidence, it is not resistance, it is not factious, it is not even disrespectful, to treat it as not having yet quite established a settled doctrine for the country." Quoting a hero of Senator Douglas, Democratic President Andrew Jackson, Lincoln reminds his rival, "Mere precedent is a dangerous source of authority." Congress, therefore, and hence the people they represent, were not bound by the decision on subsequent questions of national policy.[32]

Lincoln would go on in his First Inaugural Address of 1861 to place his juridical philosophy regarding Supreme Court rulings in the context of self-government properly understood:

> At the same time the candid citizen must confess that if the policy of the government, upon vital questions, affecting the whole people, is to be irrevocably fixed by decisions of the Supreme Court, the instant they are made, in ordinary litigation between parties, in personal actions, the people will have ceased, to be their own rulers, having, to that extent, practically resigned their government, into the hands of that eminent tribunal.[33]

So, while individual court decisions or laws may be bad, and the people are free to change them according to established procedures, the lesson of the Lyceum Address of 1838 remains, "for the sake of example, they should be religiously observed." Needless to say, this requires faith or trust on the part of the community struggling as a minority to repeal laws it considers bad. They must have faith that their continued obedience to a government that countenances some bad laws will benefit them until those laws get changed.

Lincoln hastens to add that bad laws and grievances with no existing legal redress will arise even in a free government. Just a few sentences earlier he had exhorted "all sexes and tongues, and colors and conditions, [to] sacrifice unceasingly upon" the altars of civil obedience. Women and slaves could not vote and, therefore, would have to bear the burden of bad laws more helplessly, and perhaps more grudgingly, than the enfranchised part of the community. Their faith in what Lincoln called "a political edifice of liberty and equal rights" becomes the faith that St. Thomas lacked upon hearing of the resurrection of Jesus: "blessed are they that have not seen, and yet have believed" (John 20:29b). Although women and slaves "have not seen" their liberties and rights secured by their own actions, their obedience to the laws and government show they "have believed" or trusted that the full blessings of self-government will come to them in time. This constitutes their "sacrifice." As Lincoln described the American regime as "conducing more essentially to the ends of civil and religious liberty, than any of which the history of former times tell us," he hopes that those most tempted to disregard the laws will join the rest in observing all the laws "if not too intolerable."

Lincoln acknowledges the tension between a religious observance of the laws—to ensure the rule of law—and the occasional need to repeal bad laws—to protect more fully the rights of the entire community. After all, one could only promote "reverence for the laws" if they secure the safety and happiness of the community. For "bad laws" to be "religiously observed" requires that a higher or long-term end be served: namely, "for the sake of example," that better laws might be instituted in time. In this last case, it is not the law that is good but the act of obeying it as one seeks to repeal it. This requires that a person inform his reverence for the laws with a judgment of their general beneficence.

The need to transcend or look beyond the laws in order to determine which ones should be repealed produces the tension between strict law-abidingness and occasional efforts to repeal the few bad laws. This transcendence of the laws may at first appear similar to the action of a mob, which determines outside of the law how to secure justice in a particular situation. However, judgment of a law as bad does not allow one to refuse obedience to it; it only lends one moral authority to seek its repeal through the existing government and laws. This Lincoln would do in 1862, when as president he signed a law forbidding slavery in the federal territories notwithstanding the Supreme Court's earlier holding in the *Dred Scott* case. Law-abidingness and lawful repeal efforts pay due homage to the existing law's authority while seeking its reform.

Given Lincoln's counsel for obedience to the laws, good and bad, one finds little room for justifiable civil disobedience. Nevertheless, he admits indirectly that some grievances that have no legal redress may be "too intolerable" to bear: "If such arise, let proper legal provisions be made for them with the least possible delay; but, till then, let them if not too intolerable, be borne with."[34] He does not elaborate on this exception, for that would distract his audience from his main teaching that civil obedience and not moral grandstanding will protect free government from the unruly. Lincoln goes so far as to repeat his main teaching in the next paragraph, saying that no grievance "is a fit object of redress by mob law." By emphasizing the threat that mobs pose to free government and the rule of law, Lincoln disregards almost any claim a citizen may have to civil disobedience. In doing so, he makes practically no distinction between civil disobedience and mob law, thereby keeping his gospel of law-abidingness on the forefront of his listeners' minds.

In his First Inaugural Address, Martin Van Buren stated that the fifty years since the drafting of the Constitution have proven false the worst fears of America's naysayers. Similarly, the retiring Andrew Jackson in his Farewell Address stated: "We have now lived almost fifty years under the Constitution framed by the sages and patriots of the Revolution.... We encountered ... trials with our Constitution yet in its infancy ... But we have passed triumphantly through all these difficulties. Our Constitution is no longer a doubtful experiment ..."[35] Lincoln counters: "But, it may be asked, why suppose danger to our political institutions? Have we not preserved them for more than fifty years? And why may we not for fifty times as long?" Lincoln suggests that while there is no "*sufficient* reason" for expecting imminent danger, to presume this "would itself be extremely dangerous"—precisely the presumption President Van Buren makes in his Inaugural Address.

This is similar to Lincoln's earlier effort to awaken the public, who in the "proneness" of their minds see the direct effects of mob rule as the only consequences. He states that to suppose no danger would be to fall prey to the same lack of foresight that sees mob action as efficient albeit irregular justice. Presuming that popular government would always succeed in America is particularly ominous, given the existence of "many causes, dangerous in their tendency, which have not existed heretofore."[36]

Lincoln cites two "props" that previously aided the perpetuation of the American system but that now "are decayed, and crumbled away": first, "men of ambition and talents" at the American Founding, who satisfied their ambition in the establishment of a self-governing nation; second, "the passions of the people," which were either subdued or vented through their rebellion against British rule.[37]

Lincoln argues that at the time of the American Founding, "all that sought celebrity and fame, and distinction, expected to find them in the success of that experiment": namely, "the capability of a people to govern themselves." While President Van Buren noted the "capacity of the people for self-government," as well as "their willingness ... to submit to all needful restraints and exactions of municipal law,"[38] he does not comment on the motives of the Founders in attempting to establish a new form of government. Lincoln suggests that the Founders had everything to gain and little to lose in the pursuit of immortal fame. Indeed, this fame was all the more enduring as it gave ambition a legitimate outlet for satisfaction. Men "of ambition and talents," however, now pose a threat because "they will as naturally seek the

gratification of their ruling passion, as others have *so* done before them."
Here Lincoln alludes to *Federalist* No. 72, which describes "the love of
fame" as "the ruling passion of the noblest minds."[39] Not surprisingly,
Federalist No. 72 defends the re-eligibility of the executive magistrate in
the proposed Constitution of 1787, which at minimum sought to avoid
the proliferation of former presidents "wandering among the people like
discontented ghosts, and sighing for a place which were destined never
more to possess."[40] While the majority of ambitious men will aspire to
nothing more than a congressional, gubernatorial, or even presidential
office, there remain those few whose ambitions match that of "an
Alexander, a Caesar, or a Napoleon." They are precisely those men who
find little satisfaction in running a government set up by others, let alone
obeying laws set down by others. These are, in short, the makers and
manipulators of mobs. Because the prop of "distinction" will not entice a
Caesar to serve in a regime of someone else's making, Lincoln offers an
alternative: a united people, "attached to the government and laws" and
with adequate intelligence, thus equipped to prevent the schemes of a
"towering genius" from coming to fruition.[41]

He then turns to the second prop that formerly aided the founding of
free government in the United States but now endangers it: "the *passions*
of the people." Van Buren viewed this threat to the American republic
with less apprehension: "Fifty years ago its rapid failure was boldly
predicted. Latent and uncontrollable causes of dissolution were supposed
to exist even by the wise and good, and . . . the fears of many an honest
patriot overbalanced his sanguine hopes." He reports that "in every
instance" the predictions "have completely failed," and he attributes their
misguided "forebodings" to "imperfect experience." "Party
exasperation," Van Buren adds, "often carried to its highest point," has
only served to strengthen the nation. In the estimation of this early
promoter of political parties, "The alleged causes of danger have long
surpassed anticipation, but none of the consequences have followed."
This leads him to conclude: "Present excitement will at all times magnify
present dangers, but true philosophy must teach us that none more
threatening than the past can remain to be overcome . . ."[42]

Lincoln disagrees. He foresees dangers equally if not "more
threatening than the past" that "remain to be overcome" if only because
the future threat to the American system springs from a source that
originally helped establish the national government. Lincoln will
conclude that "Passion has helped us; but can do so no more. It will in
future be our enemy."[43]

Both props mentioned by Lincoln relate to passion. The first prop was the thirst for distinction, what he called "their ruling passion." The second prop—described as "jealousy, envy, and avarice," along with "hate" and "revenge"—Lincoln calls "the *passions* of the people." Again, these popular passions, like the ruling passion of the American founders, found legitimate expression in the revolt against Great Britain and therewith "the advancement of the noblest of cause[s]—that of establishing and maintaining civil and religious liberty." Nevertheless, "the force of circumstances" and not the "judgment" of the people impelled them forward, suppressing "the basest principles of our nature," which would otherwise destroy a community.

Lincoln comments that "this state of feeling," community passions either lying dormant or directed "exclusively against the British nation," must fade away with "the circumstances that produced it." With the passing of the revolutionary generation passes a *"living history,"* no longer the aid to free government it once was, and presaging a turning inward of those passions that hitherto had benefited the struggle for independence. Lincoln concludes: "They *were* the pillars of the temple of liberty; and now, that they have crumbled away, that temple must fall, unless we, their descendants, supply their places with other pillars, hewn from the solid quarry of sober reason. Passion has helped us; but can do so no more. It will in future be our enemy." Lincoln most likely borrowed "the pillars of the temple of liberty" from Van Buren's reference to the revolutionary heroes as "the earliest and firmest pillars of the republic."[44] Or he could have gleaned the metaphor from George Washington's 1783 Circular Address to the States, which proposes a union of the newly independent American states, sound public credit, a strong and orderly militia, and a "pacific and friendly Disposition" among the citizens of the several states as "the Pillars on which the glorious Fabrick of our Independency and National Character must be supported."[45]

Van Buren adds that "the Revolution that gave us existence as one people was achieved at the period of my birth; . . . I feel that I belong to a later age and that I may not expect my countrymen to weigh my actions with the same kind and partial hand." Van Buren predicts he will not receive the degree of sympathy that Americans gave to members of the Founding generation. This illustrates Lincoln's claim that the passing of this "living history" poses a threat to American self-government that "invading foe-men" could never present. Perhaps Van Buren's observation prompted Lincoln to develop a substitute for those revolutionary pillars that have "crumbled away."

Apparently, though the ruling passion of the Founders combined with the base passions of the people to erect a "temple of liberty," they now must be replaced with other props to support and maintain the structure of American self-government. "Reason, cold, calculating, unimpassioned reason," Lincoln declares, "must furnish all the materials for our future support and defense." Instead of passion, reason must produce a regime characterized by *general intelligence, sound morality, and, in particular, a reverence for the constitution and laws*." Van Buren also acknowledged his "unwavering reliance on the patriotism, the intelligence, and the kindness of a people who never yet deserted a public servant honestly laboring in their cause."[46] However, he offered no exposition of the pending vulnerabilities of the nation comparable to Lincoln's analysis. As a result, his call to patriotism, intelligence, and kindness lacks the gravity of Lincoln's exhortation.

Lincoln closes the penultimate paragraph of his address by extolling George Washington as the only name "revered . . . to the last." He predicts that if the American people add "reverence for the constitution and laws" to their reverence for Washington, no towering genius will be able to subvert the American establishment of self-government: "that we improved to the last; that we remained free to the last; that we revered his name to the last; [tha]t, during his long sleep, we permitted no hostile foot to pass over or desecrate [his] resting place; shall be that which to le[arn the last] trump shall awaken our WASH[INGTON]."[47] Lincoln draws from the New Testament to picture Washington's "long sleep" and "the last trump" that shall "awaken" him:

> Behold, I shew you a mystery: We shall not all sleep, but we shall all be changed, In a moment, in the twinkling of an eye, at the last trump: for the trumpet shall sound, and the dead shall be raised incorruptible, and we shall be changed. (1 Cor. 15:51-52)

> For if we believe that Jesus died and rose again, even so them also which sleep in Jesus will God bring with him. . . . For the Lord himself shall descend from heaven with a shout, with the voice of the archangel, and with the trump of God: and the dead in Christ shall rise first: Then we which are alive and remain shall be caught up together with them in the clouds to meet the Lord in the air: and so shall we ever be with the Lord." (1 Thess. 4:14, 16-17)

Washington becomes one of the "dead in Christ" who will awaken "at the last trump" (or, "with the trump of God") to see that his founding work—maintained by succeeding generations of Americans—stood the test of time. In other words, as the people "remained free to the last," they proved their mettle by frustrating the schemes of men bent on satisfying their thirst for distinction by undermining the work of the American founding.

Of course, the people would only do so by heeding Abraham Lincoln's present advice. Nevertheless, at first glance what looms largest is the message, not the messenger. But this begs a closer look at Lincoln's portrayal of the Founding "props," for does not his praise of Washington, his call for a "reverence" for the Constitution and laws, and his appeal to the patriotic and filial attachments of the nation to vivify his political religion embody a "state of feeling" that likens to passion rather than reason—a prop he regards as no longer a boon to the American regime?

Lincoln proposes that the nation adopt a "political religion," comprising "reverence for the laws." This reverence, like any other type of reverence, is not directly rational or calculating in its operation. Instead, it derives its practice from tradition and habit. For example, Lincoln asks his audience to "swear by the blood of the Revolution" to obey every law of the nation. He even states that a violation of a single law would be to "trample on the blood" of one's father. Simply telling them not to disobey any law is not enough; Lincoln must conjure up images of war and sacrifice to inspire reverent civic obedience in his audience. This does not mean that reverence is necessarily irrational or inconsistent with the dictates of reason, only that tradition and habit contribute more to its daily practice than do mere reflection and choice. By recalling the scenes of the revolution to hearten men to their duty of law-abidingness, only to conclude later that "the scenes of the revolution" are gone and can avail little or no assistance in perpetuating our free political institutions, presents an apparent contradiction that demands further examination.

Lincoln speculated that founding a self-governing regime does not ensure its perpetuation: the American founding produced a government that did not guarantee its own long-term success. But Lincoln says, "They succeeded. The experiment is successful . . ." It is ironic that the truth the Founders supposedly established, "the capability of a people to govern themselves," is the very subject at risk from mob rule. Upon investigation it appears that Lincoln intends his "political religion" to suffice for the mass of mankind, but "men of ambition and talent" remain a problem.[48] As they will seek to gratify "their ruling passion," and, therefore, not be satisfied by merely obeying laws, Lincoln must supplement his "political religion" to prevent the tyrannous exploits of those few of "the family of the lion, or the tribe of the eagle."[49]

To be sure, political religion constitutes the protection of the sheep from the rapacious wolves in their midst. As Lincoln explained during the Civil War:

> The shepherd drives the wolf from the sheep's throat, for which the sheep thanks the shepherd as a *liberator*, while the wolf denounces him for the same act as the destroyer of liberty, especially as the sheep was a black one. Plainly the sheep and the wolf are not agreed upon a definition of the word liberty; and precisely the same difference prevails to-day among us human creatures, even in the North, and all professing to love liberty.[50]

And yet, the national flock still needs a shepherd like Lincoln to ensure that the wolves do not assume the shepherd's garb in their pursuit of glory. But how can the sheep tell a real shepherd from a false one? How can the sheep identify a shepherd who will repudiate what Lincoln calls "the wolf's dictionary"? Understanding Lincoln's "towering genius" thesis is the key to understanding the relationship between "political religion" and its true preachers—especially its founder, Abraham Lincoln.

The threat of a "towering genius" is premised on the belief that this person "thirsts and burns for distinction" above all else, even moral virtue or right. In other words, for these individuals, to tower is more important than how this stature is achieved and toward what ends they are devoted. But as Harry V. Jaffa points out, true genius—the truly magnanimous man—disdains not a "beaten path" but the path of mere popular approval.[51] True genius towers by actions worthy of greatness, whether or not the people recognize them as such. Any "distinction" gained by ignoble means—for example, "at the expense of emancipating slaves [through unconstitutional means], or enslaving freemen"—even by exploring "regions hitherto unexplored," is shallow if not ignoble distinction and, therefore, not the kind of fame that satisfies the truly great-souled individual. Lincoln admits that the "loftiest genius" would "willingly, perhaps more so," acquire distinction by "doing good." Nevertheless, distinction remains the object and not necessarily the pursuit of a noble end. If all the fame attained by pursuing noble ends has been achieved, as Lincoln appears to contend through the Founders' establishment of self-government, then fame will be had by other means.

This new and peculiar danger requires a new and peculiar solution. Hence, Lincoln discovers a new region "hitherto unexplored," whereby another lofty and ambitious soul can rise nobly to the occasion to satisfy his desire for distinction while promoting the public good. In truth, the opportunity is not "past" to do good and not evil in the pursuit of glory. To frustrate the potential destroyers of the American republic, the people need someone to cultivate their general intelligence, sound morals, and a firm attachment to the government and laws—the likely product of Lincoln's counsel to unify under a common reverence for the Constitution and laws. Simply put, the people need the guidance and wisdom of an Abraham Lincoln to defend against the threat of a towering genius.[52]

When Lincoln first ran for the Illinois General Assembly in 1832, he stated that education was "the most important subject which we as a people can be engaged in." He added: "That every man may receive at least, a moderate education, and thereby be enabled to read the histories of his own and other countries, by which he may duly appreciate the value of our free institutions, appears to be an object of vital importance . . ."[53] The towering genius who makes a pretense of the people's good must be countered by an equally towering genius who really intends to secure the people's good, which Lincoln indicates here by encouraging popular education and especially knowledge of America's self-governing way of life. As the people did not themselves foresee the threat to their liberty from towering geniuses, for the people by implication are not geniuses, they must depend on those rare individuals who are a match for this threat but who will gratify their ambition by defending the people. Lincoln himself proves to be this towering but noble genius, seeing something "left to be done in the way of building up," where the towering but ignoble genius sets "boldly to the task of pulling down."[54]

The evidence that Lincoln believes such noble geniuses exist lies, paradoxically, in his depreciation of the American Founders' accomplishments: "That our government should have been maintained in its original form from its establishment until now, is not much to be wondered at." On the other hand, he had only a few paragraphs earlier extolled the sacrifices of the American revolutionaries to inspire reverence for a constitution and laws that they had established. These divergent statements show that Lincoln's purpose for praising, then diminishing, the achievements of the Founders must lie beyond the isolated statements. Had Lincoln not believed the Founders' accomplishments worthy of continuation, he would not have delivered an address entitled "The Perpetuation of Our Political Institutions."

In speaking of the self-evident truths of the Declaration of Independence in his senatorial campaign of 1858, Lincoln referred to the political philosophy of the "Wise statesmen" of the Founding as "their lofty, and wise, and noble understanding of the justice of the Creator to His creatures" and "their enlightened belief."[55] In his Lyceum Address,

Lincoln sought to reconcile the nobility of their cause with a lowered estimation of their enterprise (if his call for law-abidingness through appeals to the Founding was to succeed). Lincoln needed to show how someone could undermine even the legitimate fame of the American Founders. This would show how vulnerable their fame was to the schemes of the ambitious, and therewith the precarious footing of the American regime of popular government. If the Founders no longer received the praise and respect of a later generation of Americans, the experiment in self-government would be short-lived.

In the paragraphs describing the two props "which now are decayed, and crumbled away," Lincoln establishes the need for someone who holds such fame in contempt—because he recognizes how easily it may be subverted—in order to secure a true defense of the people without the expectation of their praise. Only this type of towering genius could forgo the ephemeral praises of the people and remain clear-sighted enough to accomplish the actual perpetuation of self-government.

As succeeding statesmen can never legitimately surpass the honors of those who established free government, their lot remains to satisfy their ambition by aiding the people to defend self-government from its enemies—enemies recognizable only to future statesmen. Herein lies their claim to fame, if only a fame worthy of if not necessarily bestowed by the people. Interestingly enough, Lincoln began his first campaign for public office in 1832 with the hope that his political accomplishments would not go unnoticed. Speaking of his own "peculiar ambition," he remarked, "I can say for one that I have no other so great as that of being truly esteemed of my fellow men, by rendering myself worthy of their esteem."[56] At the start of his 1858 campaign for the U.S. Senate, Lincoln confessed "pretending no indifference to earthly honors," but also professed "to be actuated in this contest by something higher than an anxiety for office."[57]

Finally, with respect to divine providence and the noble aspirations of mortal human beings, Lincoln praised the departed Henry Clay as the "man the times have demanded, and such, in the providence of God was given to us." He then concludes: "Let us strive to deserve, as far as mortals may, the continued care of Divine Providence, trusting that, in future national emergencies, He will not fail to provide us the instruments of safety and security."[58] Here is a prescient admission of Lincoln's own aspiration to be a like instrument in the hands of his Maker. On the way to his first presidential inauguration, he would say of himself, "I shall be most happy indeed if I shall be an humble instrument in the hands of the Almighty . . ."[59] As for the Lyceum Address, Lincoln aims to tie any future acclaim to his building up of the people. Where the American Founders established a free government, Lincoln contents himself to build upon their foundation by establishing a free people.

Now Lincoln can conclude his address by comparing the success of the American regime with "the only greater institution," the church. As the American people fortify self-government through general intelligence, sound morality, and, most important, a political religion of law-abidingness, the American nation joins the church in becoming impervious to "the gates of hell." On the way to his first inauguration as president, Lincoln likened the vigilance of the American people to the strength of the church: "When the people rise in masses in behalf of the Union and the liberties of their country, truly may it be said, 'The gates of hell shall not prevail against them.'"[60] In "the hearts of a people like yours," Lincoln reposes "the salvation of this Union." The allusion to the biblical notion of "the gates of hell" confirms the initial hypothesis of Lincoln's Lyceum Address: "As a nation of freemen, we must live through all time or die by suicide." As the "author and finisher" of its fate, the American regime will "live through all time," and, therefore, "the gates of hell shall not prevail against it," if it withstands the temptations of mob rule.

The history of the American Revolution, thus, should be read "as long as the bible shall be read," as both serve to nurture the faith and hence the obedience of their adherents. Of course, a careful reading has shown that a nation's history is only as edifying as its historians are virtuous—especially its public ones, like Lincoln and other opinion-makers who remind the community of the achievements of their forebears. Just as the church cannot survive without the aid of its divine Author and Finisher, so, too, a self-governing United States cannot perpetuate itself without its earthly "author and finisher" in the American people. While Lincoln cannot legitimately claim to be the author of the American regime, he can act as a finisher by vivifying the principles and practices of the Founding era. As a preacher of the gospel of law-abidingness, Lincoln sustains the work of the American Founding and thereby finishes or at least perfects the national faith.

In the Lyceum Address, religion plays a supporting role in the success of a republic. Simply put, seminaries and preachers serve republics by teaching church folk to be good and obey the law. Lincoln does not develop the connection between religion and the pillar of "sound morality" required for the future support of self-government. Though the connection exists, the crux of Lincoln's argument remains the promotion of law-abidingness. An explanation of the role of religion in shaping the moral character of a community would detract from the central message of obedience to the Constitution and the laws, however promoted. Furthermore, Lincoln's emphasis on the priority reason must have if America is to survive requires the subordination of religion to reason in perpetuating American self-government.

But what about the closing hyperbole in his ode to "the solid quarry of reason"? Lincoln's exhortation, that "Reason, cold, calculating, unimpassioned reason, must furnish all the materials for our future support and defence," depreciates in part the influence religion has on a republic. But this exaggerated reliance on pure reason serves to contrast the previous section, which describes the forgone pillars furnished by the passions of America's statesmen and revolutionary community. In his Temperance Address of 1842, Lincoln would tout reason with even more florid rhetoric. There it serves as an ironic critique of reason as understood by perfectionist, reform, and communitarian movements, which inflated expectations of what imperfect human beings could accomplish if only the right environment (administered by the right people) were established. For now, in frontier Illinois reeling from the Panic of 1837, Lincoln lauds reason above all as a moderating influence on a passion-stirred populace.

Lincoln's call for support from seminaries and pulpits shows that religion has a place in the public square. It has a specific public role, however, which Lincoln defines with precision: the promotion of law-abidingness. If religion were encouraged to have an unrestrained influence on free government, history shows that fanaticism in the public councils would ensue. Therefore, Lincoln finds sufficient cause to promote reason, albeit with purple prose, as the primary guide for the public mind—the last thing on the "mind" of a mob.

Gettysburg Address (1863)

Lincoln's Gettysburg Address stands out as his most famous appeal to the nation's revealed religion to invigorate the nation's civil religion. As Garry Wills observes in his thoroughgoing treatment of the address, *Lincoln at Gettysburg* (1992), Lincoln employed a "biblical vocabulary for a chosen nation's consecration and suffering and resurrection."[61] Wills, nevertheless, highlights the influence of the Transcendentalists and "rural cemetery" movement at the expense of elaborating the biblical elements of the Gettysburg Address. The interpretation that follows, therefore, will focus on the biblical imagery and allusions of Lincoln's brief but poignant eulogy to the dead at Gettysburg.

The dedication of the battlefield at Gettysburg, Pennsylvania, provided a logical venue and occasion for Lincoln to draw upon the spiritual resources of the nation. David Wills, a Gettysburg judge put in charge of burial arrangements following the July 1-3, 1863, battle, asked that Lincoln "formally set apart these grounds to their Sacred use by a few appropriate remarks."[62] Judge Wills also mentioned that Edward Everett, the famed orator and elder statesman from Massachusetts, would be the keynote speaker. Although Lincoln would not headline the event, his presence and "few appropriate remarks" would lend the dignity of the chief executive of the nation to the cemetery dedication.

Despite receiving second billing, Lincoln invited an old law partner from his Springfield days to attend the upcoming dedication. "It will be an interesting ceremony," Lincoln wrote, and he went on to invite Stephen T. Logan to "remain through the meeting of Congress" in early December, when he would send his state of the union address to Congress.[63] In addition, Lincoln made sure he arrived on time by rejecting a proposal that his trip to and from Gettysburg, Pennsylvania, be made in one day: "I do not like this arrangement. I do not wish to so go that by the slightest accident we fail entirely, and, at the best, the whole to be a mere breathless running of the gauntlet."[64] He, therefore, expected to make the most of his "few appropriate remarks" at the Gettysburg battlefield.

Lincoln begins his address with an archaic reference to the birth of the United States: "Four score and seven years ago our fathers brought forth on this continent, a new nation . . ."[65] The opening phrase, "Four score and seven years ago," recalls Psalms 90:10: "The days of our years are threescore years and ten; and if by reason of strength they be fourscore years, yet is their strength labour and sorrow; for it is soon cut off, and we fly away."[66] No lesser authorities on the art of writing than Messrs. Strunk and White puzzled over Lincoln's opening. In their minds, the less "fancy" the better, and so they thought Lincoln "knowingly or unknowingly, was flirting with disaster" in an effort to achieve "cadence."[67]

That Lincoln "knowingly" alluded to Psalms 90 can be shown by a letter he wrote when he heard that a lifelong Democrat, 105-year-old Deacon John Phillips, voted for him in 1864: "The example of such devotion to civic duties in one whose days have already extended an average life time beyond the Psalmist's limit, cannot but be valuable and fruitful."[68] What does Lincoln's allusion to Psalms 90 teach us about the "days" or longevity of the American nation?

Later in the address, Lincoln calls for "a new birth of freedom" for the United States to receive "under God" a new lease on life. Other verses from Psalms 90 offer fitting parallels to the nation's crisis:

Verse 3: "Thou turnest man to destruction; and sayest, Return, ye children of men."

Verse 7: "For we are consumed by thine anger, and by thy wrath are we troubled."

Verse 12: "So teach us to number our days, that we may apply our hearts unto wisdom."

Verse 17: ". . . establish thou the work of our hands upon us; yea, the work of our hands establish thou it."

The psalmist contrasts God's providence, comprising both the destruction and restoration of His people, with the finiteness of human beings, their brevity of life compared to grass (verse 6): "In the morning it flourisheth, and groweth up; in the evening it is cut down, and withereth." Given the unexpected duration and severity of the war, Lincoln alludes to Psalms 90 to counter the belief that the Union has run out of time, lucky to have lasted so long "beyond the Psalmist's limit" and now in the death throes of her fading glory.

Historian Don E. Fehrenbacher offers additional support for Lincoln's deliberate use of a biblical locution for time—"Four score and seven years ago"—by suggesting that Lincoln may have gleaned the opening sentence of his Gettysburg Address from a speech of Congressman Galusha A. Grow. When the 37th Congress first met in special session on July 4, 1861, the Pennsylvania congressman was elected Republican speaker of the House of Representatives. Early in his acceptance speech, Congressman Grow referred to the birth of the American nation in imagery strikingly similar to Lincoln's over two years later at Gettysburg: "Fourscore years ago fifty-six bold merchants, farmers, lawyers, and mechanics, the representatives of a few feeble colonists, scattered along the Atlantic sea-board, met in convention to found a new empire, based on the inalienable rights of man." Anticipating Lincoln's Gettysburg Address, Congressman Grow dates the nation's birth not to the ratification of the U.S. Constitution, but to the signing of the Declaration of Independence: "Seven years of bloody conflict ensued, and the 4th of July, 1776, is canonized in the hearts of the great and the good as the jubilee of oppressed nationalities; and in the calendar of heroic deeds it marks a new era in the history of the race."[69] Grow later refers to the time elapsed since the Declaration of

Independence as "Three quarters of a century," and, similar to Lincoln's allusion to Psalms 90, observes that the anniversary of July 4th occurs "after a period but little exceeding that of the allotted lifetime of man."[70] Given Lincoln's obvious desire to work with the newly elected Congress to put down the insurrection, it is quite likely that he read House Speaker Grow's speech. At Gettysburg Lincoln would adopt Grow's biblical reference to the nation's founding in a way that invested America's birth and present struggle with spiritual significance. In a speech that makes no explicit reference to the Bible or Christianity, Lincoln still manages from the outset to imbue the dedication at Gettysburg with theological import.

A few days after the Battle of Gettysburg, Lincoln spoke briefly to Union well-wishers about the birth of the nation: "How long ago is it— eighty odd years?—since on the Fourth of July for the first time in the history of the world a nation by its representatives, assembled and declared as a self-evident truth that 'all men are created equal.' That was the birthday of the United States of America." Lincoln dates the birth of the nation more precisely in a speech of July 10, 1858, during his run for the U.S. Senate: "We run our memory back over the pages of history for about eighty-two years and we discover that we were then a very small people in point of numbers . . . We find a race of men living in that day whom we claim as our fathers and grandfathers; they were iron men, they fought for the principle that they were contending for . . ."[71] On both occasions, Lincoln traced the nation's origin to the Declaration of Independence and hence to its affirmation that "all men are created equal."

In his July 7th response to serenaders celebrating the victory at Gettysburg, Lincoln refers to the Confederate forces defeated at Gettysburg as "the cohorts of those who opposed the declaration that all men are created equal." He suggests that the cause of the Civil War could somehow boil down to a disagreement over human equality and its role in the American regime. But Lincoln cut short any elaboration of his initial reflections on that momentous battle and the respective causes for which the contesting armies fought, saying, "Gentlemen, this is a glorious theme, and the occasion for a speech, but I am not prepared to make one worthy of the occasion."[72] He left that for the dedication of the Soldiers' National Cemetery at Gettysburg, Pennsylvania, on November 19, 1863.

To dedicate something is to set it apart for some sacred purpose, which makes Lincoln's reverential speech all the more fitting. Lincoln provides a definition of "dedicate" by way of the synonyms "consecrate" and "hallow." He refers to the work of the American Founders ("our fathers") in dedicating the "new nation" to human equality. But instead of simply dedicating a portion of the battlefield as a cemetery for the military dead, which is the declared purpose of the gathering, he exhorts the nation to dedicate *itself* to "the unfinished work" of the Union war effort. "We have come to dedicate a portion of that field," and "we should do this." Nevertheless, "in a larger sense, we can not dedicate—we can not consecrate—we can not hallow—this ground."

Lincoln and those in attendance "should" dedicate the grounds because those who died there deserve the honor: "It is altogether fitting and proper that we should do this." Lincoln repeats this sentiment various ways. Regarding Everett's oration and Lincoln's remarks delivered at the dedicatory ceremony, Lincoln observes, "The world will little note, nor long remember what we say here, but it can never forget what they did here." He also comments on the nobility of the efforts of the soldiers who died at the Battle of Gettysburg, which left an "unfinished work" for the living to complete. Finally, Lincoln calls the departed "these honored dead," and calls their struggle to the death on behalf of freedom "the last full measure of devotion." In short, Lincoln leaves no doubt that the dead at the Gettysburg battlefield have more than earned the memorial of November 19, 1863.

The rhetorical twist in the address, of course, is Lincoln's transition from dedicating the battlefield cemetery to dedicating himself, his listeners, and hence the nation to "the unfinished work which they who fought here have thus far so nobly advanced." Commentators have long noted the irony in Lincoln's statement that the world "will little note, nor long remember what we say here, but it can never forget what they did here." Charles Sumner, an antislavery senator from Massachusetts, remarked that Lincoln's Gettysburg Address "will live when the memory of the battle will be lost or only remembered because of the speech."[73] Even though Lincoln hopes the world will honor the dead and the cause for which they fought more so than those who commemorated it, the world will only do so—or do so for long—if the events are made memorable by the elocutions of men like Lincoln and Everett. As much as Lincoln himself appreciates the bravery and sacrifice of those "who struggled here,"[74] apparently their struggle will not in and of itself keep the memory alive for future generations. It needs a memorial in the form of words, not just a designated cemetery, that can be more easily recalled, if not memorized, than a mere record of the battle.

To no one's surprise, it is Lincoln's 272-word "remarks" that succeeding generations remember, and not Edward Everett's two-hour keynote "oration," which closely chronicled the three-day battle. In a letter written to Lincoln the day after the dedication at Gettysburg, the renowned Edward Everett acknowledged the brilliance of Lincoln's achievement: "Permit me also to express my great admiration of the thoughts expressed by you, with such eloquent simplicity & appropriateness, at the consecration of the cemetery. I should be glad, if I could flatter myself that I came as near to the central idea of the occasion, in two hours, as you did in two minutes."[75] In January the following year, Everett would ask Lincoln to send a copy of his Gettysburg Address for inclusion in a bound volume of the Gettysburg speeches for auction at the New York Sanitary Fair.[76]

Because "in a larger sense, we can not dedicate . . . this ground," Lincoln says that we should "rather . . . be dedicated here to the unfinished work" of those who fought at Gettysburg. Instead of just dedicating the field for the dead, who have already consecrated the grounds by their actions on behalf of the Union and the cause of freedom, the living should dedicate themselves to the cause of the dead. It is as if the living should now take the opportunity to prove their sincere wishes for the dead by joining in the work "which they who fought here have thus far so nobly advanced." The "great civil war," which produced the "great battlefield" at Gettysburg, now presents a "great task" for the living: "that from these honored dead we take increased devotion to that cause for which they gave the last full measure of devotion."

Lincoln first mentioned the "cause" earlier in the speech as the survival of a nation conceived in liberty and dedicated to human equality. Although Lincoln never mentions slavery, the address takes place in the year the Emancipation Proclamation took effect. Declaring that "all persons held as slaves" within the rebellious states or portions thereof "are, and henceforward shall be free," Lincoln went on to commit "the Executive government of the United States, including the military and naval authorities thereof" to "recognize and maintain the freedom of said persons."[77] With the peculiar institution in the South now an official target of the federal war effort, "sincerely believed to be an act of justice, warranted by the Constitution, upon military necessity," Lincoln understood the cause for which the federal army fought at Gettysburg to include the abolition of slavery in the rebellious states.

Reflecting on the sacrifice of the Union soldiers buried at the Gettysburg National Cemetery, those who "gave the last full measure of devotion," the nation should resolve to finish what their dear departed had begun on their behalf. In the closing sentence of his address Lincoln announces "the great task remaining before us." It was four-fold:

> "that from these honored dead we take increased devotion to that cause
> for which they gave the last full measure of devotion—
> "that we here highly resolve that these dead shall not have died in
> vain—
> "that this nation, under God, shall have a new birth of freedom—
> "and that government of the people, by the people, for the people shall
> not perish from the earth."

Lincoln first exhorts the nation to "take increased devotion" to the Union
cause. Why "increased" devotion? Unionists in the field and at home
were not unanimous in anti-slavery sentiment, especially not as a reason
for risking life, limb, and property against their southern brethren. With
the Emancipation Proclamation taking effect on January 1, 1863, a
March 1863 draft law only exacerbated the problem. Lincoln would
acknowledge in his Second Inaugural Address, "Neither anticipated that
the *cause* of the conflict might cease with, or even before, the conflict
itself should cease. Each side looked for an easier triumph, and a result
less fundamental and astounding."[78] His listeners, therefore, must take
"increased devotion" to the principle of human equality to bring the war
to a close through a Union victory. This victory would represent a
successful passage of the test of self-government's endurance. This "new
birth of freedom" would also signify a renewed commitment to human
equality—a commitment that certainly faltered in the South leading up to
the Civil War, but also showed signs of slackening in the North as a
result of the Emancipation Proclamation.

Next, Lincoln asks that the country "highly resolve that these dead
shall not have died in vain." Any person who counts the men who
"brought forth" a nation "dedicated to the proposition that all men are
created equal" as their "fathers" should shoulder the burden of securing
liberty and equality. Lincoln suggests that the cause for which the Union
soldiers died at Gettysburg was equality, and not just, as a common
slogan put it, "the Union as it was." In so doing he implies that only if
the living understand the sacrifice at Gettysburg in this light, can the
deaths of so many Union soldiers be seen as noble and not "vain." That
"for which they gave the last full measure of devotion" is the
perpetuation of self-government understood to be not only "conceived in
liberty," but also "dedicated to the proposition that all men are created
equal."

Garry Wills calls Lincoln's suggestion that Union soldiers died at
Gettysburg for the sake of equality "a giant (if benign) swindle."[79] He
argues that Lincoln was "a revolutionary" for placing the "central

proposition" of the Declaration of Independence "in a newly favored position as a principle of the Constitution."[80] For further proof, Wills cites the commentary of the Chicago *Times*, which assailed Lincoln's speech for misrepresenting the cause for which the dead at Gettysburg fought: "It was to uphold this constitution, and the Union created by it, that our officers and soldiers gave their lives at Gettysburg." Referring to the American Founders, the *Times* concluded: "They were men possessing too much self-respect to declare that negroes were their equals, or were entitled to equal privileges." Wills concludes that "Lincoln's clever assault on the constitutional past," by vivifying the letter of the Constitution with the spirit of the Declaration of Independence, was an act of re-founding that marks the Gettysburg Address as the nation's "new birth of freedom" in more ways than one.[81]

Noted Lincoln biographer and Civil War historian David Herbert Donald agrees with Wills that in the Gettysburg Address, Lincoln conjoined equality with Union as federal war aims. Unlike Wills, however, Donald was careful to note that the Chicago *Times* was "ultra-Democratic" and "strongly antiwar," and, therefore, no indifferent observer of Lincoln's war effort.[82] The *Times* had railed against Lincoln ever since his 1858 campaign against their favorite son, Democratic Senator Stephen A. Douglas. Only a month before the battle of Gettysburg, the Copperhead sentiments of *Times* editor Wilbur F. Storey led to a suspension of the newspaper by General Ambrose E. Burnside. Lincoln promptly revoked the order, but the damage was done.[83]

More important, because Wills interprets Lincoln's use of the Declaration of Independence in the Gettysburg Address as "correcting the Constitution itself without overthrowing it,"[84] he ends up confusing constitutional means with ends. By juxtaposing Union and equality as opposing federal war aims, Wills creates a false dichotomy between the goal of the war and the goal of the federal union.[85] Lincoln prosecuted the war to suppress a domestic insurrection—citizens in rebellion against their federal government. But the ultimate goal of the war was not a Union without purpose or meaning. A few days after the battle at Gettysburg, Lincoln shared this purpose with jubilant serenaders: "I would like to speak in terms of praise due to the many brave officers and soldiers who have fought in the cause of the *Union and liberties* of the country from the beginning of the war."[86] (Emphasis added.) By appending "liberties" to "Union," he reminded the nation of the purpose that the constitutional union serves.

Moreover, the liberty for which Americans fought the Revolutionary War is precisely what Lincoln interprets the Founders to have recognized as the *equal* endowment of all human beings. To say, "All men are created equal," is to declare a truth about the nature of human beings as self-governing creatures. The Declaration of Independence affirms that among the rights individuals possess by nature are "life, liberty, and the pursuit of happiness," and that "to secure these rights, governments are instituted among men." In short, Thomas Jefferson and the Second Continental Congress were careful to distinguish the rights individuals possessed by nature and the need for a government to protect the exercise of those natural rights.

Lincoln's best explication of this Jeffersonian premise of the American Founding can be found in an 1857 speech in which he criticized Senator Stephen A. Douglas's defense of the Supreme Court's *Dred Scott* decision. Taking aim at Douglas's agreement with Chief Justice Roger B. Taney's reading blacks out of the Declaration of Independence, Lincoln exclaimed:

> I think the authors of that notable instrument intended to include *all* men, but they did not intend to declare all men equal *in all respects.* They did not mean to say all were equal in color, size, intellect, moral developments, or social capacity. They defined with tolerable distinctness, in what respects they did consider all men created equal— equal in "certain inalienable rights, among which are life, liberty, and the pursuit of happiness." This they said, and this they meant.

Lincoln goes on to explain the limited intentions and authority of the Second Continental Congress in drawing up the Declaration of Independence: "They did not mean to assert the obvious untruth, that all were then actually enjoying that equality, nor yet, that they were about to confer it immediately upon them. In fact they had no power to confer such a boon. They meant simply to declare the *right*, so that the *enforcement* of it might follow as fast as circumstances should permit."[87] The last two sentences show that Lincoln understood the Declaration of Independence not to be a constitution but the reason for a constitution.

A people constitute themselves under a government for the sake of protecting their natural rights—rights that would otherwise be exposed to the wiles and wills of those of greater strength or ingenuity. A person may have the equal rights to life, liberty, or pursuit of happiness possessed by the rest of humanity, but those rights remain insecure unless a social contract establishes a safe arena for their exercise.

A note containing Lincoln's thoughts on the connection between the American union and individual liberty offers a telling description of the principle of equality that informed Lincoln's political philosophy. Lincoln wrote that "the principle of 'Liberty to all,'" expressed in the self-evident truth of the Declaration of Independence that "All men are created equal," was "the primary cause of our great prosperity." He thought that the American colonists could have declared independence from England without that principle, "but *without* it, we could not, I think, have secured our free government, and consequent prosperity." Lincoln distinguishes "independence" from "our free government, and consequent prosperity" to point out that separation from Great Britain would not have prospered the American people unless they had established their new government on the principle of human equality. Without freedom as the goal—government by the consent of the governed—"our fathers" would not have fought for "a mere change of masters."[88] What Lincoln called "a philosophical cause" was the very heart of American self-government.

Alluding to Proverbs 25:11—"A word fitly spoken is like apples of gold in pictures of silver"—Lincoln adds: "The assertion of that *principle*, at *that time*, was *the* word, *'fitly spoken'* which has proved an 'apple of gold' to us. The *Union*, and the *Constitution*, are the *picture* of *silver*, subsequently framed around it. The picture was made, not to *conceal*, or *destroy* the apple; but to *adorn*, and *preserve* it. The *picture* was made *for* the apple—*not* the apple for the picture." On December 30, 1860, president-elect Lincoln received a letter from an anxious Alexander Stephens, who had spoken against secession (to no avail) in his home state of Georgia and would nevertheless be elected vice president of the Confederate States of America. He asked Lincoln to "do what you can to save our common country," and added, "A word fitly spoken by you now would be like 'apples of gold in pictures of silver.'"[89] Lincoln's repeated emphases of words and phrases in his note on constitutional union and liberty, especially in reference to Proverbs 25:11, shows that he believed the word fitly spoken had already been uttered—in the Declaration of Independence. All Lincoln could do was to point the nation back to it as a way of moving forward so that "neither *picture*, or *apple* shall ever be blurred, or bruised or broken."

He expressed this understanding of American self-government en route to his first inauguration as president: "I am exceedingly anxious that this Union, the Constitution, and the liberties of the people shall be perpetuated in accordance with the original idea for which that struggle was made . . ."[90] The "original idea" for Lincoln was always the self-evident truth of the equal rights of humanity as expressed in the Declaration of Independence. He repeated this sentiment the next day at Independence Hall in Philadelphia, Pennsylvania, when he remarked that "all the political sentiments I entertain have been drawn, so far as I have been able to draw them, from the sentiments which originated, and were given to the world from this hall in which we stand. I have never had a feeling politically that did not spring from the sentiments embodied in the Declaration of Independence."[91]

Two years earlier, Lincoln's court schedule in Bloomington, Illinois, obliged him to turn down an invitation to speak at a Republican festival in Boston celebrating the birthday of Thomas Jefferson. Even though he lost his 1858 campaign to unseat Senator Stephen Douglas, his debates with Douglas brought him fame throughout Illinois and the northeast, as well as many an invitation to speak.[92] Expressing his regrets, which were soon reprinted in Republican newspapers, Lincoln portrayed the Republican Party as the true political heir of Thomas Jefferson. He added, "But soberly, it is now no child's play to save the principles of Jefferson from total overthrow in this nation." Lincoln called these principles "the definitions and axioms of free society," and worried aloud over their depreciation by some Democrats as "glittering generalities," or worse, "self-evident lies" that could only be true for "superior races." He closed with rousing praise for the author of the Declaration of Independence:

> All honor to Jefferson—to the man who, in the concrete pressure of a struggle for national independence by a single people, had the coolness, forecast, and capacity to introduce into a merely revolutionary document, an abstract truth, applicable to all men at all times, and so to embalm it there, that to-day, and in all coming days, it shall be a rebuke and a stumbling-block to the very harbingers of re-appearing tyranny and oppression.[93]

As president, Lincoln soon found himself playing a similar role as Jefferson: leading the nation "in the concrete pressure of a struggle," if not for "national independence," for national survival against the forces of secession. He would do so by holding fast to the "abstract truth" of human equality.

On the way to his first presidential inauguration, and a day before his Independence Hall speech, Lincoln spoke to the mayor and citizens of Philadelphia: "All my political warfare has been in favor of the teachings coming forth from that sacred hall. May my right hand forget its cunning and my tongue cleave to the roof of my mouth, if ever I prove false to those teachings."[94] Here he quotes Psalms 137:5-6: "If I forget thee, O Jerusalem, let my right hand forget her cunning. If I do not remember thee, let my tongue cleave to the roof of my mouth; if I prefer not Jerusalem above my chief joy." The psalmist recounts Israel's lament while in captivity in Babylon. Seven states seceded to form the

Confederate States of America as Lincoln made his way to the nation's capital for his inauguration, but Lincoln did not consider the United States falling yet into the ways of a modern-day Babylon. The nation as a whole had not renounced the American Founders' vision of a self-governing nation based on the principle of human equality. Lincoln's reference to Old Testament Israel's singing the Lord's song in a strange land (Ps. 137:4), therefore, is not a political prophecy, but rather an expression of his pious devotion to the original understanding of American self-government. By saying, "I shall do nothing inconsistent with the teachings of those holy and most sacred walls," and employing a biblical allusion, he turns Independence Hall into a "sacred hall" of civil and religious liberty. He thereby fostered a civil religion that calls for reverence of the nation's political principles.

Lincoln explains to the mayor of Philadelphia that if he could tarry there just a while longer, he would "listen to those breathings rising within the consecrated walls where the Constitution of the United States, and, I will add, the Declaration of American Independence was originally framed." With the nation dividing over the future of slavery, Lincoln inserts "American" when referring to the Declaration of Independence to remind the country that its political prosperity depends on their remaining one United States of America. As the incoming president, he did not wish to give any implicit justification for crude declarations of independence by groups of individuals in the southern states.

A Union victory hastened by the renewed efforts of listeners inspired by Lincoln's Gettysburg Address will result only from the actions of those determined not to let self-government die at the hands of what can now be deemed political unbelievers. The Union cause must win, not only to prove the practicality of the American experiment in self-government, but also to hold out the promise that "any nation so conceived and so dedicated, can long endure." As he stated in his 1861 address to Congress in special session: "And this issue embraces more than the fate of these United States. It presents to the whole family of man, the question, whether a constitutional republic, or a democracy—a government of the people, by the same people—can, or cannot, maintain its territorial integrity, against its own domestic foes."[95] By showing that an appeal from the ballot to the bullet,[96] as Lincoln understood rebellious citizens in the southern states to have done, would only prove fruitless, he hopes to demonstrate that the "new birth of freedom" stands a good—nay, the best—chance of producing a government "of the people, by the people, for the people" that "shall not perish from the earth." If this is not a "great task," Lincoln does not know what is.

But this cannot take place without divine assistance. Lincoln does not presume that the determinations of mere mortals can guarantee the success of this "great task" that remains for the American citizenry. "So true is it," Lincoln wrote in 1864, "that man proposes, and God disposes."[97] Similarly, Lincoln appeals to divine providence in the final sentence of his Gettysburg Address—"that this nation, under God, shall have a new birth of freedom"—as a reminder that the nation's best efforts still need the approbation of the Almighty for eventual success. The death of Union soldiers, interpreted as an expression of the fullest devotion to the cause of equal human liberty, can result in "a new birth of freedom" if the living adopt the same motive for siding with the Union in the Civil War.

Associate Justice Clarence Thomas called the "Dedicatory Remarks" at Gettysburg Lincoln's "Great Commission."[98] They evoke a religious spirit that is difficult to miss. This is all the more remarkable for their lack of direct biblical references. He mentions "God" only once, and there is considerable debate as to whether he inserted the reference in the final draft of the speech, or while he listened to Everett's oration, or even as he delivered the famous last sentence of his own address. Nevertheless, his was no simple or crude appeal to a national civil religion. Lincoln displayed an uncanny ability to meet the solemnity of the occasion with a panegyric calling forth the Christian sensibilities of his audience.

Abraham Lincoln interpreted the Civil War, the Battle of Gettysburg, and the sacrifices of the dead through a biblical ethos. He hoped to inspire his listeners to continue fighting for the high cause of securing, under divine providence, the equal rights of human liberty—the bedrock principle upon which a free people establishes government. With all thoughts fixed on the death of loved ones, comrades in arms, and fellow citizens, Lincoln at Gettysburg draws attention to the departed in an effort to renew the resolve of the living to a course of action that gives the national life meaning. For the nation to experience "a new birth of freedom," the American people under the smiles of heaven must be its author.

First Inaugural Address (1861)

In addition to appealing to religion for support of the American system of government, Lincoln also made frequent reference to providence as an immanent guide to "this-worldly" human action. No event required his greatest effort in this regard than his first inauguration as president.[99]

Lincoln appeals to religion in the First Inaugural Address most explicitly in the closing paragraphs, where he focuses on the reaction of his audience to his preceding argument. He asks, "Why should there not be a patient confidence in the ultimate justice of the people?"[100] This follows his earlier defense of the Constitution as offering the best hope for those who wish to maintain self-government, even "where the moral sense of the people imperfectly supports the law itself." There Lincoln cites opposing constitutional issues dealing with slavery—"the fugitive slave clause of the Constitution, and the law for the suppression of the foreign slave trade"—to make a connection between the moral sense of the community and the words of the U.S. Constitution: "The great body of the people abide by the dry legal obligation in both cases, and a few break over in each. This, I think, cannot be perfectly cured . . ."[101] He continues, "Is there any better, or equal hope, in the world?" Lincoln suggests that a constitutional regime, despite the occasional lapses it cannot cure in the people, remains the best practical means of preserving their liberties. For Lincoln, whoever rejects constitutional government "does, of necessity, fly to anarchy or to despotism."[102]

He concludes this paragraph by commenting on the judgment of God as it involves the opposing states of the Union: "If the Almighty Ruler of nations, with his eternal truth and justice, be on your side of the North, or on yours of the South, that truth, and that justice, will surely prevail, *by the judgment of this great tribunal, the American people.*" (Emphasis added.) Lincoln believes that a God of truth and justice will avail himself of human agency to accomplish His purposes as those same humans act according to their understanding of what His truth and justice is. After meeting with a synod comprising loyal, New School Presbyterians, Lincoln shared, "He could only do his duty by the assistance of God and *the means which He has supplied, of which the reverend gentlemen around him were noble examples.*"[103] (Emphasis added.) To be sure, the action or inaction of human beings can scarcely hinder their Maker. Nevertheless, Lincoln believes that if God favors either side of the American conflict, His truth and His justice will manifest itself as the American people resolve their differences within the constitutional structure of the Union.

Lincoln seeks to manifest God's will through the just intentions and actions of the American people. By linking providence with the actions of the opposing sides of the Union, each having "faith in being in the right," he points not only to the justice of God but to the significance of political action by those who seek to carry out God's justice. This likens to the Old Testament model that King Jehoshaphat set for his governors: "And he set judges in the land throughout all the fenced cities of Judah, city by city, And said to the judges, Take heed what ye do: for ye judge not for man, but for the Lord, *who is with you in the judgment.* Wherefore now let the fear of the Lord be upon you; take heed and do it . . ." (2 Chron. 19:5-7a; emphasis added). Worldly justice will bear the mark of divine approbation as individuals take political action with pious humility.

Lincoln expressed the same sentiment in an address to the New York legislature as he was making his way to the nation's capital for his first inauguration:

> In the mean time, if we have patience; if we restrain ourselves; if we allow ourselves not to run off in a passion, I still have confidence that the Almighty, the Maker of the Universe will, *through the instrumentality of this great and intelligent people*, bring us through this as He has through all the other difficulties of our country.[104] (Emphasis added.)

This, of course, begs the question of what God's justice is. In Lincoln's mind, given the inscrutableness of the will of God, one does well to exercise "a patient confidence" in pursuit of this good. Lincoln can still call the American people to judge as a "great tribunal," while reminding them implicitly that their judgment must be tempered by respect for a God who may favor the policies of one's rivals.[105] While human judgment in the First Inaugural Address serves to manifest God's superintending work, that judgment or political action is essential for those who claim to secure the will of God in their country.

Glen E. Thurow interprets Lincoln as not simply equating "the voice of the people" with "the voice of God." However, Thurow asks, "is it surprising that Lincoln asserts the people will decide justly when it is Lincoln who is in a position to lead and guide them? Would he have said the same thing had he lost the election?"[106] He thereby suggests that Lincoln believed the American people to speak (or vote) with the voice of God only when Lincoln was in office. But this contradicts both Lincoln's humility and direct statements on the subject. As an incumbent state legislator, Lincoln included the following statement in his party's newspaper when he ran for re-election: "While acting as their representative, *I shall be governed by their will,* on all subjects upon which I have the means of knowing what their will is; and upon all others, I shall do what my own judgment teaches me will best advance their interests."[107] Even in his First Inaugural Address, Lincoln asks, "In our present differences, is either party without faith of being in the right?" He goes on to suggest that providence, "with his eternal truth and justice," will ultimately weigh into the conflict and produce justice through the very contest of public opinions.[108] Thus, while Lincoln does not categorically equate popular opinion with the will of God, he also does not presume that equation whenever the public agrees with him.

The next two paragraphs, each just one sentence, continue this theme but emphasize the role of both moderation and conviction in the pursuit of justice:

> By the frame of the government under which we live, this same people have wisely given their public servants but little power for mischief; and have, with equal wisdom, provided for the return of that little to their own hands at very short intervals.
>
> While the people retain their virtue, and vigilence, no administration, by any extreme of wickedness or folly, can very seriously injure the government, in the short space of four years.[109]

Lincoln again focuses on the actions of the people, and especially the wisdom of constituting their government with limited powers exercised for a limited duration. Animated by a people vigilant over their government, a self-governing regime offers the best hope for peaceful and lasting government under God.

This idea of constitutional self-government under the beneficence of God stands as a running theme for Lincoln. A chief example is his well-known reference to the American people as God's "almost chosen people," which he made in an address to the New Jersey Senate as he was traveling to his first presidential inauguration. In relating the early revolutionary efforts of New Jersey to his present objective as president-elect, Lincoln remarks, "I shall be most happy indeed if I shall be an humble instrument in the hands of the Almighty, and of this, his almost chosen people, for perpetuating the object of that great struggle."[110] Here he provides a political parallel for the biblical representative of God's will, the Hebrew nation. But where the Jews of the Old Testament were chosen by God to be a spiritual "light unto the nations," Lincoln suggests that the American people could very well be God's elect to offer political light unto the world.

To take an obvious example, Lincoln saw the existence of slavery in a self-governing nation as contrary to divine intention:

> We [northerners] think Slavery a great moral wrong, and while we do not claim the right to touch it where it exists, we wish to treat it as a

wrong in the Territories, where our votes will reach it. We think that a respect for ourselves, a regard for future generations and for the God that made us, require that we put down this wrong where our votes will properly reach it.[111]

That the injustice of slavery would "require" men to treat it as "a great, moral wrong" follows the Declaration of Independence as it called Americans to revolt from despotic government not only out of "right" but out of "duty."[112] In another reflection on the basis of self-government found in the Declaration of Independence, Lincoln said:

> This was their majestic interpretation of the economy of the Universe. This was their lofty, and wise, and noble understanding of the justice of the Creator to His creatures. Yes, gentlemen, to *all* His creatures, to the whole great family of man. In their enlightened belief, nothing stamped with the Divine image and likeness was sent into the world to be trodden on, and degraded, and imbruted by its fellows.[113]

He would say just one month later, "Our reliance is in the *love of liberty* which God has placed in our bosoms."[114]

Lincoln does not substitute the American people for the biblical chosen. He calls them God's "almost" chosen people, at minimum respecting the religious sensibilities of Jewish Americans. In a political sense, moreover, the American people could only be God's "chosen" if they succeeded in perpetuating "this Union, the Constitution, and the liberties of the people" according to "the original idea for which that struggle was made": an idea "that held out a great promise to all the people of the world to all time to come."[115] With the nation divided over slavery, Lincoln could scarcely call them God's chosen people without qualification. Recall the Old Testament promise to Abram, the original "chosen" one: "And I will make thee a great nation, and I will bless thee, and make thy name great; and thou shalt be a blessing: And I will bless them that bless thee, and curse him that curseth thee: and in thee shall all families of the earth be blessed" (Gen. 12:2-3). Lincoln hoped to be the instrument of God and the American people in leading them to secure the principle of human equality for themselves and hence for mankind, thereby blessing all the families or nations of the earth.

Before the Senate of New Jersey, a state that split its electoral college votes between Stephen Douglas and himself,[116] Lincoln goes on to develop the requirements for self-government:

> I learn that this body is composed of a majority of gentlemen who, in the exercise of their best judgment in the choice of a Chief Magistrate, did not think I was the man. I understand, nevertheless, that they came

forward here to greet me as the *constitutional* President of the United States—as citizens of the United States, to meet the man who, for the time being, is the representative man of the nation, united by a purpose to perpetuate the Union and liberties of the people. As such, I accept this reception more gratefully than I could do did I believe it was tendered to me as an individual.[117] (Emphasis added.)

Lincoln affirms the majority's votes for Douglas as following from "their best judgment" and hence worthy of respect. Although Lincoln did not receive all of their state's electoral college votes, he acknowledges that differences of opinion are to be expected in politics and are especially not to be condemned by those who win.[118] The votes of the people must be considered by all as faithfully cast and, therefore, faithfully to be respected, regardless of who wins or loses.

This leads to his next point: even though the majority of the New Jersey state senators voted for a man who eventually lost the election, they abided by the results of the election and paid deference to President-elect Lincoln. Lincoln does not take for granted that a great portion of his audience were not "sore losers." Lincoln could think of no greater proof of the practical demonstration of self-government than being hosted at a reception of men who did not vote for him. Their peaceful submission to "the *constitutional* President of the United States" (emphasis added), unlike the armed aggression of southern citizens he sought to resist, shows an adherence to the rule of law and the principle of majority rule necessary for the successful perpetuation of a republican government. For this, Lincoln accepts their reception "more gratefully than I could do did I believe it was tendered to me as an individual."

Republics rise or fall on the principle that elections must produce neither sore losers nor spiteful winners. As Lincoln put it to a Republican congressman from Pennsylvania:

We have just carried an election on principles fairly stated to the people. Now we are told in advance, the government shall be broken up, unless we surrender to those we have beaten, before we take the offices. . . . [I]f we surrender, it is the end of us and of the government. They will repeat the experiment upon us *ad libitum*.[119]

Lincoln would restate this principle in his First Inaugural Address: "If the minority will not acquiesce, the majority must, or the government must cease. There is no other alternative; for continuing the government, is acquiescence on one side or the other."[120]

On the other hand, the victor in a constitutional election must consider, as Lincoln did, all of the electorate his constituents. Lincoln's most explicit profession of this idea was published in a political advertisement from his 1836 campaign for a second term in the Illinois House of Representatives: "If elected, I shall consider the whole people of Sangamon my constituents, as well those that oppose, as those that support me."[121] By further observing that his tenure as president would only be "for the time being," Lincoln graces his electoral victory with the political moderation or humility he thinks necessary for the perpetuation of a regime wholly reliant on active participation—which means judgment—by the people at large.

Without knowing the entire will of God, Lincoln charts a course for the country between the political paralysis of pious resignation and the jeremiads of the self-righteous. The former leads to the accident and force that befalls those who choose not to act, while the latter identify their cause as God's cause to the detriment of deliberative politics. The third paragraph from the end of his First Inaugural Address expresses his hope. Following another call for patience—"Nothing valuable can be lost by taking time"—and moderation—"If there be an object to *hurry* any of you, in hot haste, to a step which you would never take *deliberately*, that object will be frustrated by taking time; but no good object can be frustrated by it"—he states: "If it were admitted that you who are dissatisfied, hold the right side in the dispute, there still is no single good reason for precipitate action. Intelligence, patriotism, Christianity, and a firm reliance on Him, who has never yet forsaken this favored land, are still competent to adjust, in the best way, all our present difficulty."[122] Lincoln repeats the theme of the preceding paragraphs, referring explicitly to Christianity and a reliance on God as part of the successful American experiment in republican government. He also adds "intelligence" and "patriotism," which recalls his Lyceum Address of 1838, wherein he exhorted Americans to forge new pillars for the republic out of "general intelligence" and "a reverence for the constitution and laws."[123] Lincoln cites the natural and the supernatural, one's worldly intellect and otherworldly faith, as proven and divinely ordained means of solving the nation's problems.

Following this reference to earthly action and heavenly reflection, he concludes in the next (and penultimate) paragraph that responsibility for any imminent civil war lies with his "dissatisfied fellow countrymen" and not with the incoming administration. The federal government will not strike the first blow, as Lincoln aims only to "preserve, protect and defend" it. This reference to the presidential oath of office places the discussion of culpability in the context of piety: "*You* have no oath registered in Heaven," Lincoln charges, "to destroy the government, while *I* shall have the most solemn one to 'preserve, protect and defend' it."[124] This contrast of religious integrity highlights both the earthly duty to abide by one's word—in this case, to abide by the Constitution—as well as to fulfill one's pledge to God. By using an oath as a measure for determining just action, Lincoln shows that his actions as president will fulfill the natural expectation of one who takes his oaths seriously.

On the other hand, any action to destroy the federal government represents not only an earthly breach of contract but also a gross affront to a just God. Lincoln gave his clearest statement on this subject in an 1864 newspaper article he entitled "The President's Last, Shortest, and Best Speech": "I am not much of a judge of religion, but that, in my opinion, the religion that sets men to rebel and fight against their government, because, as they think, that government does not sufficiently help *some* men to eat their bread in the sweat of *other* men's faces, is not the sort of religion upon which people can get to heaven!"[125] As the duly elected president, Lincoln has a constitutional and sworn obligation to defend the nation. Those seeking to undermine this obligation, therefore, stand as lawless aggressors before God and the American people. Again, Lincoln's running argument on behalf of constitutional government favors both earthly and heavenly justice, while incriminating those who would renege on their obligation to their fellow citizens as well as presume upon the expectation of a just God.[126] Without a constitutional oath, which seals the acceptance of a responsibility delegated by the citizenry, those in rebellion have no pressing requirement to do anything but obey the constitutional powers that be.

Lincoln's original draft of his First Inaugural Address did not include what became the concluding paragraph. He added a paragraph written by William H. Seward, his Secretary of State, with a few noteworthy emendations. Seward's text and his corrections read as follows:

> I close. We are not we must not be aliens or enemies but ~~countrym~~ fellow countrymen and brethren. Although passion has strained our bonds of affection too hardly they must not ~~be broken they will not~~, I am sure they will not be broken. The mystic chords which proceeding from ~~every ba~~ so many battlefields and ~~patriot~~ so many patriot graves ~~bind~~ pass through all the hearts and ~~hearths~~ all the hearths in this broad continent of ours will yet ~~harmon~~ again harmonize in their ancient music when ~~touched as they surely~~ breathed upon ~~again~~ by the ~~better angel~~ guardian angel of the nation.[127]

Lincoln edited the new paragraph to read as follows:

> I am loth to close. We are not enemies, but friends. We must not be enemies. Though passion may have strained, it must not break our

bonds of affection. The mystic chords of memory, stretching from every battle-field, and patriot grave, to every living heart and hearthstone, all over this broad land, will yet swell the chorus of the Union, when again touched, as surely they will be, by the better angels of our nature.[128]

A comparison of these two paragraphs illustrates the importance Lincoln placed on the nation's capacity to rise to the challenge set before them as opposed to a passive expectation of the intervention of God on behalf of those who see themselves and their cause as righteous.

Beginning with the first sentence, Lincoln chooses not to begin the concluding paragraph of his address with the solemn, "I close." While the somberness of the occasion and impending crisis may have called for a terse announcement of the end of his address, Lincoln wished to express his reluctance to end on a note that finds the country still divided. To be sure, the preceding paragraph identified Lincoln's "dissatisfied fellow countrymen" as the culprits if a civil war broke out: it is *their* "hands" that will decide, *they* would be the "aggressors," and any action against the federal government would be *their* attempt to "destroy the government." Following this unflattering portrait of his rebellious countrymen, any closing comment by Lincoln must serve at least to lessen the adversarial tone of the penultimate paragraph. He, therefore, concludes with an appeal to the rebellious states not as potential enemies but as present, and he hopes future, friends.

Nevertheless, keeping southerners as friends depends on persuading them that the nation's first Republican president intends them no harm— the central thesis of the First Inaugural Address. Lincoln is "loth to close," as the end of his address would mean (rhetorically, as least) the end of his singular attempt to persuade, to befriend, his dissatisfied brethren at the beginning of his presidential tenure. One would be wary to finish a conversation intended on mending differences with others if one were unsure of the success of the attempt. Lincoln conveys a sense of hopeful hesitancy. He wants to assure southern loyalists that although differences exist, these should not be allowed to disturb what affinity had formerly existed. As he has called them not to act rashly, he follows his own advice by not concluding his address too hastily.

The brevity of Lincoln's next two sentences, in place of Seward's long-winded sentence, emphasizes the gravity of any state's decision to rebel from the Union. After a lengthy and detailed explanation of the forthcoming Republican administration of the United States, Lincoln summarizes his intentions by moving from prospective policy to present identity: "We are not enemies, but friends. We must not be enemies."

The present fruits of friendship, scarce as they may appear to those defeated in the recent national election, must be seen as too good to hazard a future as enemies. Lincoln already explained this when he pointed out how those who seek greater enforcement of the fugitive slave clause of the Constitution, or of the foreign slave trade prohibition, would find it more difficult upon the break up of the Union: "Can aliens make treaties easier than friends can make laws? Can treaties be more faithfully enforced between aliens than laws can among friends?"[129] The bottom-line for Lincoln? "We must not be enemies." This outcome would cast serious doubt upon the possibility of self-government, a theme Lincoln expounded throughout his public career.

Lincoln then revisits a theme of the Lyceum Address: the tension between reason and passion. Where Seward states emphatically that "passion *has* strained our bonds of affection too hardly," Lincoln qualifies this judgment by saying, "Though passion *may have* strained, it must not break our bonds of affection." (Emphases added.) Lincoln has already made his case against rebellious southerners in the central arguments of his address and thus concludes on a more ambivalent but hopeful and conciliatory note. His concern lies rather with the future conduct of the separating and separated citizens of the Union: how they will choose to act, now that they have heard the intentions and plans of the incoming administration.

The final sentence of the Inaugural Address presents the listener with Lincoln's parting message on the issue that divides the country. Like the preceding sentences of the concluding paragraph, Lincoln keeps for the most part Seward's suggestion. Significantly, though, Lincoln amends it to focus entirely on the action his listeners must take and not that of a divine being or supernatural force: "The mystic chords of memory . . . will yet swell the chorus of the Union, when again touched, as surely they will be, by the better angels of our nature." By replacing "the guardian angel of the nation" with "the better angels of our nature," he places the burden of America's prosperity not upon divine intervention but with the will of each soul who hears or reads his speech.

In an 1863 letter written for a gathering of Union supporters in Springfield, Illinois, Lincoln briefly described the dual nature of man's responsibility before God: "Let us diligently apply the means, never doubting that a just God, in his own good time, will give us the right result."[130] Lincoln has already appealed in his First Inaugural Address to "the Almighty Ruler of nations," "Christianity," and "a firm reliance on Him, who has never yet forsaken this favored land." Having already referred to the Creator as desirous for men to be self-governing, Lincoln concludes his First Inaugural Address with a reminder of the citizenry's "this-worldly" responsibility for the future course of the nation. Ben Franklin may have originated the aphorism, "God helps those who help themselves," but no American statesman ever staked as much political success on its practical truth as Abraham Lincoln.[131]

*   *   *   *   *

Two years after President Zachary Taylor died in office, Lincoln campaigned as a presidential elector for the new Whig candidate, General Winfield Scott. During the 1852 campaign, Lincoln responded to a comment of Stephen Douglas regarding the role of providence in politics:

> But Judge Douglas alluding to the death of General Taylor says it was the hand of Providence which saved us from our first and only military administration. This reminds me of Judge Douglas' so much wanted [vaunted?] confidence in the people. The people had elected Gen. Taylor; and, as is appointed to all men once to do, he died. Douglas chooses to consider this a special interference of Providence, against the people, and in favor of Locofocoism."[132]

Lincoln points out the error of blithely interpreting worldly events as the expression of God's will for or against a particular public policy. He reminds his listeners that all men will die eventually, not merely those who are alleged to oppose the will of God. Hebrews 9:27 reads: "And as it is appointed unto men once to die, but after this the judgment." Lincoln concludes that Douglas's trust in the people "seems to go no farther than this, that they may be safely trusted with their own affairs, provided Providence retains, and exercises a sort of veto upon their acts . . ." Douglas thinks of providence as a cosmic second-guesser, Lincoln argues, whenever the people vote for a candidate "contrary to the dictation of a democratic [i.e., Democratic Party] convention." Were the Whig candidate to win the presidential election, Lincoln comments, "I much doubt if we do not perceive a slight abatement in Judge Douglas' confidence in Providence, as well as in the people."

This is not to say that Lincoln ruled out the hand of providence in President Taylor's or any man's death. In fact, two weeks after Taylor's death, Lincoln delivered a eulogy that invoked providence as working of its own accord as well as through the actions of the people:

> I fear the one *great* question of the day, is not now so likely to be partially acquiesced in by the different sections of the Union, as it

would have been, could Gen. Taylor have been spared to us. Yet, under all circumstances, trusting to our Maker, and through his wisdom and beneficence, to the great body of our people, we will not despair, nor despond.[133]

Here Lincoln implies that "our Maker," for reasons unknown, "spared" not President Taylor. But one could not discern, as Stephen Douglas would claim two years hence, any sign of God's intention for resolving the growing crisis over sectionalism and slavery.

Lincoln disclosed another aspect of his understanding of providence in an 1843 campaign circular to Illinois Whigs. Remonstrating against the late Whig habit of supporting like-minded candidates of the opposing party, Lincoln exclaimed: "If it be the will of Heaven that such men shall politically live, be it so, but never, never again permit them to draw a particle of their sustenance from us."[134] While acknowledging that God sets the ultimate courses of human beings, he also affirms a person's ability this side of the grave to order his actions according to his own best judgment.

Lincoln's most explicit pronouncement on the will of God with respect to the cause of the Union during the Civil War appears in the conclusion of his 1862 Annual Message to Congress. It came only ten weeks after the most controversial action of his administration, the Emancipation Proclamation (announced on September 22, 1862, to take effect on January 1, 1863). In the preliminary Emancipation Proclamation, he declared that on January 1, 1863, "all persons held as slaves within any state, or designated part of a state, the people whereof shall then be in rebellion against the United States shall be then, thenceforward, and forever free . . ."[135] What he will describe in the Final Emancipation Proclamation of 1863 as "a fit and necessary war measure,"[136] Lincoln extols in his 1862 Annual Address to Congress as a sure means of ending the Civil War. Referring to the emancipation decree and his proposed constitutional amendments regarding state emancipation and colonization of free blacks, he declares:

> We know how to save the Union. The world knows we do know how to save it. We—even *we here*—hold the power, and bear the responsibility. In *giving* freedom to the *slave*, we *assure* freedom to the *free*—honorable alike in what we give, and what we preserve. We shall nobly save, or meanly lose, the last, best hope of earth.[137]

Here, saving the Union means not only a federal victory over southern secession forces, but also the perpetuation of American self-government without slavery. What is most striking is not the certainty with which he recommends these war measures and amendments to Congress, but the certainty with which he recommends them to the approval of God. His concluding sentence, which follows immediately upon the previous citation, states: "Other means may succeed; this could not fail. The way is plain, peaceful, generous, just—a way which, if followed, the world will forever applaud, *and God must forever bless.*" (Emphasis added.) Not only does Lincoln believe that nations will praise the goodness of his recommendations, but God could not do otherwise!

Shortly after the Emancipation Proclamation, Lincoln responded to a letter from the Religious Society of Friends in the State of Iowa: "I am conscious of no desire for my country's welfare, that is not in consonance with His will, and of no plan upon which we may not ask His blessing."[138] This sentence lays great stress on godly confirmation of the dictates of human reason. Just as future generations will recognize the merits of Lincoln's proposal, the working of providence will—in coordination with a Congress agreeable to Lincoln's suggestions— "bless" or prosper the proposals. As Lincoln put it one year before his election to the presidency:

> "Our position," says Mr. L., "is right—our principles are good and just, but I would desire to impress on every Republican present to have patience and steadiness under all circumstances—whether defeated or successful. But I do hope that as there is a just and righteous God in Heaven, our principles will and shall prevail sooner or later."[139]

Lincoln had begun his 1862 Annual Address to Congress by acknowledging the "health and bountiful harvests" the country had seen. In the previous year's address to Congress, Lincoln also began by acknowledging that they had "cause of great gratitude to God for unusual good health, and most abundant harvests," especially since they were in "the midst of unprecedented political troubles."[140] Now a year later, Lincoln calls attention to the continued aid of providence and exhorts the Congress to "press on, guided by the best light He gives us, trusting that in His own good time, and wise way, all will yet be well." This hopeful introduction and the bold conclusion mentioned above reflect the strength of Lincoln's conviction that the cause of the Union, now fortified by a federal commitment to emancipation, must find favor with the Almighty.[141] While victory in the war will come "in His own good time, and wise way" (over two years later and with much more sacrifice), God cannot but approve federal measures conducive of freedom. Lincoln's explicit statement of what God "must" do in response to certain actions by an earthly government lends great weight to the premise of his original thesis as espoused in his Lyceum Address of 1838: under the favor of a divine superintending being, citizens can use their reason to direct the course of their community and nation, with religion playing a supporting role.

Lincoln took care in appealing to revealed religion for political purposes in a speech delivered two months before his nomination for president: "Public opinion at the South regards slaves as property and insists upon treating them like other property." He adds: "On the other hand, the free states carry on their government on the principle of the equality of men. We think slavery is morally wrong, and a direct violation of that principle. We *all* think it wrong. It is clearly proved, I think, by natural theology, apart from revelation."[142] Lincoln makes clear his opinion that the evil of slavery need not be determined necessarily, and especially not sufficiently, by the authority of the Bible or any other religious text. He expressed a like sentiment when responding to resolutions presented by a religious committee supportive of his war policies in 1864. Reflecting on "the effective and almost unanamous [*sic*] support which the Christian communities are so zealously giving to the country, and to liberty," he comments, "it is difficult to conceive how it could be otherwise with one professing christianity, *or even having ordinary perceptions of right and wrong.*"[143] (Emphasis added.)

Of course, there is his most explicit reflection on the Bible and slavery:

> The sum of pro-slavery theology seems to be this: "Slavery is not universally *right*, nor yet universally *wrong*; it is better for *some* people to be slaves; and, in such cases, it is the Will of God that they be such.
>
> Certainly there is no contending against the Will of God; but still there is some difficulty in ascertaining, and applying it, to particular cases. For instance we will suppose the Rev. Dr. Ross has a slave named Sambo, and the question is 'Is it the Will of God that Sambo shall remain a slave, or be set free?' The Almighty gives no audable answer to the question, and his revelation—the Bible—gives none—or, at most, none but such as admits of a squabble to it's [*sic*] meaning.[144]

While Lincoln did not share this last reflection publicly, it contains the kernel of his belief that arguments against slavery based simply on the Bible would not suffice in the political arena. With men like the Reverend Frederick A. Ross, who in 1857 authored *Slavery Ordained of God*, one sees the futility in appealing to a sacred text that is open to conflicting interpretations. Even when Lincoln said, "Our reliance is in the *love of liberty* which God has placed in our bosoms,"[145] he did so to highlight the innate freedom of human beings and, hence, the need to direct that freedom according to the dictates of a reason endowed by the Creator.

Notes

1. "Communication to the People of Sangamo County (9 March 1832)," in *The Collected Works of Abraham Lincoln*, Roy P. Basler, ed., 9 vols. (New Brunswick: Rutgers University Press, 1955), 1: 8. Hereinafter cited as *Collected Works*; all emphases in original except where otherwise noted.

2. "The Northwest Ordinance (13 July 1787)," in *Documents of American History*, 8th ed., Henry Steele Commager, ed., 2 vols. (New York: Meredith Corporation, 1968), 1: 131. Lincoln showed a close familiarity with the Northwest Ordinance in his "Address at Cooper Institute, New York City (27 February 1860)," in *Collected Works*, 2: 523-27.

3. Thomas F. Schwartz, "The Springfield Lyceums and Lincoln's 1838 Speech," *Illinois Historical Journal* 83 (Spring 1990): 49. See also Carl Bode, *The American Lyceum: Town Meeting of the Mind* (New York: Oxford University Press, 1956), 96-98.

4. Contrasting Lincoln's realism with Van Buren's optimism, Major L. Wilson argues for a reading of the Lyceum Address that places "Lincoln's Whiggish sentiment" in the foreground: "A 'political' reading of the Lyceum Address, in sum, sees Lincoln as a politician and not a prophet of dire evils to come. His phrasing reflected nothing more than the rhetorical excesses of a young and partisan Whig mocking the Democratic incumbent." "Lincoln and Van Buren in the Steps of the Fathers: Another Look at the Lyceum Address," *Civil War History* 29 (September 1983): 209, 204. Wilson quickly adds, "But there are problems with such a narrow political interpretation." He, therefore, concludes with a discussion of Lincoln's "ideology," with its standard of "right and wrong," which invites the American people to improve—and not simply venerate—the work of the American Founders ("Lincoln and Van Buren," 205-11). See also Major L. Wilson, "Lincoln on the Perpetuation of Republican Institutions: Whig and Republican Strategies," *Journal of the Abraham Lincoln Association* 18 (Winter 1997): 15-25.

5. "To the Editor of the *Sangamo Journal* (13 June 1836)," in *Collected Works*, 1: 48: "If alive on the first Monday in November, I shall vote for Hugh L. White for President." The other two Whigs were William H. Harrison (who defeated Van Buren in the 1840 presidential election) and Daniel Webster.

6. "Inaugural Address (4 March 1837)," in *A Compilation of the Messages and Papers of the Presidents*, James D. Richardson, ed., 20 vols. (Washington, D.C.: Government Printing Office, 1896), 3: 315. Hereinafter cited as *Messages and Papers of the Presidents*. Van Buren's address reflects many of the sentiments of the Farewell Address of Andrew Jackson, who delivered his speech the day of Van Buren's inauguration. See "Farewell Address (4 March 1837)," in *Messages and Papers of the Presidents*, 3: 292-308.

7. "Address before the Young Men's Lyceum of Springfield, Illinois (27 January 1838)," in *Collected Works*, 1: 108.

8. *Collected Works*, 1: 109. In his Farewell Address the previous year, Andrew Jackson offered a similar caution: "You have no longer any cause to fear danger from abroad; . . . It is from within, among yourselves—from cupidity, from corruption, from disappointed ambition and inordinate thirst for power—that factions will be formed and liberty endangered." "Farewell Address (4 March 1837)," in *Messages and Papers of the Presidents*, 3: 307-308.

9. "Address before the Wisconsin State Agricultural Society, Milwaukee, Wisconsin (30 September 1859)," in *Collected Works*, 3: 481.

10. See David Grimsted, *American Mobbing, 1828-1861: Toward Civil War* (New York: Oxford University Press, 1998); Max Berger, *The British Traveller in America, 1836-1860* (New York: Columbia University Press, 1943), 71-72; and Albert J. Beveridge, *Abraham Lincoln, 1809-1858*, 2 vols. (Cambridge, Mass.: Riverside Press, 1928), 1: 227.

11. *Lincoln Day by Day: A Chronology, 1809-1865*, Earl Schenck Miers, ed., 2 vols. (Washington: Lincoln Sesquicentennial Commission, 1960), William E. Baringer, vol. 1: *1809-1848*, "October 23" entry, 81. David Grimsted argues that the "most obvious precipitant of these 'various excitements' [i.e., mobs] was the growing effectiveness of abolition organization in the North and the sending of abolitionist literature southward." "Rioting in Its Jacksonian Setting," *The American Historical Review* 77 (April 1972): 375.

12. "Protest in Illinois Legislature on Slavery (3 March 1837)," in *Collected Works*, 1: 75.

13. "[W]henever the vicious portion of population shall be permitted to gather in bands of hundreds and thousands, and burn churches, ravage and rob provision stores, throw printing presses into rivers, shoot editors, and hang and burn obnoxious persons at pleasure, and with impunity; depend on it, this Government cannot last." "Address before the Young Men's Lyceum of Springfield, Illinois (27 January 1838)," in *Collected Works*, 1: 111. See Harry V. Jaffa, *Crisis of the House Divided: An Interpretation of the Issues in the Lincoln-Douglas Debates* (Seattle: University of Washington Press, 1973; reprint ed., Chicago: University of Chicago Press, 1982, © 1959), 199, for a more extended discussion of why "Lincoln could not afford to be identified with Lovejoy's cause." See also Neil Schmitz, "Murdered McIntosh, Murdered Lovejoy: Abraham Lincoln and the Problem of Jacksonian Address," *Arizona Republic* 44, no. 3 (Autumn 1988): 15-39.

14. "Speech in the Illinois Legislature Concerning the State Bank (11 January 1837)," in *Collected Works*, 1: 69, 67.

15. "Inaugural Address (4 March 1837)," in *Messages and Papers of the Presidents*, 3: 316, 318.

16. See Major L. Wilson, *The Presidency of Martin Van Buren* (Lawrence: University Press of Kansas, 1984), chap. 1, "A Restless Nation," 1-20, 39-42,

and Rush Welter, *The Mind of America, 1820-1860* (New York: Columbia University Press, 1975), chap. 7, "The Politics of Democracy," 165-89.

17. Aristotle, *The Politics*, trans. Carnes Lord (Chicago: University of Chicago Press, 1984), bk. 5, chap. 8, 163 (1308a30).

18. "To Marquis de Lafayette (10 May 1786)," in *George Washington: A Collection*, W. B. Allen, ed. (Indianapolis: Liberty Fund, Inc., 1988), 320.

19. "Address before the Young Men's Lyceum of Springfield, Illinois (27 January 1838)," in *Collected Works*, 1: 111. Cf. the Apostle Paul: "But we know that the law is good, if a man use it lawfully; knowing this, that the law is not made for a righteous man, but for the lawless and disobedient, for the ungodly and for sinners, for unholy and profane, for murderers of fathers and murderers of mothers, for manslayers . . ." (1 Tim. 1:8-9).

20. "Address before the Young Men's Lyceum of Springfield, Illinois (27 January 1838)," in *Collected Works*, 1: 110-12.

21. *Collected Works*, 1: 112.

22. Speaking of the new federal government in which he served twice as its chief magistrate, Washington said: "Respect for its authority, compliance with its Laws, acquiescence in its measures, are duties enjoined by the fundamental maxims of true Liberty. . . . But the Constitution which at any time exists, 'till changed by an explicit and authentic act of the whole People, is sacredly obligatory upon all." "Farewell Address (19 September 1796)," *George Washington: A Collection*, 518.

23. "Inaugural Address (4 March 1837)," in *Messages and Papers of the Presidents*, 3: 314, 315, 316, and 319.

24. *Messages and Papers of the Presidents*, 3: 314.

25. "Address before the Young Men's Lyceum of Springfield, Illinois (27 January 1838)," in *Collected Works*, 1: 112.

26. An exhortation to law-abidingness can be found in the Bible in 1 Timothy 2:1-4, among other places, which gives Christians the hope that their obedience to the government will produce both peace for them and salvation for others:

> I exhort therefore, that, first of all, supplications, prayers, intercessions, and giving of thanks, be made for all men; For kings, and for all that are in authority; that we may lead a quiet and peaceable life in all godliness and honesty. For this is good and acceptable in the sight of God our Saviour; Who will have all men to be saved, and to come unto the knowledge of the truth.

27. "Address before the Young Men's Lyceum of Springfield, Illinois (27 January 1838)," in *Collected Works*, 1: 112.

28. Wayne C. Temple, *Abraham Lincoln: From Skeptic to Prophet* (Mahomet, Ill.: Mayhaven Publishing, 1995), 23.

29. Cf. William S. Corlett, Jr., "The Availability of Lincoln's Political Religion," *Political Theory* 10 (November 1982): 520-40, which presents Lincoln's "political religion" as an expression of a "civic humanism" having nothing to do with revealed religion.

30. One is reminded of a similar discussion of the necessity of "veneration" for "stability" in even "the wisest and freest governments" in *Federalist* No. 49. James Madison writes: "In a nation of philosophers, . . . reverence for the laws, would be sufficiently inculcated by the voice of enlightened reason. But a nation of philosophers is as little to be expected as the philosophical race of kings wished for by Plato. And in every other nation, the most rational government will not find it a superfluous advantage, to have the prejudices of the community on its side." *The Federalist*, Jacob E. Cooke, ed. (Middletown, Conn.: Wesleyan University Press, 1961), 340.

31. 19 How. (60 U.S.) 393 (1857). The Court held that Dred Scott, a Missouri slave, could not sue for his freedom in a federal court because he was a Negro slave and, therefore, not a Missouri citizen. Justice Taney went on to rule, in a fit of *obiter dicta*, that the Missouri Compromise of 1820 was an unconstitutional act of Congress. See Don E. Fehrenbacher, *The Dred Scott Case: Its Significance in American Law and Politics* (New York: Oxford University Press, 1978).

32. "Speech at Springfield, Illinois (26 June 1857)," in *Collected Works*, 2: 401, 402. For a lucid discussion of this aspect of Lincoln's constitutional jurisprudence, see John Agresto, *The Supreme Court and Constitutional Democracy* (Ithaca, N.Y.: Cornell University Press, 1984), 86-95.

33. "First Inaugural Address—Final Text (4 March 1861)," in *Collected Works*, 4: 268. Responding to a speech by Senator Stephen A. Douglas, sponsor of the Kansas-Nebraska Act of 1854 (which repealed the Missouri Compromise of 1820), Lincoln declared: "I insist that if there is ANY THING which it is the duty of the WHOLE PEOPLE to never entrust to any hands but their own, that thing is the preservation and perpetuity, of their own liberties, and institutions." "Speech at Peoria, Illinois (16 October 1854)," in *Collected Works*, 2: 270.

34. "Address before the Young Men's Lyceum of Springfield, Illinois (27 January 1838)," in *Collected Works*, 1: 113.

35. "Farewell Address (4 March 1837)," in *Messages and Papers of the Presidents*, 3: 293.

36. "Address before the Young Men's Lyceum of Springfield, Illinois (27 January 1838)," in *Collected Works*, 1: 113.

37. *Collected Works*, 1: 114.

38. "Inaugural Address (4 March 1837)," in *Messages and Papers of the Presidents*, 3: 316.

39. *The Federalist*, No. 72, 488.

40. *The Federalist*, No. 72, 489.

41. "Address before the Young Men's Lyceum of Springfield, Illinois (27 January 1838)," in *Collected Works*, 1: 114.

42. "Inaugural Address (4 March 1837)," in *Messages and Papers of the Presidents*, 3: 315, 316, 317, and 319.

43. "Address before the Young Men's Lyceum of Springfield, Illinois (27 January 1838)," in *Collected Works*, 1: 115.

44. "Inaugural Address (4 March 1837)," in *Messages and Papers of the Presidents*, 3: 313.

45. "Circular to the States (14 June 1783)," in *George Washington: A Collection*, 242. Cf. "To Marquis De Lafayette (29 January 1789)," in *George Washington: A Collection*, 428: "Nothing but harmony, honesty, industry and frugality are necessary to make us a great and happy people. Happily the present posture of affairs and the prevailing disposition of my countrymen promise to co-operate in establishing those four great and essential pillars of public felicity." Compare as well Rev. 3:12: "Him that overcometh will I make a pillar in the temple of my God . . ."

46. "Inaugural Address (4 March 1837)," in *Messages and Papers of the Presidents*, 4: 1530.

47. "Address before the Young Men's Lyceum of Springfield, Illinois (27 January 1838)," in *Collected Works*, 1: 115.

48. Cf. Michael P. Zuckert, "Lincoln and the Problem of Civil Religion," in *Law and Philosophy: The Practice of Theory—Essays in Honor of George Anastaplo*, John A. Murley, Robert L. Stone, and William T. Braithwaite, eds., 2 vols. (Athens: Ohio University Press, 1992), 2: 726: "But just as Lincoln cannot have expected the political religion to work for princes, so he cannot have expected it to work for the people either. The feelings prompted by the Revolution depended on the living experiences he recited; he gave no reason to expect that his political religion would be exempt from the fate of all dead history."

49. Cf. 2 Samuel 1:23, where David laments the fall of Saul and Jonathan before the invading Philistine army: "Saul and Jonathan were lovely and pleasant in their lives, and in their death they were not divided: they were swifter than eagles, they were stronger than lions."

50. "Address at Sanitary Fair, Baltimore, Maryland (18 April 1864)," in *Collected Works*, 7: 302.

51. Jaffa, *Crisis of the House Divided*, 216-19. I am indebted to Jaffa's articulation of the magnanimous man as the key to understanding Lincoln's warning against "towering geniuses." For evidence that the "towering genius" Lincoln had in mind was Stephen A. Douglas, see Michael Burlingame, "Appendix: Stephen A. Douglas as a Target of Lincoln's Lyceum Address," *The Inner World of Abraham Lincoln* (Urbana: University of Illinois Press, 1994), 365-68. Cf. Major L. Wilson, who recounts the Whig portrayal of Martin Van Buren as feigning deference to President Andrew Jackson while yearning for the power of the presidency: "His protest of a 'sufficient glory' serving under 'such a chief,' along with the vow to tread in the 'footsteps' of Jackson, quickly entered the public domain and were made to appear, not as the phrases of a concerned and dutiful son but rather as the flattery of a time server questing for preferment and power." "Lincoln and Van Buren in the Steps of the Fathers," 203.

52. This puts the lie to Edmund Wilson's suggestion that Lincoln "projected himself into the role against which he is warning them." *Patriotic*

Gore: Studies in the Literature of the American Civil War (New York: Oxford University Press, 1962), 106-108, 115.

53. "Communication to the People of Sangamo County (9 March 1832)," in *Collected Works*, 1: 8.

54. "Address before the Young Men's Lyceum of Springfield, Illinois (27 January 1838)," in *Collected Works*, 1: 114.

55. "Speech at Lewiston, Illinois (17 August 1858)," in *Collected Works*, 2: 546.

56. "Communication to the People of Sangamo County (9 March 1832)," in *Collected Works*, 1: 8. His law partner William Herndon commented famously on Lincoln's drive and ambition: "That man who thinks Lincoln calmly sat down and gathered his robes about him, waiting for the people to call him, has a very erroneous knowledge of Lincoln. He was always calculating, and always planning ahead. His ambition was a little engine that knew no rest." William H. Herndon and Jesse W. Weik, *Herndon's Life of Lincoln: The History and Personal Recollections of Abraham Lincoln*, introduction and notes by Paul M. Angle, with new introduction by Henry Steele Commager (Cleveland: World Pub. Co., 1942; reprint edition, New York: Da Capo Press, Inc., 1983), 304.

57. "Speech at Lewistown, Illinois (17 August 1858)," in *Collected Works*, 2: 547.

58. "Eulogy on Henry Clay (6 July 1852)," in *Collected Works*, 2: 132.

59. "Address to the New Jersey Senate at Trenton, New Jersey (21 February 1861)," in *Collected Works*, 4: 236. See also "Reply to Eliza P. Gurney (26 October 1862)," in *Collected Works*, 5: 478.

60. "Reply to [Governor] Oliver P. Morton at Indianapolis, Indiana (11 February 1861)," in *Collected Works*, 4: 193-94.

61. Garry Wills, *Lincoln at Gettysburg: The Words That Remade America* (New York: Simon & Schuster, 1992), 89.

62. "'A Few Appropriate Remarks': The Summons to Gettysburg (2 November 1863)," in *Dear Mr. Lincoln: Letters to the President*, Harold Holzer, ed. (Reading, Mass.: Addison-Wesley Publishing Company, 1995), 287. The closing two paragraphs of Wills's invitation, from which Lincoln gleaned some ideas for his brief remarks, read as follows:

> It will be a source of great gratification to the many widows and orphans that have been made almost friendless by the Great Battle here, to have you here personally! and it will kindle anew in the breasts of the comrades of these brave dead, who are now in the tented field or nobly meeting the foe in the front, a confidence that they who sleep in death on the Battle Field are not forgotten by those highest in authority; and they will feel that, should their fate be the same, their remains will not be uncared for.
>
> We hope you will be able to be present to perform this last solemn act to the Soldiers dead on the Battle Field.

63. "To Stephen T. Logan (9 November 1863)," in *Collected Works*, 7: 7.

64. "To Edwin M. Stanton [17 November 1863]," in *Collected Works*, 7: 16. Garry Wills notes that Lincoln left for Gettysburg the day before the

cemetery dedication, a trip that took six hours: "If Lincoln had not changed the schedule, he would very likely not have given his talk." *Lincoln at Gettysburg*, 26.

65. "Address Delivered at the Dedication of the Cemetery at Gettysburg—Final Text (19 November 1863)," in *Collected Works*, 7: 23. All subsequent references to the text of the Gettysburg Address refer to this volume and page.

66. Other scholars have noted the allusion to Psalms 90. See Eva Brann, "A Reading of the Gettysburg Address," in *Abraham Lincoln, The Gettysburg Address, and American Constitutionalism*, Leo Paul S. de Alvarez, ed. (Irving, Tex.: University of Dallas Press, 1976), 21-22; Garry Wills, *Lincoln at Gettysburg*, 78; and Glenn LaFantasie, "Lincoln and the Gettysburg Awakening," *Journal of the Abraham Lincoln Association* 16 (Winter 1995): 74.

67. William Strunk, Jr., and E. B. White, *The Elements of Style*, 3rd ed. (New York: Macmillan Publishing Company, Inc., 1979), 77.

68. "To John Phillips (21 November 1864)," in *Collected Works*, 8: 118. Cf. Michael Burlingame, "New Light on the Bixby Letter," *Journal of the Abraham Lincoln Association* 16 (Winter 1995): 70, n. 45. Burlingame suggests that Lincoln did not write the letter to John Phillips: "It hardly strains credulity to believe that [Lincoln's secretary John] Hay wrote this routine letter." He notes that the letter was written the same day as the famous letter to Mrs. Lydia Bixby, which bears the earmarks of Hay's ghostwriting.

69. Don E. Fehrenbacher, *Lincoln in Text and Context: Collected Essays* (Stanford, Calif.: Stanford University Press, 1987), 285 and 347, n. 53.

70. 37th Congr., 1st sess., *Congressional Globe* (4 July 1861), 4.

71. "Speech at Chicago, Illinois (10 July 1858)," in *Collected Works*, 2: 499.

72. "Response to a Serenade (7 July 1863)," in *Collected Works*, 6: 319, 320.

73. Ward Hill Lamon, *Recollections of Abraham Lincoln, 1847-1865*, Dorothy Lamon Teillard, ed. (Lincoln: University of Nebraska Press, 1994; originally published by A. C. McClurg & Co., 1895, 2nd ed. expanded in 1911, Washington, D.C.), 179.

74. One well-known remark of Lincoln's about the sufferings of the Civil War came upon his hearing of Major General Joseph "Fighting Joe" Hooker's defeat at Chancellorsville, Virginia (May 1-3, 1863): "My God! my God! What will the country say!" Noah Brooks, *Washington in Lincoln's Time* (New York: The Century Co., 1896), 58. General Hooker led the Army of the Potomac at the peak of its fighting strength, 130,000 men against General Robert E. Lee's Confederate army of 60,000. The Union forces lost 17,000 men to Lee's 12,800, the highest loss for the Union until the battle at Gettysburg two months later. Although Lee lost Lieutenant General Stonewall Jackson to a mortal wounding at Chancellorsville, the battle constituted the greatest victory of the war for the Confederate cause.

75. Cited in n. 1 from "To Edward Everett (20 November 1863)," in *Collected Works*, 7: 25. Lincoln wrote Everett to return the compliment: "Of course I knew Mr. Everett would not fail; and yet, while the whole discourse was eminently satisfactory, and will be of great value, there were passages in it which transcended my expectation." *Collected Works*, 7: 24.

76. Cited in n. 1 from "To Edward Everett (4 February 1864)," in *Collected Works*, 7: 168. Everett also asked Lincoln to include a copy of his November 20th reply to Everett's original complimentary letter, "as its insertion would greatly enhance the value of the volume."

77. "Emancipation Proclamation (1 January 1863)," in *Collected Works*, 6: 29-30.

78. "Second Inaugural Address (4 March 1865)," in *Collected Works*, 8: 333.

79. Wills, *Lincoln at Gettysburg*, 38.

80. Wills, *Lincoln at Gettysburg*, 145. Wills later concludes that Lincoln came to Gettysburg not "to present a theory, but to impose a symbol . . . He came to change the world, to effect an intellectual revolution. . . . In his brief time before the crowd at Gettysburg he wove a spell that has not, yet, been broken—he called up a new nation out of the blood and trauma." Wills, *Lincoln at Gettysburg*, 174, 175. Historian Pauline Maier qualifies Wills's account by adding, "The act of reinterpreting the Declaration, moreover, did not stop with Lincoln; it goes on today, expanding the story's cast from hundreds to millions." *American Scripture: Making the Declaration of Independence* (New York: Alfred A. Knopf, 1997), xx. More to her point, Maier argues that "Lincoln and those who shared his convictions did not therefore give the nation a new past or revolutionize the Revolution. But as descendants of the revolutionaries and of their English ancestors, they felt the need for a document that stated those values in a way that could guide the nation, a document that the founding fathers had failed to supply." *American Scripture*, 208.

81. Wills, *Lincoln at Gettysburg*, 38-39. Note the subtitle of the book, "The Words That Remade America."

82. David Herbert Donald, *Lincoln* (New York: Simon & Schuster, 1995), 421, 465-66. The Chicago *Times* also condemned the Emancipation Proclamation as "a monstrous usurpation, a criminal wrong, and an act of national suicide." Donald, *Lincoln*, 421.

83. "To Edwin M. Stanton (4 June 1863)," in *Collected Works*, 6: 248.

84. Wills, *Lincoln at Gettysburg*, 147.

85. To Wills's credit, he recognizes the logic behind Lincoln's appreciation of American union and, therefore, does not agree with Alexander H. Stephens's oft quoted remark about Lincoln's devotion to the Union: "The Union with him, in sentiment, rose to the sublimity of a religious mysticism." Alexander Stephens cited in Wills, *Lincoln at Gettysburg*, 125.

86. "Response to a Serenade (7 July 1863)," in *Collected Works*, 6: 320.

87. "Speech at Springfield (26 June 1857)," in *Collected Works*, 2: 405-406. Taney's opinion for the Supreme Court asserted that the descendants of

slaves in the United States were "so far inferior" to the white race that "they had no rights which the white man was bound to respect." *Dred Scott v. Sandford*, 60 U.S. 393 (1857), at 407.

88. "Fragment on the Constitution and the Union [c. January 1861?]," in *Collected Works*, 4: 169.

89. Cited in n. 1 from "To Alexander H. Stephens (22 December 1860)," in *Collected Works*, 4: 161.

90. "Address to the New Jersey Senate at Trenton, New Jersey (21 February 1861)," in *Collected Works*, 4: 236.

91. "Speech in Independence Hall, Philadelphia, Pennsylvania (22 February 1861)," in *Collected Works*, 4: 240.

92. Turning down another invitation to speak just a week earlier, Lincoln replied: "I regret to say I can not do so now; I must stick to the courts awhile." "To William Morris (28 March 1859)," in *Collected Works*, 3: 374.

93. "To Henry L. Pierce and Others (6 April 1859)," in *Collected Works*, 3: 375-76. Ironically, only ten days after his tribute to Jefferson, he would flatly refuse the offer of an editor to organize a state-wide announcement of his candidacy for the presidency: "I do not think myself fit for the presidency." "To Thomas J. Pickett (16 April 1859)," in *Collected Works*, 3: 377. He repeats the sentiment three months later; see "To Samuel Galloway (28 July 1859)," in *Collected Works*, 3: 395. David Herbert Donald, *Lincoln*, 235-37, describes newspaper editorials in several states that called for Lincoln's presidential candidacy as the denouement of the U.S. Senate campaign of 1858.

94. "Reply to Mayor Alexander Henry at Philadelphia, Pennsylvania (21 February 1861)," in *Collected Works*, 2: 239.

95. "Message to Congress in Special Session (4 July 1861)," in *Collected Works*, 4: 426.

96. See his "Message to Congress in Special Session (4 July 1861)," in *Collected Works*, 4: 439:

> It is now for them [the American people] to demonstrate to the world, that those who can fairly carry an election, can also suppress a rebellion—that ballots are the rightful, and peaceful, successors of bullets; and that when ballots have fairly, and constitutionally, decided, there can be no successful appeal, back to bullets; that there can be no successful appeal, except to ballots themselves, at succeeding elections. Such will be a great lesson of peace; teaching men that what they cannot take by an election, neither can they take it by a war—teaching all, the folly of being the beginners of a war.

97. "Address at Sanitary Fair, Baltimore, Maryland (18 April 1864)," in *Collected Works*, 7: 301.

98. Clarence Thomas, "The Virtue of Practical Wisdom," Remarks delivered at the Third Annual Claremont Institute Lincoln Day Colloquium and Dinner in Washington, D.C., on February 9, 1999 (Claremont, Calif.: Claremont Institute for the Study of Statesmanship and Political Philosophy, 1999).

99. For a comparison of the respective tasks facing Abraham Lincoln and Jefferson Davis, see James R. Andrews, "Oaths Registered in Heaven:

Rhetorical and Historical Legitimacy in the Inaugural Addresses of Jefferson Davis and Abraham Lincoln," in *Doing Rhetorical History: Concepts and Cases*, Kathleen J. Turner, ed. (Tuscaloosa: University of Alabama Press, 1998), 95-117.

100. "First Inaugural Address—Final Text (4 March 1861)," in *Collected Works*, 4: 270.

101. *Collected Works*, 4: 269.

102. *Collected Works*, 4: 268.

103. "Remarks to New School Presbyterians (22 October 1863)," in *Collected Works*, 6: 531.

104. "Address to the Legislature at Albany, New York (18 February 1861)," in *Collected Works*, 4: 226. He repeated this theme in a letter to Eliza P. Gurney: "being a humble instrument in the hands of our Heavenly Father, as I am, and as we all are, to work out his great purposes . . ." "Reply to Eliza P. Gurney (26 October 1862)," in *Collected Works*, 5: 478. Lincoln delivered a more emphatic declaration of his intention to fulfill God's will for his life when he spoke against President Martin Van Buren's sub-treasury scheme before the Illinois House of Representatives:

> If ever I feel the soul within me elevate and expand to those dimensions not wholly unworthy of its Almighty Architect, it is when I contemplate the cause of my country, deserted by all the world beside, and I standing up boldly and alone and hurling defiance at her victorious oppressors. Here, without contemplating consequences, before High Heaven, and in the face of the world, I swear eternal fidelity to the just cause, as I deem it, of the land of my life, my liberty and my love.

"Speech on the Sub-Treasury ([26] December 1839)," in *Collected Works*, 1: 178-79.

105. Cf. Glen E. Thurow, *Abraham Lincoln and American Political Religion* (New York: State University of New York Press, 1976), 42-44, who interprets Lincoln as not simply equating "the voice of the people" with "the voice of God." Thurow is correct in stating that "Lincoln does not assert that the voice of the people is always the voice of God." However, Thurow asks rhetorically, "is it surprising that Lincoln asserts the people will decide justly when it is Lincoln who is in a position to lead and guide them? Would he have said the same thing had he lost the election?" He thereby suggests that Lincoln believed the American people to speak (i.e., vote) with the voice of God only when Lincoln was in office. But this contradicts both Lincoln's humble character and direct statements on the subject. As an incumbent state legislator, Lincoln included the following statement in his party's newspaper when he ran for re-election: "While acting as their representative, *I shall be governed by their will*, on all subjects upon which I have the means of knowing what their will is; and upon all others, I shall do what my own judgment teaches me will best advance their interests." "To the Editor of the *Sangamo Journal* (13 June 1836)," in *Collected Works*, 1: 48. (Emphasis added.) Even in his First Inaugural Address, Lincoln asks, "In our present differences, is either party

without faith of being in the right?" He goes on to suggest that providence, "with his eternal truth and justice," will ultimately weigh into the conflict and produce justice through the very contest of public opinions. "First Inaugural Address–Final Text (4 March 1861)," in *Collected Works*, 4: 270. See also "To Peter H. Silvester (22 December 1860)," in *Collected Works*, 4: 160: "The political horizon looks dark and lowering; but the people, under Providence, will set all right." Thus, while Lincoln does not categorically equate popular opinion with the will of God, he also does not presume that equation whenever the public agrees with him.

106. Thurow, *Abraham Lincoln and American Political Religion*, 42-44.

107. "To the Editor of the *Sangamo Journal* (13 June 1836)," in *Collected Works*, 1: 48. (Emphasis added.)

108. "First Inaugural Address—Final Text (4 March 1861)," in *Collected Works*, 4: 270.

109. "First Inaugural Address—Final Text (4 March 1861)," in *Collected Works*, 4: 270.

110. "Address to the New Jersey Senate at Trenton, New Jersey (21 February 1861)," in *Collected Works*, 4: 236. See also John Dos Passos, "Lincoln and His Almost Chosen People," in *Lincoln and the Gettysburg Address: Commemorative Papers*, Allan Nevins, ed. (Urbana: University of Illinois Press, 1964), 15-37.

111. "Speech at New Haven, Connecticut (6 March 1860)," in *Collected Works*, 4: 16.

112. The relevant sentence of the Declaration of Independence reads: "But when a long train of abuses and usurpations, pursuing invariably the same Object evinces a design to reduce them under absolute Despotism, it is their right, it is their duty, to throw off such Government, and to provide new Guards for their future security."

113. "Speech at Lewistown, Illinois (17 August 1858)," in *Collected Works*, 2: 546.

114. "Speech at Edwardsville, Illinois (11 September 1858)," in *Collected Works*, 3: 95.

115. "Address to the New Jersey Senate at Trenton, New Jersey (21 February 1861)," in *Collected Works*, 4: 236.

116. New Jersey gave four electoral votes to Lincoln and three to Stephen Douglas. John Niven, *The Coming of the Civil War, 1837-1861* (Arlington Heights, Ill.: Harlan Davidson, Inc., 1990), 120.

117. "Address to the New Jersey Senate at Trenton, New Jersey (21 February 1861)," in *Collected Works*, 4: 236.

118. Recall Alexander Hamilton's admonition in *Federalist* No. 1, 4: "So numerous indeed and so powerful are the causes, which serve to give a false bias to the judgment, that we upon many occasions, see wise and good men on the wrong as well as on the right side of questions, of the first magnitude to society."

119. "To James T. Hale (11 January 1861)," in *Collected Works*, 4: 172.

120. "First Inaugural Address—Final Text (4 March 1861)," in *Collected Works*, 4: 267.

121. "To the Editor of the *Sangamo Journal* (13 June 1836)," in *Collected Works*, 1: 48.

122. "First Inaugural Address—Final Text (4 March 1861)," in *Collected Works*, 4: 271.

123. "Address before the Young Men's Lyceum of Springfield, Illinois (27 January 1838)," in *Collected Works*, 1: 115. See also his "Speech at Lafayette, Indiana (11 February 1861)," in which states: "Still we are bound together, I trust in christianity, civilization and patriotism, and are attached to our country and our whole country." *Collected Works*, 4: 192.

124. "First Inaugural Address—Final Text (4 March 1861)," in *Collected Works*, 4: 271.

125. "Story Written for Noah Brooks [6 December 1864?]," in *Collected Works*, 8: 155.

126. For a recent exploration of the South's theological self-understanding just prior to, during, and immediately following the Civil War, see Eugene D. Genovese, *A Consuming Fire: The Fall of the Confederacy in the Mind of the White Christian South* (Athens: University of Georgia Press, 1999).

127. "First Inaugural Address (4 March 1861)," in *Abraham Lincoln: Speeches and Writings*, Don E. Fehrenbacher, ed., 2 vols. (New York: The Library of America, 1989), 1: 735, n. 224.5-11.

128. "First Inaugural Address—Final Text (4 March 1861)," in *Collected Works*, 4: 271.

129. *Collected Works*, 4: 269.

130. "Letter to James C. Conkling (26 August 1863)," in *Collected Works*, 6: 410. David Herbert Donald records that the letter was cheered by the gathering of 50,000 to 75,000 Unionists, and reprinted in nearly every major newspaper in the country. *Lincoln*, 456-57.

131. For recent studies that argue more for Lincoln's fatalism than his activity in the face of providence, see Allen C. Guelzo, "Abraham Lincoln and the Doctrine of Necessity," *Journal of the Abraham Lincoln Association* 18 (Winter 1997): 57-81, and Donald, *Lincoln*, 14-15.

132. "Speech to the Springfield Scott Club (14, 26 August 1852)," in *Collected Works*, 2: 150. The "Loco-focos" were a radical faction of Jacksonian Democrats.

133. "Eulogy on Zachary Taylor (25 July 1850)," in *Collected Works*, 2: 89. See also "Resolutions on the Death of David B. Campbell ([17] April 1855)," in *Collected Works*, 2: 310: "WHEREAS, it has pleased Almighty God in the dispensations of his Providence, to cut down at meridian of life, and in the vigor of his usefulness, a most esteemed member of this bar, David B. Campbell . . ."

134. "Campaign Circular from Whig Committee (4 March 1843)," in *Collected Works*, 1: 314.

135. "Preliminary Emancipation Proclamation (22 September 1862)," in *Collected Works*, 5: 434.

136. "Emancipation Proclamation (1 January 1863)," in *Collected Works*, 6: 29.

137. "Annual Message to Congress (1 December 1862)," in *Collected Works*, 5: 537. In his preliminary Emancipation Proclamation, Lincoln announced that he would recommend certain measures to Congress for compensating the loyal state populations for losses imposed by the United States' prosecution of the war, "including the loss of slaves." *Collected Works*, 5: 436. He follows through in his 1862 Annual Address to Congress by proposing three amendments to the U.S. Constitution: the first would compensate slave states that abolished slavery prior to January 1, 1900; the second would legally free slaves who became free "before the end of the rebellion" as a result of the war, and compensate owners loyal to the United States; and the third would authorize Congress to fund colonization programs for "free colored persons." "Annual Message to Congress (1 December 1862)," in *Collected Works*, 5: 530.

138. "To Caleb Russell and Sallie A. Fenton (5 January 1863)," in *Collected Works*, 6: 39-40 and n. 2. Roy P. Basler notes that this sentence was marked for deletion but remained in the letter when sent.

139. "Speech at Clinton, Illinois (14 October 1859)," in *Collected Works*, 3: 488. Cf. Isaac Kramnick and R. Laurence Moore, *The Godless Constitution: The Case against Religious Correctness* (New York: W. W. Norton & Company, 1996), 171, which exaggerates Lincoln's humility before the inscrutable ways of God in arguing that Lincoln "wondered constantly about what God might expect of him but never imagined that he really knew." At minimum Lincoln understood that God expected civil societies to pursue justice. For example, in response to a tribute Lincoln received from the Christian Commission for his support of their effort to provide material and spiritual comfort to Union soldiers, he wrote: "we are both alike working in the same cause, and it is because of the fact of its being a just one which gives us our mutual joy and reward in its service." "Reply to Delegation of Christian Commission (27 January 1865)," in *Collected Works* 8: 241.

140. "Annual Message to Congress (1 December 1862)," in *Collected Works*, 5: 518 and "Annual Message to Congress (3 December 1861)," in *Collected Works*, 5: 35, respectively.

141. Mark A. Noll rightly associates what little we know about Lincoln's religious faith with "his belief that American ideals reflected the principles of divine morality." *One Nation under God? Christian Faith and Political Action in America* (San Francisco: Harper & Row, Publishers, 1988), 94. But while Noll acknowledges that Lincoln's "civil religion resulted in greater good for the nation than the activities of many who have abandoned the idea of America's uniqueness under God," he ultimately rejects Lincoln's public understanding of America's providential place in history: "Surely Lincoln overestimated both the eternal value of American ideals and the godly potential of the American

people"; and "Lincoln and the Puritans were wrong about America being a unique manifestation of God's presence" (Noll, *One Nation under God?*, 103, 102). Cf. Andrew Delbanco, *The Death of Satan: How Americans Have Lost the Sense of Evil* (New York: Farrar, Straus & Giroux, 1995), 132, which describes Lincoln as "a man whose scripture was the Declaration of Independence, and the Union his church," and the Civil War as "the logical outcome of his *religious* commitments."

142. "Speech at Hartford, Connecticut (5 March 1860)," in *Collected Works*, 4: 9.

143. "To George B. Ide, James R. Doolittle, and A. Hubbell (30 May 1864)," in *Collected Works*, 7: 368.

144. "Fragment on Pro-Slavery Theology (1 October 1858?)," in *Collected Works*, 3: 204. Jack P. Maddox writes: "In their controversy with the Northern abolitionists, Southern Presbyterian theologians insisted that the Bible recognized slavery as a legitimate system without hinting that it was bad or transient." "Proslavery Millenialism: Social Eschatology in Antebellum Southern Calvinism," *American Quarterly* 31 (Spring 1970): 49. See also Mitchell Snay, *Gospel of Division: Religion and Separatism in the Antebellum South* (Chapel Hill: University of North Carolina Press, 1997; orig. publ. Cambridge University Press, 1993), esp. chap. 2, "Slavery Defended: The Morality of Slavery and the Infidelity of Abolitionism," 53-77, and chap. 3, "Slavery Sanctified: The Slaveholding Ethic and the Religious Mission to the Slaves," 113-50.

145. "Speech at Edwardsville (11 September 1858)," in *Collected Works*, 3: 95.

Chapter 3

The Political Accommodation of Religion

In the summer of 1864, Lincoln invited his long-time friend, Joshua F. Speed, to spend the night at his retreat at Soldiers' Home, just three miles north of the White House. Speed wrote of his stay at Soldiers' Home years later, and it gives perhaps the clearest indication of Lincoln's religious faith late in life:

> As I entered the room, near night, he was sitting near a window intently reading his Bible. Approaching him I said, "I am glad to see you so profitably engaged." "Yes" said he, "I am profitably engaged." "Well," said I, "If you have recovered from your skepticism, I am sorry to say that I have not." Looking me earnestly in the face, and placing his hand on my shoulder, he said, "You are wrong Speed, take all of this book upon reason that you can, and the balance on faith, and you will live and die a happier and better man."[1]

Speed notes that Lincoln had come a long way from his early days of religious "skepticism."[2] For our purposes, this famous recollection of Lincoln's dearest friend reveals an appreciation of religion that transcends its mere usefulness to the government. For Lincoln, religion *qua* religion had a purpose far beyond that of simply supporting the government: it existed to fulfill a divine purpose between an individual and God and ought not to be viewed solely in light of its political utility. Because religion's reason for being stands independent of political necessity, Lincoln made sure to enlist its services to the regime without subverting its own reason for being. He saw to it that government, while he was at the helm, accommodated religion as the citizenry saw to its higher end.

This understanding of religion's ambivalent support of the state has only recently been revived in scholarly circles.[3] For example, historian Mark Y. Hanley argues that "Protestant spiritual discourse, anchored by religious jeremiads and regular sermons, . . . placed faith's temporal benefits on a fulcrum that gave weighted advantage to a transcendent spirituality beyond the Commonwealth." In other words, while some religious leaders saw a close affinity of purpose between Christianity and the American republic, others presented "faith's capacity to improve society as a subordinate aim" to its highest priority: pointing men and women toward "a spiritual destiny beyond the commonwealth."[4]

Not unlike these Protestant critics, Lincoln spoke and acted publicly so as to protect religion's transcendent aims. Lincoln certainly appealed to revealed religion to support the American republic, and many commentators have explored his motives and reasons for doing so.[5] However, his protection of religious liberty for its own sake, for the spiritual well-being of the citizenry, has received little commentary. While Lincoln promoted a civil religion in support of the federal government, he did so without supplanting the claim of revealed religion upon American citizens. His policies during the Civil War reflect a concern to conduct government business in a manner that preserved the religious freedom of the American people. Lincoln, in short, protected the religious liberties of the people in a manner consistent with republican principles but with an eye toward fostering a due dependence on the God who makes nations.

Handbill Replying to Charges of Infidelity (1846)

A telling example of Lincoln's respect for revealed religion, especially as a principal influence on society, is his "Handbill Replying to Charges of Infidelity." In his run for Congress in 1846, Lincoln campaigned against the well-known Methodist circuit rider Peter Cartwright. Friends told Lincoln that Cartwright "was whispering the charge of infidelity" against him,[6] suggesting that Lincoln held unorthodox views about religion. Lincoln, therefore, responded with a handbill explaining his understanding of the controversy.

"Infidelity" with regards to religion, if one refers solely to its Latin root, means a lack of faith (the Latin root being *fides* or "faith," *fidelis* or "faithful"). During the nineteenth century, however, infidelity took a much looser definition. According to biographer William E. Barton, "If Lincoln was regarded as an infidel, and if he ever was tempted to think himself one, we should not be justified in accepting that judgment as final until we knew and considered what was required in that time and place to constitute a man an infidel." He relates that Baptist ministers in general would have considered the belief in a round—as opposed to a flat—earth "sufficient to brand a man as an infidel." Barton bolstered this assessment by relating his experience in 1881 with a student whose father removed him from Barton's tutelage because the boy had learned that the earth was round. As for the Methodist Cartwright, he "would probably have considered a man an infidel who believed that the earth was not created in seven literal days."[7]

A clearer case for the charge of infidelity derives from the appearance of "rationalism" in Lincoln's statements. As explained by C. Bruce Staiger, conservative theologians and preachers criticized those who would argue "the sufficiency of human reason in matters of religion" because of its affiliation with "the ancient heathen philosophers." The "spirit of rationalism," especially as seen in the New School Presbyterians (influenced by the Congregationalists and Unitarians), seemed to introduce "a new gospel, and with it a new system of moral obligation, and a new scale of human rights."[8] The Reverend Frederick A. Ross, a pro-slavery preacher and contemporary of Lincoln's, published that a belief in the "truths" of the Declaration of Independence as "self-evident" was an "old infidel averment." Accordingly, "The time has come when civil liberty, as revealed in the Bible and in Providence, must be re-examined, understood, and defended against infidel theories of human rights."[9] Because Thomas Jefferson argued for the equal rights of human beings without explicit reference to the Bible, and with express reliance on the Enlightenment philosopher John Locke, Ross found the Declaration of Independence too rationalistic for his religious sensibilities. In contrast, Lincoln saw the Declaration of Independence as "the sheet anchor of our republican liberties." Here was more than enough material to convict him in Ross's court without exploring the issue of Lincoln's sporadic church attendance or life-long practice of not pledging church membership.

As the 1846 handbill contains the most direct expression of Lincoln's view of religion and public life, at least to that point in his life, we quote it in its entirety:

To the Voters of the Seventh Congressional District.
FELLOW CITIZENS:

A charge having got into circulation in some of the neighborhoods of this District, in substance that I am an open scoffer at Christianity, I have by the advice of some friends concluded to notice the subject in this form. That I am not a member of any Christian Church, is true; but I have never denied the truth of the Scriptures; and I have never spoken with intentional disrespect of religion in general, or of any denomination of Christians in particular. It is true that in early life I was inclined to believe in what I understand is called the "Doctrine of Necessity"—that is, that the human mind is impelled to action, or held in rest by some power, over which the mind itself has no control; and I have sometimes (with one, two or three, but never publicly) tried to maintain this opinion in argument. The habit of arguing thus however, I have, entirely left off for more than five years. And I add here, I have always understood this same opinion to be held by several of the Christian denominations. The foregoing, is the whole truth, briefly stated, in relation to myself, upon this subject.

I do not think I could myself, be brought to support a man for office, whom I knew to be an open enemy of, and scoffer at, religion. Leaving the higher matter of eternal consequences, between him and his Maker, I still do not think any man has the right thus to insult the feelings, and injure the morals, of the community in which he may live. If, then, I was guilty of such conduct, I should blame no man who could condemn me for it; but I do blame those, whoever they may be, who falsely put such a charge in circulation against me.[10]

Lincoln admits that he is not a member of any Christian church. As a state legislator, Lincoln did not attend church services regularly. Soon after he moved to Springfield, the new state capital, he wrote to Mary Owens, "I've never been to church yet, nor probably shall not be soon. I stay away because I am conscious I should not know how to behave myself."[11] In the midst of the Civil War he would confess, "I have often wished that I was a more devout man than I am."[12] His closest friend, Joshua F. Speed, also recalled Lincoln's personal struggle of faith during his early years in Springfield: "When I knew him, in early life, he was a skeptic." Speed added, however, that Lincoln "was very cautious never to give expression to any thought or sentiment that would grate harshly upon a Christian's ear."[13] The exoneration implicit in his handbill—"I have never denied the truth of the Scriptures"—lies with his belief that infidelity or lack of faith lies primarily in one's view of the Holy Scriptures and not with membership at a particular church congregation.

Most important, Lincoln wishes to address the political relevance of a candidate's religious beliefs and practice. He adds that he never spoke "with intentional disrespect" of religion or any particular denomination. His concern not to show disrespect toward the faith of others can be seen in a draft of a speech comparing Thomas Jefferson and Zachary Taylor (the Whig presidential candidate in 1848) on the presidential veto power: "They are more alike than the accounts of the crucifixion, as given by any two of the evangelists—more alike, or at least as much alike, as any two accounts of the inscription, written and erected by Pilate at that time."[14] In his only term as congressman, Lincoln omitted the biblical reference in his final draft. He knew enough not to stir up controversy over apparent inconsistencies in the Bible.

Hans J. Morgenthau interpreted Lincoln's reticence in the 1846 handbill to profess "a single positive assertion" about his religious beliefs as "a testimony both to his indifference to religious dogma and organization and to his intellectual honesty."[15] To be sure, Lincoln had little time for religious doctrines and sectarian institutions derived from the Holy Scriptures by fallible human minds[16] and was careful not to misrepresent himself religiously on the stump. But the interpretation places too great an emphasis on Lincoln's "political expediency," for he only intended to clarify his rumored "infidelity." Lincoln felt no obligation to share personal religious views that he believed bore little or no relevance to the campaign at hand. He therefore shows that his avoidance of sins of commission is the only relevant political consideration, not any sins of omission. The latter may have "eternal consequences" to be worked out "between him and his Maker," but this bears no import to political affairs. Lincoln chose to explain his understanding of religion and civil society to help his constituents know the legitimate expectations they should have regarding a candidate's public attitude toward religion.

This is why Lincoln does not state explicitly what he thinks about the Bible or any particular Christian doctrine. Like George Washington, James Madison, and other American Founders, Lincoln did not think the public profession of one's religious convictions contributed much for the community to consider when deciding on a candidate for office or when discussing the merits of a specific public policy. An undue emphasis on one's religious beliefs, moreover, could easily lead to factious politics, with no easy means of resolving disagreements. Here religion in the public square could give rise to factious majorities ruling according to their numerical might, as opposed to principled right, and therefore threaten the perpetuation of American self-government.

In the handbill, Lincoln volunteers an account of his belief "in early life" in the doctrine of necessity, which seems to deny the free will of man. However, he emphasizes that five years had passed since he last made these arguments, they were never made in public, and they were understood by him to be shared by several Christian denominations. A case in point would be his own parents' church in Kentucky, Little Mount Separate Baptist Church. They were part of the "Separate" Baptist movement, otherwise known as primitive or "hard-shell" Baptists for their strict predestination doctrines.[17] In short, Lincoln's belief in the doctrine of necessity was a private matter not intended for the public ear and one that did not threaten Christian orthodoxy because none existed on the subject. He offers this personal information in the event that it might have been the source of the rumor of his religious infidelity. In the second paragraph, Lincoln shares his understanding of how the rumor might trouble the consciences of some of his constituents—hence, the reason for his no longer debating said belief even privately "with one, two or three."

Lincoln states that he doubts he could be moved to support a political candidate whom he knew to be "an open enemy of, and scoffer at, religion." Lincoln defends the community's "feelings" connected with religion; they should be immune from public "insult." While the private insult of a neighbor's religion is hardly intended by Lincoln, his emphasis on the feelings of "the community" leaves room for *discussing* the truth of a particular religion with one's neighbor without the malice and recklessness accompanying the intentional slight of a fellow citizen's convictions. Religion deals with a man's conscience and hence should be handled with care—especially if that man is a neighbor and fellow citizen.

During his first run for Congress in 1842, Lincoln showed respect for a community's religious sensibilities—despite personally experiencing "the strangest church influence" against him—in a letter written to a delegate to the Seventh Congressional District convention after the campaign was over:

> Baker is a Campbellite, and therefore as I suppose, with few exceptions got all that church. My wife has some relatives in the Presbyterian and some in the Episcopal Churches, and therefore, wherever it would tell, I was set down as either the one or the other, whilst it was every where contended that no ch[r]istian ought to go for me, because I belonged to no church, was suspected of being a deist, and had talked about fighting a duel. With all these things Baker, of course had nothing to do. *Nor do I complain of them. As to his own church going for him, I think that was right enough*, and as to the influences I have spoken of in the other, though they were very strong, it would be grossly untrue and unjust to charge that they acted upon them in a body or even very nearly so. I only mean that those influences levied a tax of a considerable per cent. upon my strength throughout the religious community.[18] (Emphasis added.)

In the eyes of church-goers, his dueling episode with James Shields the previous year,[19] lack of church membership, and suspected deism crippled his campaign to be nominated as the Whig candidate of Sangamon County. Lincoln confesses that he found his campaign hampered by public doubts over his religious inclinations; yet, he does not begrudge his opponent (and close friend) for drawing the support of his own community church. Here, Lincoln grants not only the likelihood but the propriety of winning the support of those most acquainted with you. For example, in his first run for the Illinois State House, the twenty-three-year-old Lincoln received 277 out of 300 votes from his hometown precinct—the political equivalent of a congregation.[20] Even though it turned out to be a losing bid, Lincoln's first campaign for public office demonstrated the power of proximity or affection for what is near and dear, which he extends to one's church.

He also guards the "morals" fostered by the religious sentiments of the community from public "injury." To disregard the consequences of undermining a community's religious beliefs is to place too sanguine a confidence in the principles and practices of what one would substitute in their place. As George Washington expressed this in his Farewell Address:

> Of all the dispositions and habits which lead to political prosperity, Religion and morality are indispensable supports. In vain would that man claim the tribute of Patriotism, who should labour to subvert these great Pillars of human happiness, these firmest props of the duties of Men and citizens. The mere Politician, equally with the pious man ought to respect and cherish them.[21]

Lincoln leaves "the higher matter of eternal consequences" to the offending party "and his Maker," and preserves religious freedom, on the one hand, and promotes social responsibility, on the other. George Washington set the example:

> The liberty enjoyed by the people of these states of worshipping Almighty God agreeably to their consciences, is not only among the choicest of their *blessings*, but also of their *rights*. While men perform their social duties faithfully, they do all that society or the state can with propriety demand or expect; and remain responsible only to their Maker for their religion, or modes of faith, which they may prefer or profess.[22]

As president, Lincoln explicitly acknowledged the nation's debt to the Almighty through proclamations of days of religious observance. Lincoln called for national days of thanksgiving, fasting, and prayer eleven times. In his last public address, following Lee's surrender at Appomattox, Lincoln states: "In the midst of this [celebration], however, He, from Whom all blessings flow, must not be forgotten. A call for a national thanksgiving is being prepared, and will be duly promulgated."[23] These proclamations, as well as other speeches involving religion in the public sphere, show the mutual benefit Lincoln believed religion and government could have on each other.

Most important, his speeches and writings reflect a penchant for drawing on religion for public purposes, as well as facilitating the natural and rightful expression of man's desire to worship the Creator. Lincoln, therefore, preserved the status of religion, independent of the needs of government, as worthy of the adherence of democratic citizens.

Order for Sabbath Observance (1862)

"I sincerely wish war was an easier and pleasanter business than it is," Lincoln wrote the son of Henry Clay, "but it does not admit of holy-days."[24] Indeed, the Battle of Bull Run (at Manassas, Virginia, July 21, 1861), the first battle between the Union and Confederate armies, began at dawn on a Sunday. Ironically, only five weeks after Lincoln's letter to Thomas H. Clay, Lincoln issued an order for the military to observe the Sabbath. That noted sage of Lincolniana, Carl Sandburg, cautioned against inferring too much about Lincoln's religious sympathies from his Sabbath Day order. He suggested it came from Secretary of War Edwin M. Stanton. Relying on the statement of an assistant adjutant general, who claims to have taken the order from Stanton's hand to Lincoln's for the latter's approval, Sandburg concludes: "The text and tone of this order indicate definitely it was composed by someone else than Lincoln."[25] Roy P. Basler, editor of the authoritative *Collected Works of Abraham Lincoln*, qualifies this account somewhat. He cites a New York *Tribune* article reporting that gentlemen "representing religious bodies in New-York City, called upon the President and heads of departments today to urge upon him the propriety of enforcing a better observance of the Sabbath in the army. The interviews are represented as agreeable and satisfactory." Lincoln issued the order two days after this interview.[26] Even if the order was not Lincoln's composition, his decision to issue it settles the matter regarding his agreement with its aim as well as its stated rationale. Lincoln was too careful a writer, especially when it dealt with religious matters, to approve public statements—let alone issue orders—unless he agreed wholeheartedly with their sentiments.

Lincoln began the order with a clear statement of his constitutional authority for doing so, as well as the limited scope of its application: "The President, *Commander-in-Chief* of the Army and Navy, desires and enjoins the orderly observance of the sabbath by the officers and men in the military and naval service."[27] Because government should not ordinarily direct the religious expression of the community, Lincoln is careful to note his authority for doing so in this instance. He both "desires and enjoins" this observance, making clear that the order derives from personal preference in addition to constitutional prerogative. He then lists four reasons for the order:

> The importance for man and beast of the prescribed weekly rest, the sacred rights of Christian soldiers and sailors, a becoming deference to the best sentiment of a Christian people, and a due regard for the Divine will, demand that Sunday labor in the Army and Navy be reduced to the measure of strict necessity.

The first reason draws on the well-known biblical command of a weekly day of rest to fall on the last day of the week. Lincoln alludes to God in "the *prescribed* weekly rest" (emphasis added), so as not to rob the recuperative effect of a day of rest of its divine sanction.[28] But note that both "man and beast" gain from its observance. Lincoln's inclusion of beasts both satisfies the biblical intention of the command—"Six days thou shalt do thy work, and on the seventh day thou shalt rest: that thine ox and thine ass may rest, and the son of thy handmaid, and the stranger, may be refreshed" (Ex. 23:12)—as well as the dictates of common sense. Lincoln, therefore, pays deference to the Originator of the practice, while emphasizing the benefit that a Sabbath rest bestows to those who observe it.

The second reason highlights an important distinction Lincoln makes that few scholars today acknowledge: religion is a good in and of itself, regardless of its usefulness to government. Because each individual possesses a natural right to believe in God, government must protect its exercise as much as any other right. By referring to the freedom of religion as "sacred rights," Lincoln acknowledges that human beings must be secure in their freedom to worship God without undue government interference. A government that acted otherwise would be denying the exercise of a right as natural, and therefore deserving of government protection, as any other that man has. William B. Allen explains that "man's religious life is independent of the needs of the state. Accordingly, the state *never* has any business taking a man under coercion and forcing him to enter into any practice whatever without the reasonable exercise and accoutrements of his faith."[29] (Emphasis in original.)

For Lincoln, the end of government always consisted of protecting civil *and* religious liberty.[30] Inasmuch as religious liberty finds its fulfillment in the worship of a divine being, transcending the world of man and government, its sacredness bestows on it an importance greater than any other right man possesses by nature. James Madison gave the clearest expression of this principle in his "Memorial and Remonstrance" of 1785:

> It is the duty of every man to render to the Creator such homage, and such only, as he believes to be acceptable to him. This duty is precedent both in order of time and degree of obligation, to the claims of Civil Society. . . . We maintain therefore that in matters of Religion, no man's right is abridged by the institution of Civil Society, and that Religion is wholly exempt from its cognizance. [31]

If government is to fulfill its duty to secure all the rights of the citizenry, it must accommodate the Sabbath observance not as a favor but as an obligation to religious citizens.[32] Lincoln's protection of "the sacred rights of Christian soldiers and sailors" serves as a reminder that government exists to serve the people, not the other way around.

The third reason for proscribing "Sunday labor in the Army and Navy" is "a becoming deference to the best sentiment of a Christian people." Except in cases of "strict necessity," Lincoln believes that government should accommodate the religious practices of the citizenry. This both facilitates their piety while enabling them to fulfill their civic duties. Government sanction of the Sabbath befits an authority that aims to support its citizens' best impulses: respect for and obedience to both God and country.[33]

Finally, Lincoln argues that "a due regard for the Divine will" requires that government accommodate the religious obligations of the community.[34] Presiding over a nation well read in the Bible, he treats the Old Testament command for a Sabbath day's rest as a truth amenable to all of his listeners regardless of their religious beliefs. George Anastaplo explains that "a substantial uniformity in the literary tastes and in the orthodox religious sentiments of his community—tastes and sentiments which the respectable literature and the influential intellectuals of his day did not openly challenge," allowed Lincoln to speak to the nation in such boldly religious terms without exceeding the powers of his office. At the time, the "religious devotion" of the American people was "not too strong to resent an exploitation of religious sentiment for political purposes; not too weak to make such a dedication of religious sentiment ineffective."[35]

This puts too fine a point, however, on Lincoln's cultivation of America's civil religion. Why would firm believers in the Christian God "resent" Lincoln's call for a Sabbath among the Union ranks, or his many other appeals to the "religious sentiment" of the American people? It should be no surprise that Lincoln or any other government official would do so for political reasons. What is worth noting is that Lincoln sought a political objective while enlisting "the best sentiment of a Christian people." Americans, in short, remember him so fondly to this day precisely because *Lincoln's* practice of civil religion as president accomplished political objectives without interfering with the public's pursuit of religious ones. He showed Americans how to bring their religion with them into the public arena without embroiling the country in theological disputes.

. Lincoln continues in his order for a Sabbath observance by explaining that the "discipline and character" of the military would suffer if the Sabbath observance or the sanctity of God's name were disregarded. Furthermore, "the cause they defend" would likewise be "imperiled" as the disfavor of God would fall upon a nation that failed to obey His express commands. He then quotes George Washington verbatim in support of his order for a military Sabbath: "At this time of public distress . . . men may find enough to do in the service of God and their country without abandoning themselves to vice and immorality."[36] Lincoln continues: "The first General Order issued by the Father of his Country after the Declaration of Independence, indicates the spirit in which our institutions were founded and should ever be defended: 'The General hopes and trusts that every officer and man will endeavor to live and act as becomes a Christian soldier defending the dearest rights and liberties of his country.'"

Dated July 9, 1776, George Washington's order called for the appointment of chaplains for the regiments and an exhortation to religious observance.[37] Lincoln followed his example throughout his presidency. For instance, the U.S. Christian Commission, a volunteer organization that supplied blankets, clothing, books, and spiritual consolation to Union soldiers, once asked to preside over a public meeting to "give the meeting in Washington the greatest possible weight for the Sacred interests involved." The press of his presidential duties forced Lincoln to decline, but in a gracious letter he notes, "The birth-day of Washington, and the Christian Sabbath, coinciding this year, and suggesting together, the highest interests of this life, and of that to come, is most propitious for the meeting proposed."[38] Two months into the war, he had directed General Benjamin F. Butler—"if in his discretion he shall deem it necessary and advisable"—to appoint a chaplain to a volunteer hospital in the field.[39] He would later recommend that Congress appoint chaplains for hospitals, in addition to those already appointed to the military.[40] In his 1862 Order for Sabbath Observance, Lincoln enlists the support of the religious sentiments of the nation for the sake of both man and government, with the "sacred rights" of man taking precedence. As government exists to secure the equal rights to life, liberty, and the pursuit of happiness, and as worship of the Creator constitutes part of one's pursuit of happiness and a natural right equal to that of any other, Lincoln exercises his authority as president and commander in chief to protect this freedom.

Annual Message to Congress (1863)

If ever Lincoln appeared to presume too much upon a religious consensus in the nation, he did so in his 1863 Annual Address to Congress. In this "state of the union" address, as in all his annual addresses to Congress, Lincoln reflects on the condition of the Indian nations. He briefly recounts treaties drawn up since the previous session of Congress that sought "the establishment of permanent friendly relations with such of these tribes as have been brought into frequent and bloody collision with our outlying settlements and emigrants."[41] Lincoln then outlines a policy of beneficence toward the Indian tribes:

> Sound policy and our imperative duty to these wards of the government demand our anxious and constant attention to their material well-being, to their progress in the arts of civilization, and, above all, to that moral training which, under the blessing of Divine Providence, will confer upon them the elevated and sanctifying influences, the hopes and consolation of the Christian faith.[42]

In addition to promoting their "material well-being" and "progress in the arts of civilization," Lincoln draws the attention of Congress "above all" to the "moral training" of the Indians. While moral character need not follow from any particular religious creed or revealed religion in general, Lincoln praises this training of the soul because "under the blessing of Divine Providence" the training will endow Indians with divine favor: "the elevated and sanctifying influences, the hopes and consolation of the Christian faith." Nevertheless, Lincoln appears to make an explicit appeal to its revelatory claims about itself: namely, that it can bring men to a saving knowledge of God. Although Christianity was by far the predominant religion of America, Lincoln's proposed policy toward the Indians appears to favor one religion over others.

One difficulty lies with the concept of sanctification. It means setting something or someone aside for a holy purpose, but this implies exclusion. The "hopes and consolation" of Christianity are at minimum directed toward eternal life hereafter, which implies exclusion even more so. These seem to have nothing to do with civil religion, which denotes a common, public understanding of a nation's relation to God. For example, Jean-Jacques Rousseau listed the following set of precepts for a neutral civil religion:

> The existence of an omnipotent, intelligent, benevolent divinity that foresees and provides; the life to come; the happiness of the just; the punishment of sinners; the sanctity of the social contract and the law—these are the positive dogmas. As for the negative dogmas, I would limit them to a single one: no intolerance.[43]

Rousseau concluded sharply: "But anyone who dares to say 'Outside the church there is no salvation' should be expelled from the state . . ."[44] As the peace of civil society depends on a social bond that excludes no citizen from its fellowship, Lincoln's praise of "the Christian faith" would appear to exclude Americans who do not see Christianity as holding man's "hopes and consolation."

Two learned editor-scholars of the Lincoln corpus, Roy P. Basler and Don E. Fehrenbacher, both question the composition of Lincoln's Indian policy. They note that the preliminary draft of the address bears Lincoln's handwriting beginning four paragraphs *after* the statement regarding "the elevated and sanctifying influences, the hopes and consolation of the Christian faith." They conclude that his cabinet drafted the preceding portion of the address (except for the opening paragraph, which does not appear in the preliminary draft).[45] All told, Lincoln endorsed the entire address but almost certainly did not pen the section regarding the instruction of the Indians in the Christian faith. While he agreed with its sentiments in general, the prevalence of the Christian religion in America begs grace for Lincoln's rare accommodation of an explicit endorsement of it.

Reply to Loyal Colored People of Baltimore upon Presentation of a Bible (1864)

To judge from his stated opinion of the Bible in an altogether different setting, Lincoln as president did implicitly defend the veracity of the Christian religion. Upon receiving a Bible from a delegation of "the Loyal Colored People of Baltimore," given in appreciation for his Emancipation Proclamation, Lincoln closed his brief reply with a reflection on the Bible:

In regard to this Great Book, I have but to say, it is the best gift God has given to man.

All the good the Saviour gave to the world was communicated through this book. But for it we could not know right from wrong. All things desirable for man's welfare, here and hereafter, are to be found portrayed in it. To you I return my most sincere thanks for the very elegant copy of the great Book of God which you present.[46]

The press reported the event and his response the following day, but Lincoln originally gave his opinion of the Bible to a private audience. In it the president shares a religious conviction that, outside the context of a small, sympathetic audience, might offend non-Christian Americans. Lincoln, however, made no reference to any public policy and, thus, was free to his speak his mind about the Bible without jeopardizing the religious freedom of non-Christian Americans. The president of the United States need not surrender his religious freedom in order to secure that of the nation.

Given his audience, he makes a somewhat exaggerated claim that except for the Bible, "we could not know right from wrong." Contrast this statement with one from the summer of 1858, where Lincoln referred to the central truth of the Declaration of Independence—"that all men are created equal"—as the "father of all moral principle."[47] Also, when commenting on the support of churches for his prosecution of the Civil War, Lincoln wrote: "Indeed it is difficult to conceive how it could be otherwise with any one professing christianity, or even having ordinary perceptions of right and wrong."[48] Moreover, the Bible itself affirms the ability of human beings to discern right from wrong apart from biblical revelation.[49] Earlier in his political career, Lincoln commented on truths that both the Bible and human experience validated: "The Bible says somewhere that we are desperately selfish. I think we would have discovered that fact without the Bible."[50] All of these statements must be read together to understand Lincoln's moral epistemology, which at minimum suggest that he found the moral directives of Scripture to jibe with the dictates of human reason.

The same holds true for his acknowledgment of the Christian church as God's or "His" church and Jesus as "the Saviour." In responding to resolutions presented by the American Baptist Home Mission Society, Lincoln called attention to "those professedly holy men of the South" who appealed for support of the Confederacy from "the christian world" abroad:

[T]o my thinking, they contemned God and His church, far more than did Satan when he tempted the Saviour with the Kingdoms of the earth.

The devils [*sic*] attempt was no more false, and far less hypocritical. But let me forbear, remembering it is also written "Judge not, lest ye be judged."[51]

Lincoln shares his personal belief that there exists a church of God and that Jesus is the Saviour of mankind, but this comes in a private reply to a committee of the American Baptist Home Mission Society. Given that he had thanked the committee earlier for "adding to the effective and almost unanamous [*sic*] support which the Christian communities are so zealously giving the country, and to liberty," his biblical reference was in keeping with the support churches gave to his prosecution of the war. Lincoln comments, "Indeed it is difficult to conceive how it could be otherwise with any one professing christianity [*sic*]," expressing his wonderment that men of the cloth would not only favor slavery but also seek support from other Christians to protect it.

He applied the same principle to foreign affairs by proposing an anti-slavery resolution for adoption at public meetings in England. Faced with the possible recognition of the Confederacy by Great Britain (if the war turned against the Union), on professedly biblical grounds no less, Lincoln wrote:

> Whereas, while *heretofore*, State, and Nations, have tolerated slavery, *recently*, for the first in the world, an attempt has been made to construct a new Nation, upon the basis of, and with the primary, and fundamental object to maintain, enlarge, and perpetuate human slavery, therefore,
> Resolved, That no such embryo State should ever be recognized by, or admitted into, the family of christian and civilized nations; and that all ch[r]istian and civilized men everywhere should, by all lawful means, resist to the utmost, such recognition or admission.[52]

Lincoln hoped British citizens would adopt the resolution to affirm publicly that pro-slavery regimes are not only uncivilized but also un-Christian. Thus in sharing his opinion about the consistency of southern church leaders to their own religion, Lincoln could speak the language of his listeners without hiding his own beliefs on the subject.

Garry Wills missed this point in his book, *Under God: Religion and American Politics* (1990), when he addressed Lincoln's public use of religion. In a chapter entitled, "Lincoln's Black Theology," Wills refers to Lincoln's appeal to religion in support of the Union as the expression of "an emotional artist," asserting that "this controlled politician" could *not* have believed his public statements regarding God and religion. He adds that Lincoln "even went so far, in identifying himself with blacks, as to use 'the Saviour' in thanking the Baltimore freedmen who presented him with a Bible—a locution common to them, but not to him."[53] Lincoln certainly did not use the term publicly as often as a preacher would, but how often would an American president or any other politician need to refer publicly to Jesus Christ? Moreover, as far as "the Saviour" being a black locution, Lincoln used the same term in an 1864 letter to the (non-black) American Baptist Home Mission Society.[54]

Lincoln also referred to "the Saviour" in speeches and debates in his 1858 campaign against Senator Stephen A. Douglas—a campaign where Lincoln made every effort to distinguish his defense of the natural rights of American slaves from the claim that he sought the immediate elevation of blacks in American society. Here are a few examples: "language of the Saviour"; "The Saviour, I suppose, did not expect that any human creature could be perfect as the Father in Heaven"; "The application is made by the Saviour in this parable"; and "the maxim which was put forth by the Saviour is true."[55] Douglas called Lincoln's party "the Black Republican party" throughout the campaign. Lincoln could not afford this moniker to stick in Illinois, a state comprising many citizens who had migrated from the bordering slave-holding state of Kentucky, and whose citizens had recently passed a law prohibiting the emigration of free blacks into Illinois.[56] Even as early as 1839, when addressing in the Illinois State House of Representatives, he refers to the "Saviour of the world" and "the Saviour and his disciples."[57]

Appointment of Hospital Chaplains

"Having been solicited by Christian Ministers, and other pious people," Lincoln wrote the Reverend F. M. Magrath,

> to appoint suitable persons to act as Chaplains at the hospitals for our sick and wounded soldiers, and feeling the intrinsic propriety of having such persons to so act, and yet believing there is no law conferring the power upon me to appoint them, I think fit to say that if you will voluntarily enter upon, and perform the appropriate duties of such position, I will recommend that Congress make compensation therefor at the same rate as Chaplains in the army are compensated.[58]

The Rev. Magrath was one of at least seven ministers Lincoln encouraged to volunteer as hospital chaplains with expectation of federal compensation in the not too distant future. The president would follow through on his proposal on December 3, 1861, in his first annual address to Congress.[59] In the mean time, seeing the need of "our sick and wounded soldiers" but "no law conferring the power upon me to appoint them," Lincoln did what he could to accommodate their wishes.

Lincoln had made the same offer nine days earlier in response to Archbishop John J. Hughes's request for the appointment of Catholic chaplains for hospitals:

> I find no law authorizing the appointment of Chaplains for our *hospitals*, and yet the services of chaplains are more needed, perhaps, in the hospitals, than with the healthy soldiers in the field. With this view, I have given a sort of quasi appointment . . . to each of three protestant ministers . . . I will thank you to give me the name or names of one or more suitable persons of the Catholic Church, to whom I may with propriety, tender the same service.[60]

The Rev. Magrath was one of two priests Archbishop Hughes assigned to be hospital chaplain following Lincoln's suggestion, which resulted in Magrath's request of Lincoln discussed earlier.[61]

Lincoln was careful not to promote a policy, even one that would receive popular approval, in a manner inconsistent with the powers of his office. He, therefore, wrote out a form letter that followed verbatim his earlier letter to the Rev. Magrath to encourage interested ministers to volunteer with the hope of eventually receiving compensation from Congress.[62] Lincoln then appended the form letter as "Schedule A" to his 1861 Annual Address to Congress.

In his address, Lincoln states, "By mere omission, I presume, Congress has failed to provide chaplains for hospitals occupied by volunteers."[63] He goes on to describe his form letter and how it was sent to solicit volunteers to work in the hospitals. He continues: "These gentlemen, I understand, entered upon the duties designated, at the times respectively stated in the schedule, and have labored faithfully therein ever since. I therefore recommend that they be compensated at the same rate as chaplains in the army. I further suggest that general provision be made for chaplains to serve at hospitals, as well as with regiments." Lincoln thereby makes possible the religious support of the war by loyalists, while ensuring that its accommodation takes place according to the settled will of the people as stipulated in the Constitution they sought so fervently to preserve. More important, Lincoln understands that the primary reason for hospital chaplains as well as army chaplains is to enable enlisted men to continue in their respective faiths. Given that many would see their last days on earth from a hospital bed, chaplains would perform an invaluable service to the country.

Even though the nation is at war, Lincoln as president recognizes that the government has an obligation not to interfere unduly with its citizens' exercise of their natural rights, the foremost of them being one's duty to the Creator. This is why Lincoln commented to the archbishop that "the services of chaplains are more needed, perhaps, in the hospitals, than with the healthy soldiers in the field," for men in hospitals need religion primarily for solace in and of itself—not so they can get back into action as soon as possible. Lincoln understands that religion, while a good thing regardless of one's circumstances, is all the more beneficial and, hence, necessary in situations that produce despair rather than hope.

Lincoln dealt with a host of other issues related to the appointment of chaplains to hospitals and the military. For example, he strove for a nonsectarian policy in Congress regarding chaplain appointments. As mentioned earlier, after a few Protestant ministers accepted his suggestion to volunteer their services, Archbishop Hughes wrote Lincoln in kind. Lincoln replied, "If you perceive no objection, I will thank you to give me the name or names of one or more suitable persons of the Catholic Church, to whom I may with propriety, tender the same service."[64] Two months later, Lincoln accommodated interested Jews: "I shall try to have a new law broad enough to cover what is desired by you in behalf of the Israelites."[65] Dr. Arnold Fischel had asked to be appointed chaplain of a predominantly Jewish regiment from New York, but was informed by the secretary of war, Simon Cameron, that two recent acts of Congress required that a military chaplain be a "regular ordained minister of some Christian denomination." Three months later, Congress revised the law (effective July 17, 1862) to include Jewish chaplains, and on September 18, 1862, the Reverend Jacob Frankel became the first rabbi appointed to an American military chaplaincy.[66]

Late in the war, Lincoln expressed "no objection" to having a woman confirmed as chaplain by a regiment that had unanimously elected her. Secretary of War Edwin M. Stanton had "declined to recognize the mustering on account of her sex, not wishing to establish a precedent."[67] Veteran captain of the Black Hawk War that he was, Lincoln merely adapted the common practice of troops electing their own captains to the situation of regiment chaplains. Unlike Stanton, Lincoln did not impose any particular biblical proscription against female preachers upon the regiment. Following the acceptance of blacks as Union soldiers, Lincoln arranged for the compensation of a black chaplain who had been denied wages duly commissioned to him.[68] His statements regarding chaplain appointments thus reflect a penchant for including all interested faiths as he encouraged the religious expression of the people, while adhering to the rule of law and constitutional supremacy in civil matters.

Lincoln's famous response to an address by a committee of the Methodist Episcopal Church illustrates his inclusionary policy even toward particular denominations. "Nobly sustained as the government has been by all the churches," Lincoln remarks, "I would utter nothing which might, in the least, appear invidious against any." He closes: "God bless the Methodist Church—bless all the churches—and blessed be God, Who, in this our great trial, giveth us the churches."[69] In addition, Lincoln highlights the contribution the churches and, therefore, religion in general have made toward resolving the nation's crisis. Given the severity of "our great trial," he offers thanks to God for providing the American churches to assist in bearing the load of the war effort. From providing hospital volunteers and fielding sanitary commissions to outfitting local missions of mercy, while offering, above all, spiritual consolation, the American church had proven to be a tremendous support during a time of despair.

To cite just one example, Lincoln was said to be greatly appreciative of the actions of one church in riotous New York. Its patriotic actions were prompted by the words of Dr. Joseph P. Thompson amid the draft riots of 1863:

> Of what avail are our churches if we shall no longer have a government or a country? Of what worth is our Christianity if it cannot preserve these? If the government cannot save the country, let the churches save both. Let this church call for volunteers; equip a regiment; and put it into the field, to show that *we* will never give it up.[70]

The sum of $30,000 was raised following the service, with two women sending $500 each, saying, "We cannot go: put men in our stead." According to pastor Thompson's account of the noteworthy action of Broadway Tabernacle (Congregational) of New York, "It cheered the burdened heart of the President and gave new courage to the indomitable Minister of War." By enlisting government aid for hospital chaplains on a nonsectarian basis, Lincoln demonstrated that the political usefulness of religion could coexist with government accommodation of church and synagogue involvement in the war effort.

Governing the Rebel Churches

General Benjamin F. Butler, the military governor of New Orleans known as the "Beast" throughout the South for his Remirro-de-Orco-style rule,[71] ordered that the "omission, in the service of the Protestant Episcopal Church in New Orleans, of the Prayers for the President of the

United States, would be regarded as evidence of hostility to the Government of the United States."[72] To Lincoln's chagrin, this was only the beginning of his troubles with religious liberty in the occupied South. With southern states in rebellion against federal authority, Lincoln was at pains to free his generals to prevent subversion while still protecting the right of law-abiding citizens to exercise their religious freedom.

In an effort to consolidate Union support, especially among sympathetic Southerners, another Union general issued an order stipulating that members of certain churches take an oath of loyalty before gathering at their places of worship. Lincoln viewed the order as a discriminatory interference with religious worship, for no oath was required of those taking part in non-religious, public gatherings. He wrote a letter "more social than official, containing suggestions rather than orders."[73] In it he shares his concern:

> I somewhat dread the effect of your Special Order, No. 61 dated March 7, 1864. I have found that men who have not even been suspected of disloyalty, are very averse to taking an oath of any sort as a condition, to exercising an ordinary right of citizenship. The point will probably be made, that while men may without an oath, assemble in a noisy political meeting, they must take the oath, to assemble in a religious meeting.[74]

Here Lincoln understands the right to worship as "an ordinary right of citizenship." By "ordinary" he means that one's duty to the Creator, while a sacred right, deserves government protection as much as any other right—for example, the right to assemble peacefully. He saw no distinction between religious gatherings and political ones worthy of government intervention. Religious liberty should therefore not be singled out for extraordinary precaution by the government, and thus forced to pass an additional threshold for its lawful exercise.

Lincoln's public defense of religious freedom goes back at least to 1844, when he arranged a public meeting to discuss a Philadelphia riot involving Protestants, Catholics, and the militia. Catholics had been protesting mandatory readings of the King James Bible in the public schools, while certain Protestant organizations called for stricter naturalization laws and the limitation of office-holding to American-born citizens. At the Springfield meeting, Lincoln introduced resolutions that defended the Whig Party from charges of bigotry against foreigners and Catholics, one of which summarized his thinking on the matter:

> *Resolved,* That the guarantee of the rights of conscience, as found in our Constitution, is most sacred and inviolable, and one that belongs

no less to the Catholic, than to the Protestant; and that all attempts to abridge or interfere with these rights, either of Catholic or Protestant, directly or indirectly, have our decided disapprobation, and shall ever have our most effective opposition.[75]

In fact, he explained his policy toward allegedly secessionist churches from within the general context of free speech and public order. In a series of letters to military officers and interested citizens, Lincoln explained his understanding of the problem of military intervention in church affairs. To begin with, Lincoln suspended an order that sought to expel the Reverend Samuel B. McPheeters and his wife from the state of Missouri for "unmistakeable evidence of sympathy with the rebellion."[76] Among the allegedly treasonous acts was baptizing a child with the name of a Confederate general! Dr. McPheeters, pastor of the Pine Street Presbyterian Church of St. Louis, ultimately was forced from the pastorate by unionists in his congregation but remained in the state. A few days after Lincoln suspended the order, he wrote General Samuel R. Curtis and explained his rationale, adding that Curtis could consider the suspension withdrawn "if, after all, you think the public good requires his [Dr. McPheeters's] removal."[77] Lincoln closed his letter with what became his standard policy on churches suspected of disloyalty:

> But I must add that the U.S. government must not, as by this order, undertake to run the churches. When an individual, in a church or out of it, becomes dangerous to the public interest, he must be checked; but let the churches, as such take care of themselves. It will not do for the U.S. to appoint Trustees, Supervisors, or other agents for the churches.

Lincoln explains his policy regarding military intervention in alleged "rebel" churches without any discussion of religion. Instead, he reduces the problem to a question of civil disturbance. Neither a church as such nor a preacher should constitute the focus of military attention, but rather the "individual" and the danger he may pose to "the public interest."[78] His being "in a church or out of it" makes no difference.

Upon hearing that General William Tecumseh Sherman had reinstated a loyal Presbyterian pastor who had been discharged by Confederate parishioners in Memphis, Tennessee, an exasperated Lincoln elaborated on his earlier order:

> I am now told that . . . the Military put one set of men out of and another set into the building. This, if true, is most extraordinary. I say again, if there be no military need for the building, leave it alone, neither putting any one in or out, of it, except on finding some one preaching or practicing treason, in which case lay hands upon him just

as if he were doing the same thing in any other building, or in the
streets or highways.[79]

Lincoln thought it "most extraordinary" that any general in the field
would construe his policy on southern churches as permission to appoint
church pastors.[80] By referring to the Memphis church as a "building," he
demonstrated a single-minded concern that only "military necessity"
dictate a general's treatment of churches.[81] Given "no military need for
the building," Lincoln stated his policy regarding any southern church in
three words—"leave it alone." Treat a rebel church like they would any
other building they find in the field of battle. Similarly, treat actual
treason by a preacher like they would any other person in any other
venue. Even Lincoln's use of the word "preaching," in context, referred
not to a sermon's religious doctrine but to its political content: was it
"treason" or not? With no ecclesiastical entanglement at issue, Lincoln
skirted any claim of violating the free exercise of religion. He would
finally wash his hands of this fiasco when asked a couple of months later
if he wanted to return the Memphis church to its previous pastor: "The
president declines making any further order in the case of the
Presbyterian Church in Memphis."[82]

"It will not do," Lincoln chides, "for the U.S. to appoint . . . agents
for the churches." As republican government is not a religious institution
and cannot of right be vested with ecclesiastic powers, it has no business
administering churches. Government must "let the churches take care of
themselves," just as government must let individuals take care of
themselves so long as their actions do not conflict with the peace and
order of society. "Do *not* unto others as you would *not* have them do
unto you," becomes the civil approximation of the golden rule. If church
leaders and members are obligated to follow this rule with respect to "the
public interest," and hence practice Lincoln's political religion,
government must do no less with respect to the religious interest.

The problem for Lincoln, of course, remained the excessive and
sometimes contrary measures taken by his officers in the field. Secretary
of War Edwin M. Stanton ordered that "all houses of worship belonging
to the Methodist Episcopal Church South in which a loyal minister, who
has been appointed by a loyal Bishop of said church, does not now
officiate" be placed "at the disposal of Rev. Bishop Ames."[83] The express
purpose of the order reads: "It is a matter of great importance to the
Government, in its efforts to restore tranquility to the community and
peace to the nation, that Christian ministers should, by example and
precept, support and foster the loyal sentiment of the people." Orders like
these arose in response to actions like that of the southern Episcopal

Church, which revised its Prayer Book to list prayers "for the Confederacy, instead of for the United States and its president."[84] When Lincoln heard of Stanton's order, he wrote him and included a passage he wrote the previous December regarding renewed claims of mistreatment of Dr. McPheeters: "I have never interfered, nor thought of interfering as to who shall or shall not preach in any church; nor have I knowingly, or believingly, tolerated any one else to so interfere by my authority." Under pressure from Lincoln, who was prompted by loyal parishioners in Missouri, Stanton modified his order. Just a few days later, Lincoln felt obliged to cast the original and modified order in the best light possible:

> As you see within, the Secretary of War modifies his order so as to exempt Missouri from it. Kentucky was never within it; nor as I learn from the Secretary, was it ever intended for any more than a means of rallying the Methodist people in favor of the Union, in localities where the rebellion had disorganized and scattered them. Even in that view, I fear it is liable to some abuses, but is not quite easy to withdraw it entirely, and at once.[85]

Lincoln would have to extricate himself from similar incidents time and again throughout the war. The most infamous case involves Lincoln's rescinding of Grant's General Order No. 11, which expelled Jews "as a class" from the Department of the Tennessee. The state was then fighting a losing battle against speculators in trade across the western Tennessee border. The President's reason for revoking the order, as conveyed by General Henry W. Halleck in a telegram to Grant, was that the order "proscribed an entire religious class, some of whom are fighting in our ranks . . ."[86] Lincoln saw the expulsion order not as an ethnic but a religious persecution. Without turning a blind eye to subversive conduct, Lincoln sought to respect the rights of people of faith, which included the leaders and laypersons of southern churches.

Executive Proclamations of Days of Fasting, Thanksgiving, and Prayer

About a week after he called for a national day of thanksgiving, Lincoln demonstrated the seriousness with which he considered proclamations of national days of thanksgiving and prayer in an 1864 telegram. The telegram to General John A. Dix, written by Secretary of War Stanton and signed by Lincoln, called for the arrest of certain editors and seizure of two publishing companies—ordinarily and even in times of war a questionable government action. What was the crime that deserved said punishment? The editors had allowed the printing of a "false and spurious proclamation, purporting to be signed by the President, . . . which publication is of a treasonable nature."[87] The fake proclamation called for 400,000 new recruits, enforceable by conscription if necessary, as well as "a day of fasting, humiliation and prayer." Always one to write and speak with precision, the lawyer-turned-president would not countenance the publication of words falsely attributed to him.

Lincoln's actual calls for national days of fasting, thanksgiving, and prayer illustrate his most direct efforts to encourage religious observances during the Civil War. To appraise their impact aright, one must understand that proclaiming days of thanksgiving and prayer do not necessarily support revealed religion at the expense of a civil religion amenable to citizens of all faiths. As John West explains in *The Politics of Revelation and Reason* (1996):

> One possible way to square such public devotions with a morality derived from reason is to champion the claims of natural religion—that is, a religion discoverable by human reason. . . . Hence, it is possible to regard prayer days as consistent with the morality of reason because reason itself can discover that there is a God who should be venerated.[88]

West goes on to conclude: "Days of fasting and thanksgiving serve as an acknowledgment of this critical reservation to the social compact. They constitute a symbolic recognition by the nation that religious adherents do not forfeit the higher claims of religion once they enter civil society."[89] Cicero relates the same idea in his *De Legibus* (or *Laws*):

> Therefore among all the varieties of living beings, there is no creature except man which has any knowledge of God, and among men themselves there is no race either so highly civilized or so savage as not to know that it must believe in a god, even if it does not know in what sort of god it ought to believe. Thus it is clear that man recognizes God because, in a way, he remembers and recognizes the source from which he sprang.[90]

A biblical analogy can be found in Acts 17:16-34, where Paul preaches to a meeting of the Areopagus and refers to one of their poets to support the idea that all men owe their existence to God: "For in him we live, and move, and have our being; as certain also of your own poets have said, For we are also his offspring" (Acts 17:28). A central claim of the American regime, of course, is that its separation of church and state promoted both civil and religious liberty—a claim Lincoln would defend throughout his political career. It is no surprise, then, that Lincoln's proclamations of thanksgiving days promote both civil and revealed religion. He uses these occasions to foster civil religion, for the sake of preserving the Union, while he encourages citizens to exercise their respective faith in revealed religion.

His first religious proclamation came four months to the day after Confederate forces fired upon Fort Sumter. It also followed two consecutive Union defeats in the first skirmishes of the war, Manassas and Wilson's Creek—battles that signaled a war to be prolonged beyond initial expectations. Responding to a recommendation from Congress, which followed a tradition begun by the first Congress under the U.S. Constitution,[91] Lincoln issued a Proclamation of a National Fast Day. After quoting the congressional resolution, he gives two "whereas" clauses in support of his proclamation of "a day of humiliation, prayer and fasting."[92] The first states that "it is fit and becoming in all people, at all times, to acknowledge and revere the Supreme Government of God." This shows an understanding of God derived not so much from revealed religion but from natural theology. Lincoln saw natural theology as providing moral distinctions that were discernible by human reason not tied to a personal faith in divine revelation.

For example, in 1860 Lincoln said, "We understand that the 'equality of man' principle which actuated our forefathers in the establishment of the government is right; and that slavery, being directly opposed to this, is morally wrong. I think that if anything can be proved by natural theology, it is that slavery is morally wrong."[93] Although he goes on in his fast-day proclamation to give a biblical elaboration of the relation between God and the nations—mentioning "sins and transgressions," and referring to God as "the Lord" from a direct quotation from Psalms 110:10 ("The fear of the Lord is the beginning of wisdom")—the account supports the idea of a civil religion shared by most Americans. His statement that "all people" on earth should acknowledge their dependence on "the Supreme Government of God" makes this explicit. Lincoln responded to a supportive letter from the Religious Society of Friends in Iowa with a similar note of confidence in mankind's innate sense of humility before God: "It seems to me that if there be one subject upon which all good men may unitedly agree, it is imploring the gracious favor of the God of Nations upon the struggles our people are making for the preservation of their precious birthright of civil and religious liberty."[94]

The second "whereas" clause moves from the general to the particular: "all people" becomes "our own beloved Country" as Lincoln describes the national crisis and recommends a national course of action. The country should (1) "recognize" the Civil War as God's chastisement, (2) "humble" themselves and appeal to God's mercy, and (3) "pray" that God will (a) spare them further harm, (b) prosper their military, and (c) secure their civil and religious liberties as a result.

The final paragraph states his resolution that "a day of humiliation, prayer and fasting" be set for "all the people of the nation." Asking the nation to "observe and keep that day according to their several creeds and modes of worship," Lincoln hopes that "the united prayer of the nation may ascend to the Throne of Grace and bring down plentiful blessings" upon the country. "Throne of Grace" comes from Hebrews 4:16, which reads: "Let us therefore come boldly unto the throne of grace, that we may obtain mercy, and find grace to help in time of need." Lincoln employs biblical language to proclaim a fast day, but he intends to recommend a day of humility for Americans of all faiths. The proclamation of a national fast day may incidentally promote the separate religions in America but in principle fosters a religious sentiment that unites all the faiths in support of the cause of Union. In his first national proclamation calling for pious observance, Lincoln recommends a course of action that enlists all religions to support the cause of the country. But neither the means—the nation's revealed religions—nor the end—a national or civil religion in support of the government—contradict the otherwise separate objectives of religion and government.

The shortest of Lincoln's orders regarding a religious holiday followed upon the cities of Washington and Georgetown declaring their own day of thanksgiving to take place on November 28, 1861. So on November 27, Lincoln announced that "the several Departments will on that occasion be closed, in order that the officers of the government may partake in the ceremonies."[95] Even though the closing was prompted by the action of local city governments, the president found no problem accommodating the exercise of religion by local employees of the federal government. Later in the war, Lincoln not only invited the military and the American people to set apart a day for prayer, but expressly requested all government officers to do the same. At the urging of Congress, Lincoln issued a proclamation for public servants and private citizens "to assemble in their preferred places of public worship on that day" and pray with penitent hearts.[96] Although Congress presented the idea to Lincoln, he "cordially" agreed with their request—florid with "penitential and pious sentiments"—for an executive proclamation of "a day of national humiliation and prayer." One must not forget that a call to government and citizen alike to humility before the God of nations is all the more fitting given Lincoln's eventual fear that an over-confident North might run roughshod over a conquered South if it got the chance. Finally, Lincoln "heartily" approved of "the devotional design and purpose thereof," making clear his agreement with Congress's intention.

The second national proclamation, in contrast with the first, was a call for thanksgiving as opposed to humiliation. A year into the war, and without any express congressional nudging, Lincoln declared that "at their next weekly assemblages in their accustomed places of public worship" the "People of the United States" should "especially acknowledge and render thanks to our Heavenly Father for these inestimable blessings."[97] The federal army and navy had achieved "signal victories" at Shiloh, Tennessee, and at Fort Henry and Fort Donelson, both "suppressing an internal rebellion" and avoiding "the dangers of foreign intervention and invasion." Lincoln saw fit to remind the nation that not only divine punishments but blessings ought to be recognized and, hence, the nation should thank God for these recent victories as well as "invoke the Divine Guidance for our national counsels." Here Lincoln's appeal to the nation's religious sentiments encourages support for the national government without subverting the highest aims of the separate religions practiced by the nation.

The next religious proclamation came almost a year later in response to a Senate request for the same. Repeating the introduction he wrote for his first proclamation of a national fast day, Lincoln then says that it is the duty "of nations as well as of men" to "recognize the sublime truth, announced in the Holy Scriptures and proven by all history, that those nations only are blessed whose God is the Lord."[98] The last clause comes from Psalms 33:12: "Blessed is the nation whose God is the Lord: and the people whom he hath chosen for his own inheritance." Lincoln qualifies this biblical reference, however, with the statement that its truth is "proven by all history." Even though his biblical reference breaches strict republican propriety by citing a particular religious text, his appeal to the lessons of "history" provides a nonsectarian argument for introducing the dictates of revelation into the public square. He calls on the experience and education of his listeners, as well as their Judaeo-Christian heritage, to support his national call to "prayer and humiliation." He also presents a truth for the implicit verification of his listeners: namely, that history shows Providence blesses those nations that humble themselves before God. Borrowing the language of the

Bible, Lincoln promotes a government objective using the language most familiar to Americans at the time.[99]

But what does it mean for a nation to recognize "the Lord" as God? Psalms 33:8-9 reads: "Let all the earth fear the Lord: let all the inhabitants of the world stand in awe of him. For he spake, and it was done; he commanded, and it stood fast." It continues some verses later, "Behold, the eye of the Lord is upon them that fear him, upon them that hope in his mercy. . . . Let thy mercy, O Lord, be upon us, according as we hope in thee" (Ps. 33:18, 22). The psalmist declares that all the nations should fear the one true God because He is the Almighty Creator. It appears to require that citizens of all nations should adopt the faith of Old Testament Jews. However, the command to "fear the Lord" requires only that these sundry nations humble themselves before God, not adopt or promulgate a particular theology or set of religious dogmas. "The Lord looketh from heaven; he beholdeth all the sons of men. . . . [H]e considereth all their works" (Ps. 33:13, 15b). In other words, the one true God will take it upon Himself to extend mercy on those who humble themselves. Religious pluralism does not exclude there being only one God; it simply allows disparate nations—and likewise, different groups of citizens within a nation—to acknowledge their dependence upon the Maker of heaven and earth according to their own moral lights.

While too much can be read into Lincoln's catering his rhetoric to his particular audience, he certainly understood rhetoric as a means of presenting political truth in a palatable way. Using Aristotle's typology, the reason or argument (*logos*) of his speech took into account the emotions or disposition (*pathos*) of his audience.[100] To cite just one example, when Lincoln spoke before an audience of Indian chiefs, he referred to the actions of God as "the providence of the Great Spirit, who is the great Father of us all."[101] Employing the Indian reference to God as "the Great Spirit," Lincoln conveys an understanding of God familiar to his listeners as well as supportive of the general public's belief in a Creator.

Lincoln would declare six more proclamations of thanksgiving and prayer (one of which was called informally but telegraphed nationally). One proclamation, dated October 3, 1863, became the first to fix an annual day of thanksgiving to be celebrated on the last Thursday of each November. Like the others, it promoted thanksgiving to God "with one heart and one voice by the whole American People."[102] In other words Lincoln encouraged the public faith, or civil religion, by appealing to the individual citizen's observance of his particular revealed religion. The practice of one in the service of the other did nothing to demean private faith and, hence, preserved it while benefiting the regime.

Lincoln has shown that religion should be left to its own devices and not be bothered by the government to any greater degree than the public at large. Politics must respect religion's, which means God's, claims on the citizenry. To round out this examination of Lincoln's view of religion and the American republic, the next chapter explains Lincoln's belief that religion could also pose a threat to liberty in a free society. Religion in the public square is truly a double-edged sword: it works to a nation's benefit only when guided by men beholden to, and humbled by, the principle of human equality.

Notes

1. Joshua F. Speed, *Reminiscences of Abraham Lincoln and Notes of a Visit to California* (Louisville, Ky.: John P. Morton and Company, 1884), 32-33. Don E. Fehrenbacher and Virginia Fehrenbacher, in their compilation of recollected Lincoln utterances, rank this story a "C" on a scale of "A" to "E" for reliability. ("A" denotes a Lincoln quotation recorded by the auditor within days of hearing it, and "E" denotes a quotation that "is probably not authentic.") "C" is a quotation "recorded noncontemporaneously." In Speed's case, his published account of his encounter came twenty years after the fact. *Recollected Words of Abraham Lincoln* (Stanford: Stanford University Press, 1996), 414, lii-liii. According to Mary Todd Lincoln, Lincoln "read the bible a good deal about 1864." "Mary Todd Lincoln (WHH interview [September 1866])," in *Herndon's Informants: Letters, Interviews, and Statements about Abraham Lincoln*, Douglas L. Wilson and Rodney O. Davis, eds. (Urbana: University of Illinois Press, 1998), 156. Wayne C. Temple records that Joshua F. Speed joined Trinity Methodist Church late in life. *Abraham Lincoln: From Skeptic to Prophet* (Mahomet, Ill.: Mayhaven Publishing, 1995.), 295, n. 123.

2. In an 1866 letter to William Herndon, Speed commented on Lincoln's faith: "I think that when I first knew Mr L he was skeptical as to the great truths of the Christian Religion. I think that after he was elected President, he sought to become a believer—and to make the Bible a preceptor to his faith and a guide for his conduct." "Joshua F. Speed to WHH (12 January 1866)," in *Herndon's Informants*, 156.

3. For a similar interpretation offered earlier this century, see Christopher Dawson, *Religion and the Modern State* (London: Sheed and Ward, 1935), chaps. 6, "Religion and Politics," and 7, "The Religious Solution," 102-28.

4. Mark Y. Hanley, *Beyond a Christian Commonwealth: The Protestant Quarrel with the American Republic, 1830-1860* (Chapel Hill: University of North Carolina Press, 1994), 158, 31. See also Christoph Schönborn, "The Hope of Heaven, the Hope of Earth," *First Things* (April 1995), 32-38 and George

Weigel, "The Church's Political Hopes for the World; or, Diognetus Revisited," in *The Two Cities of God: The Church's Responsibility for the Earthly City*, Carl E. Braaten and Robert W. Jenson, eds. (Grand Rapids, Mich.: Wm. B. Eerdmans Publishing Company, 1997), 59-77.

5. Harry V. Jaffa, *Crisis of the House Divided: An Interpretation of the Issues in the Lincoln-Douglas Debates* (Seattle: University of Washington Press, 1973; reprint ed., Chicago: University of Chicago Press, 1982, © 1959), 183-232; Glen E. Thurow, *Abraham Lincoln and American Political Religion* (Albany: State University of New York Press, 1976); Michael P. Zuckert, "Lincoln and the Problem of Civil Religion," in *Law and Philosophy: The Practice of Theory—Essays in Honor of George Anastaplo*, John A. Murley, Robert L. Stone, and William T. Braithwaite, eds., 2 vols. (Athens: Ohio University Press, 1992), 2: 720-43; George Anastaplo, "American Constitutionalism and the Virtue of Prudence: Philadelphia, Paris, Washington, Gettysburg," in *Abraham Lincoln, The Gettysburg Address, and American Constitutionalism*, Leo Paul S. de Alvarez, ed. (Irving, Tex.: University of Dallas Press, 1976), 113-27, 140-170.

6. "To Allen N. Ford (11 August 1846)," in *The Collected Works of Abraham Lincoln*, Roy P. Basler, ed., 9 vols. (New Brunswick: Rutgers University Press, 1955), 1: 383. Hereinafter cited as *Collected Works*; all emphases in original except where otherwise noted.

7. William E. Barton, *The Soul of Abraham Lincoln* (New York: George H. Doran Company, 1920), 63-65.

8. C. Bruce Staiger, "Abolition and the Presbyterian Schism of 1837-1838," *The Mississippi Valley Historical Review* 36 (December 1949): 393, 394.

9. Frederick A. Ross, *Slavery Ordained of God* (Philadelphia: J. B. Lippincott & Company, 1857), 123, 118.

10. "Handbill Replying to Charges of Infidelity (31 July 1846)," in *Collected Works*, 1: 382.

11. "To Mary S. Owens (7 May 1837)," in *Collected Works*, 1: 78.

12. "Remarks to Baltimore Presbyterian Synod: Two Versions [No. 1] (24 October 1863)," in *Collected Works*, 6: 535. The context for his remark, though, paints a less skeptical picture of Lincoln's faith. In the immediately preceding sentence, Lincoln states that as president he "was early brought to a living reflection that nothing in my power whatever, in others to rely upon, would succeed without the direct assistance of the Almighty, but all must fail." The sentence that follows Lincoln's wish that he was "more devout" actually affirms his piety: "Nevertheless, amid the greatest difficulties of my administration, when I could not see any other resort, I would place my whole reliance in God, knowing that all would go well, and that he would decide for the right." *Collected Works*, 6: 535, 536. Among the earliest extant writings of Lincoln's is a handwritten copybook of arithmetic, a page of which includes the following rhyme: "Abraham Lincoln/his hand and pen/he will be good but/god knows When." "Copybook Verses [1824-1826]," in *Collected Works*, 1: 1. Cf. the assessment by Francis B. Carpenter, a portrait painter who lived at the White

House for six months in 1864 as he painted a reenactment of Lincoln's first reading of the Emancipation Proclamation: "In the ordinary acceptation of the term, I would scarcely have called Mr. Lincoln a *religious* man,—and yet I believe him to have been a sincere *Christian*. (Emphasis in original.) F. B. Carpenter, *The Inner Life of Abraham Lincoln* (Lincoln: University of Nebraska Press, 1995; originally published in 1866 as *Six Months at the White House with Abraham Lincoln* by Hurd and Houghton, New York), 185-86. Biographer Ward Hill Lamon, a member of Lincoln's inner circle as president, turns Carpenter's view on its head semantically, while expressing the same sentiment: "He was not a Christian in the orthodox sense of the term, yet he was as conscientiously religious as any man." *Recollections of Abraham Lincoln, 1847-1865*, Dorothy Lamon Teillard, ed. (Lincoln: University of Nebraska Press, 1994; originally published by A. C. McClurg & Co., 1895, 2nd ed. expanded in 1911, Washington, D.C.), 334. This echoes Mary Todd's statement to William H. Herndon: "he was a religious man always, as I think," but "he was not a technical Christian." "Mary Todd Lincoln (WHH interview [September 1866])," in *Herndon's Informants*, 360.

13. Speed, *Reminiscences of Abraham Lincoln*, 32.

14. "Speech in U.S. House of Representatives on the Presidential Question (27 July 1848)," in *Collected Works*, 1: 503.

15. Hans J. Morgenthau, "The Mind of Abraham Lincoln: A Study in Detachment and Practicality," in *Essays on Lincoln's Faith and Politics*, Kenneth W. Thompson, ed. (Lanham, Md.: University Press of America, 1983), 8.

16. The passage cited most often on this subject comes from a eulogy Congressman Henry C. Deming delivered before the General Assembly of Connecticut in 1865: "He [Lincoln] said, he had never united himself to any church, because he found difficulty in giving his assent, without mental reservations, to the long complicated statements of Christian doctrine which characterize their Articles of Belief and Confessions of Faith." William J. Wolf, *The Religion of Abraham Lincoln* (New York: Seabury Press, 1963; originally published under the title *The Almost Chosen People: A Study of the Religion of Abraham Lincoln* by Doubleday & Company, Inc., 1959), 74. The Fehrenbachers rank Deming's recollection a "C" (on a scale of "A" to "E") for reliability. *Recollected Words of Abraham Lincoln*, 137.

17. Allen C. Guelzo, "Abraham Lincoln and the Doctrine of Necessity," *Journal of the Abraham Lincoln Association* 18 (Winter 1997): 66-67; Temple, *Abraham Lincoln*, 6.

18. "To Martin S. Morris (26 March 1843)," in *Collected Works*, 1: 320.

19. "To James Shields (17 September 1842)," in *Collected Works*, 1: 299-300, and "Memorandum of Duel Instructions to Elias H. Merryman [19 September 1842]," in *Collected Works*, 1: 300-302. For a brief history of Christian antagonism toward dueling in early America, see *Church and State in the United States: Historical Development and Contemporary Problems of*

Religious Freedom under the Constitution, Anson Phelps Stokes, ed., 3 vols. (New York: Harper & Brothers, 1950), 2: 5-12.

20. "Communication to the People of Sangamo County (9 March 1832)," in *Collected Works*, 1: 5, n. 1. He ran eighth out of thirteen candidates for four seats in the lower house of the Illinois General Assembly. Nevertheless, his New Salem returns were all the more impressive given that he only recently moved to the area six months prior to announcing his candidacy for Illinois State Representative. In addition, he interrupted the campaign for three months to lead a local militia brigade in the Black Hawk War, being elected captain by his men. Two years later, he would run second in a field of thirteen candidates for four Sangamon County seats, and poll first (out of seventeen candidates) in his next two re-election bids.

21. "Farewell Address (19 September 1796)," in *George Washington: A Collection*, W. B. Allen, ed. (Indianapolis: Liberty Fund, Inc., 1988), 521. Lincoln would make explicit reference to Washington's Farewell Address in his famous Cooper Institute Address of 1860; however, the context was not religion but rather sectionalism due to the slavery controversy. "Address at Cooper Institute, New York City (27 February 1860)," in *Collected Works*, 3: 536-37.

22. "To the Annual Meeting of Quakers (September 1789)," in *George Washington: A Collection*, 533.

23. "Last Public Address (11 April 1865)," in *Collected Works*, 8: 399-400.

24. "To Thomas H. Clay (8 October 1862)," in *Collected Works*, 5: 452.

25. Carl Sandburg, *Abraham Lincoln*, Sangamon ed., 6 vols. (New York: Charles Scribner's Sons, 1950), vol. 5: *The War Years— III*, 374-75.

26. "Order for Sabbath Observance (15 November 1862)," in *Collected Works*, 5: 498, n. 1.

27. *Collected Works*, 5: 497.

28. "And on the seventh day God ended his work which he had made; and he rested on the seventh day from all his work which he had made. And God blessed the seventh day, and sanctified it: because that in it he had rested from all his work which God created and made." Gen. 2:2-3. "Remember the sabbath day, to keep it holy." Ex. 20:8. "Six days may work be done; but in the seventh is the sabbath of rest, holy to the Lord . . . It is a sign between me and the children of Israel forever." Ex. 31:15a, 17a.

29. Cited from William B. Allen's draft book review of Os Guiness and James D. Hunter, eds., *Articles of Faith, Articles of Peace: The Religious Liberty Clauses and the American Public Philosophy* and Garry Wills, *Under God: Religion and American Politics* (Claremont, Calif.: By the Author, 1991), 8-9.

30. "Address before the Young Men's Lyceum of Springfield, Illinois (27 January 1838)," in *Collected Works*, 1: 108: "We find ourselves under the government of a system of political institutions, conducing more essentially to the ends of civil and religious liberty, than any of which the history of former times tells us." Lincoln goes on to say that "establishing and maintaining civil

and religious liberty" is "the advancement of the noblest of cause[s?]." *Collected Works*, 1: 114.

31. "Memorial and Remonstrance against Religious Assessments (October 1785)," in *The Mind of the Founder: Sources of the Political Thought of James Madison*, Marvin Meyers, ed. (Indianapolis: Bobbs-Merrill Company, Inc., 1973; revised ed., Hanover: University Press of New England, 1981), 7.

32. See Daniel C. Palm, "'Where Locke Stopped Short We May Go On': Religious Toleration and Religious Liberty at the Founding," in *On Faith and Free Government*, Daniel C. Palm, ed. (Lanham, Md.: Rowman & Littlefield Publishers, Inc., 1997), 29-42, for a discussion of the shift from mere toleration of religious diversity to equal protection of religious freedom as a fundamental right.

33. For an explanation of how the American regime reconciled much of the tension between the obligations to one's religion and government, see Harry V. Jaffa, *The American Founding as the Best Regime: The Bonding of Civil and Religious Liberty* (Claremont, Calif.: Claremont Institute for the Study of Statesmanship and Political Philosophy, 1990). He states: "The unprecedented character of the American Founding is that it provided for the coexistence of the claims of reason and of revelation in all their forms, without requiring or permitting any political decisions concerning them." Jaffa, *The American Founding as the Best Regime*, 15.

34. Lincoln would express a similar sentiment—that nations should follow the divine will—the next year upon hearing of the Union victory at Gettysburg: "And that for this, he [the 'President'] especially desires that on this day, He whose will, not ours, should ever be done, be everywhere remembered and reverenced with profoundest gratitude." "Announcement of News From Gettysburg (4 July 1863)," in *Collected Works*, 6: 314. Thus, the obligation that God places on men should be met, allowing the desire of both God and man to be satisfied. See also his "Announcement of Union Success in Tennessee (7 December 1863)," in *Collected Works*, 7: 35, where he takes the occasion of Confederate General Longstreet's retreat after the Battle of Chattanooga to call for a time of national thanksgiving: "esteeming this to be of high national consequence, I recommend that all loyal people do, on receipt of this, informally assemble at their places of worship and tender special homage and gratitude to Almighty God, for this great advancement of the national cause."

35. Anastaplo, "American Constitutionalism and the Virtue of Prudence: Philadelphia, Paris, Washington, Gettysburg," 168-69, n. 65. He concludes: "One must wonder what it is that the contemporary statesman has to draw upon comparable to the materials Lincoln had at hand in the Declaration of Independence, in Shakespeare, and in the Bible." Anastaplo, "American Constitutionalism and the Virtue of Prudence," 125. See also Zuckert, "Lincoln and the Problem of Civil Religion," 2: 739.

36. "Order for Sabbath Observance (15 November 1862)," in *Collected Works*, 5: 499.

37. "General Orders (9 July 1776)," in *George Washington: A Collection*, 73.

38. "To Alexander Reed (22 February 1863)," in *Collected Works*, 6: 114-15. The head of the commission had presented the meeting to Lincoln as follows:

> These meetings are doing great good for our countrys [*sic*] cause as well as for the noble men of our Army and Navy.
>
> If we may believe the united testimony of press and people their influence to check distrust and disloyalty and to restore confidence and support to the Government has been very great.

Collected Works, 6: 115, n. 1. For more information about the Christian Commission or sanitary commissions in general, see James M. McPherson, *Battle Cry of Freedom: The Civil War Era* (New York: Ballantine Books, 1989), 480-86.

39. "To Benjamin F. Butler (20 June 1861)," in *Collected Works*, 4: 413.

40. "Annual Message to Congress (3 December 1861)," in *Collected Works*, 5:40. For other letters dealing with chaplain appointments and related issues, see *Collected Works*, 4: 559-60, 5: 8-9, 40, 53-54, 69, 171, 297, 464, 464-65, 6: 44, 58, 137, 157, 193, 194, 226-27, 313-14, 420-21, 512, 7: 280, 293, 332, 8: 50, 102-103, 225. They generally comprise brief messages directing the appointment of particular men as chaplains.

41. "Annual Message to Congress (8 December 1863)," in *Collected Works*, 7: 47-48. David Donald notes that Lincoln followed custom by having a clerk read his annual addresses to Congress. David Herbert Donald, *Lincoln* (New York: Simon and Schuster, 1995), 320.

42. "Annual Message to Congress (8 December 1863)," in *Collected Works*, 7: 48.

43. Jean-Jacques Rousseau, *Social Contract*, trans. Maurice Cranston (New York: Viking Penguin, Inc., 1986), bk. 4, chap. 8, 186. Cf. Robert N. Bellah's seminal article, "Civil Religion in America," *Daedalus* 96 (1967): 1-21. For example:

> The God of the [American] civil religion is not only rather "unitarian," he is also on the austere side, much more related to order, law, and right than to salvation and love. Even though he is somewhat deist in cast, he is by no means simply a watchmaker God. He is actively interested and involved in history, with a special concern for America.

Bellah, "Civil Religion in America," 7. Michael P. Zuckert defines civil religion as "centering on the civil life of the nation and thereby providing both religious or divine support for its chief political institutions, and a set of standards in terms of which the political life of the nation may be judged . . ." Zuckert, "Locke and the Problem of Civil Religion: Bicentennial Essay No. 6" (Claremont, Calif.: Claremont Institute for the Study of Statesmanship and Political Philosophy, 1984), 2.

44. Rousseau, *Social Contract*, bk. 4, chap. 8, 187.

45. "Annual Message to Congress (8 December 1863)," in *Collected Works*, 7: 48, n. 36; *Abraham Lincoln: Speeches and Writings*, Don E. Fehrenbacher, ed., 2 vols. (New York: Literary Classics of the United States, Inc., 1989), 2: 749, n. 549.37-553.36.

46. "Reply to Loyal Colored People of Baltimore upon Presentation of a Bible (7 September 1864)," in *Collected Works*, 7: 542.

47. "Speech at Chicago, Illinois (10 July 1858)," in *Collected Works*, 2: 499.

48. "To George B. Ide, James R. Doolittle, and A. Hubbell (30 May 1864)," in *Collected Works*, 7: 368.

49. For example, Romans 2:14-15 reads: "For when the Gentiles, which have not the law, do by nature the things contained in the law, these, having not the law, are a law unto themselves: which shew the work of the law written in their hearts, their conscience also bearing witness, and their thoughts the mean while accusing or else excusing one another."

50. "Seventh and Last Debate with Stephen A. Douglas (15 October 1858)," in *Collected Works*, 3: 310.

51. "To George B. Ide, James R. Doolittle, and A. Hubbell (30 May 1864)," in *Collected Works*, 7: 368. Lincoln quotes Matthew 7:1 when he cautions his listeners not to rush to judgment against pro-slavery preachers.

52. "Resolution on Slavery [15 April 1863]," in *Collected Works*, 6: 176.

53. Garry Wills, *Under God: Religion and American Politics* (New York: Simon and Schuster, 1990), 220.

54. "To George B. Ide, James R. Doolittle, and A. Hubbell (30 May 1864)," in *Collected Works*, 7: 368: "they contemned and insulted God and His Church, far more than did Satan when he tempted the Saviour with the Kingdoms of the earth."

55. "First Lecture on Discoveries and Inventions (6 April 1858)," in *Collected Works*, 2: 442; "Speech at Chicago (10 July 1858)," in *Collected Works*, 2: 501; "Speech at Springfield, Illinois (17 July 1858)," in *Collected Works*, 2: 511; and "First Debate with Stephen A. Douglas at Ottawa, Illinois (21 August 1858)," in *Collected Works*, 3: 17, respectively.

56. Eugene H. Berwanger, *The Frontier against Slavery: Western Anti-Negro Prejudice and the Slavery Extension System* (Urbana, Ill.: University of Illinois Press, 1967), 44-46, 48-51; Don E. Fehrenbacher, *Prelude to Greatness: Lincoln in the 1850's* (Stanford: Stanford University Press, 1962), 31.

57. "Speech on the Sub-Treasury ([26] December 1839)," in *Collected Works*, 1: 167.

58. "To F. M. Magrath (30 October 1861)," in *Collected Works*, 5: 8-9. See "Form Letter to Chaplains (3 December 1861)," in *Collected Works*, 5: 53-54, for the names of the other ministers Lincoln wrote to between September 25 and November 7, 1861, to encourage their voluntary service as hospital chaplains.

59. "Annual Message to Congress (3 December 1861)," in *Collected Works*, 5: 40.

60. "To John J. Hughes (21 October 1861)," in *Collected Works*, 4: 559.

61. "To John J. Hughes (21 October 1861)," in *Collected Works*, 4: 560, n. 1. The other appointment went to the Reverend Francis X. Boyle.

62. "Form Letter to Chaplains (3 December 1861)," in *Collected Works*, 5: 53.

63. "Annual Message to Congress (3 December 1861)," in *Collected Works*, 5: 40.

64. "To John J. Hughes (21 October 1861)," in *Collected Works*, 4: 559. President James K. Polk had recommended that American bishops select two Catholic priests to serve as chaplains in the Mexican War, but they were to serve as civilians (i.e., they were not to receive military appointments). See Bertram W. Korn, *American Jewry and the Civil War* (Philadelphia: Meridian Books and the Jewish Publication Society of America, 1961), 56.

65. "To Arnold Fischel (14 December 1861)," in *Collected Works*, 5: 69.

66. Korn, *American Jewry and the Civil War*, 62, 77. Korn describes how a Jew, Michael Allen, had served as a regimental chaplain notwithstanding the original law's requirement of only ordained clergymen of Christian denominations. He adds that the appointment of chaplains who were not ordained clergymen was widespread, leading one of Lincoln's secretaries to depict military chaplains as "broken down 'reverends'" who could not find a church that would allow them to pastor. Korn, *American Jewry and the Civil War*, 58-62.

67. "To Edwin M. Stanton (10 November 1864)," in *Collected Works*, 8: 102-103 and n. 1.

68. "To Edward Bates (4 April 1864)," in *Collected Works*, 7: 280.

69. "Response to Methodists (18 May 1864)," in *Collected Works*, 7: 350-51. His "Reply to Delegation of Baptists (28 May 1864)" similarly states: "I have had great cause of gratitude for the support so unanimously given by all Christian denominations of the country. . . . This particular body is in all respects as respectable as any that have been presented to me." *Collected Works*, 7: 365. See also his "Reply to Members of the Presbyterian General Assembly (2 June 1863)," in *Collected Works*, 6: 244: "It has been my happiness to receive testimonies of a similar nature, from I believe, all denominations of Christians."

70. Stokes, *Church and State in the United States*, 2: 219.

71. McPherson, *Battle Cry of Freedom*, 623-24; Geoffrey C. Ward, with Ric Burns and Ken Burns, *The Civil War: An Illustrated History* (New York: Alfred A. Knopf, Inc., 1991), 126. For Niccolò Machiavelli's description of Remirro de Orco as "a cruel and ready man," see *The Prince*, trans. Harvey C. Mansfield, Jr. (Chicago: University of Chicago Press, 1985), 29-30.

72. Stokes, *Church and State in the United States*, 1: 220. For a similar situation in Richmond, Virginia, see "To [General] Godfrey Weitzel (12 April 1865)," in *Collected Works*, 8: 405-406.

73. "To William S. Rosecrans (4 April 1864)," in *Collected Works*, 7: 283.

74. *Collected Works*, 7: 283-84. See also "To [General] Lewis Wallace (10 May 1864)" and "To [General] Lewis Wallace (13 May 1864)," in *Collected Works*, 7: 335-36 and 339-40.

75. "Speech and Resolutions Concerning Philadelphia Riots (12 June 1844)," in *Collected Works*, 1: 338. For the historical context, see Stokes, *Church and State in the United States*, 1: 825-32; McPherson, *Battle Cry of Freedom*, 32-33.

76. "To [General] Samuel R. Curtis (27 December 1862)," in *Collected Works*, 6: 20 and n. 1.

77. "To [General] Samuel R. Curtis (2 January 1863)," in *Collected Works*, 6: 34. In his letter, Lincoln had first expressed doubt about expelling Dr. McPheeter, given that he had actually sworn an oath of allegiance to the Union, had assured Lincoln of his constant prayers for the president and his administration, was of unquestioned moral character, and was charged with no specific crime. Lincoln thought it imprudent to expel someone even known to "sympathize with the rebels" based on nothing more than a "suspicion of his secret sympathies." Lincoln repeated the charges against Dr. McPheeters as follows: "that he has a rebel wife & rebel relations, that he sympathizes with rebels, and that he exercises rebel influence." Stokes records that Dr. McPheeters had "refused to declare himself for the Union, and baptized a child with the name of a Confederate general." *Church and State in the United States*, 2: 221. His final charge to General Curtis was "to exercise your best judgment, with a sole view to the public interest, and I will not interfere without hearing you." A year later Lincoln received a petition asking that Dr. McPheeters be restored of "all his ecclesiastical rights." He replied, "I heard no further complaint from Dr. M. or his friends for nearly an entire year," and therefore believed him to be "enjoying all the rights of a civilian." "To Oliver D. Filley (22 December 1863)," in *Collected Works*, 7: 85. His concluding sentence reads: "I will not have control of any church on any side." *Collected Works*, 7: 86.

78. Lincoln returned a petition asking for Dr. McPheeters's restoration to his pulpit with a statement that reads in part: "I directed, a long time ago, that Dr. McPheeters was to be arrested, or remain at large, upon the same rule as any one else . . ." "Endorsement on Petition: Concerning Samuel B. McPheeters (22 December 1863)," in *Collected Works*, 7: 86. See also his "Memorandum about Churches (4 March 1864)," in *Collected Works*, 7: 223, which concludes: "I add if the military have military need of the church building, let them keep it; otherwise let them get out of it, and leave it and its owners alone except for causes that justify the arrest of any one."

79. "Endorsement Concerning a Church at Memphis, Tennessee (13 May 1864)," in *Collected Works*, 7: 339. After General Henry W. Halleck appointed Sherman military governor of Memphis, Tennessee, Sherman attended a local Episcopal church only to find that the minister omitted the customary prayer for the president. Sherman promptly stood up in his pew and recited the prayer

aloud. John F. Marszalek, *Sherman: A Soldier's Passion for Order* (New York: Vintage Civil War Library—Random House, Inc., 1993), 191.

80. Eight years later, the United States Supreme Court would rule that it must allow churches to decide for themselves regarding "controverted questions of faith" and "ecclesiastical government of all the individual members, congregations, and officers within the general association." See *Watson v. Jones*, 13 Wallace 679 (1872).

81. For the effect of Union war-making on southern churches, see Daniel W. Stowell, *Rebuilding Zion: The Religious Reconstruction of the South, 1863-1877* (New York: Oxford University Press, 1998), chap. 1, "God's Wrath: Disruption, Destruction, and Confusion in Southern Religious Life," 15-32.

82. "To Cadwallader C. Washburn (5 July 1864)," in *Collected Works*, 7: 427-28. See also "To Andrew Johnson (6 February 1865)," in *Collected Works*, 8: 264.

83. "To Edwin M. Stanton (11 February 1864)," in *Collected Works*, 7: 179, n. 1.

84. Stokes, *Church and State in the United States*, 2: 219, and 219-24, 226-28, generally.

85. "Endorsement to John Hogan (13 February 1864)," in *Collected Works*, 7: 182-83.

86. See McPherson, *Battle Cry of Freedom*, 620-23, and Korn, *American Jewry and the Civil War*, 126. For a thorough exploration of the men and events surrounding this incident, see Korn, *American Jewry and the Civil War*, chap. 6, "Exodus 1862," 121-55.

87. "To John A. Dix (18 May 1864)," in *Collected Works*, 7: 347-50. For an account of the incident, see *Collected Works*, 7: 348-50, n. 1; "To Edwin M. Stanton (22 August 1864)," in *Collected Works*, 7: 512-13 and n. 1; and Carl Sandburg, *Abraham Lincoln*, vol. 5: *The War Years—III*, 53-58.

88. John G. West, Jr., *The Politics of Revelation and Reason: Religion and Civic Life in the New Nation* (Lawrence: University Press of Kansas, 1996), 124.

89. West, *The Politics of Revelation and Reason*, 124-25.

90. *De Legibus*, trans. Clinton Walker Keyes (Cambridge: Harvard University Press, 1988), 323, 325.

91. Stokes, *Church and State in the United States*, 1: 486-88. Stokes notes that days of thanksgiving were observed as early as the Puritan settlement by the Plymouth Colony, and continued through the Continental Congress of the Revolutionary War era.

92. "Proclamation of a National Fast Day (12 August 1861)," in *Collected Works*, 4: 482.

93. "Speech at Hartford, Connecticut (5 March 1860)," in *Collected Works*, 4: 3.

94. "To Caleb Russell and Sallie A. Fenton (5 January 1863)," in *Collected Works*, 6: 39-40.

95. "Order for Day of Thanksgiving (27 November 1861)," in *Collected Works*, 5: 32.

96. "Proclamation of a Day of Prayer (7 July 1864)," in *Collected Works*, 7: 431-32.

97. "Proclamation of Thanksgiving for Victories (10 April 1862)," in *Collected Works*, 5: 186.

98. "Proclamation Appointing a National Fast Day (30 March 1863)," in *Collected Works*, 6: 155. He closes by exhorting the country: "let us then rest humbly in the hope authorized by the Divine teachings, that the united cry of the Nation will be heard on high, and answered with blessings . . ." *Collected Works*, 6: 156.

99. To a general disgruntled by shunted ambition, Lincoln wrote: "My belief is that the permanent estimate of what a general does in the field, is fixed by the 'cloud of witnesses' who have been with him in the field; and that relying on these, he who has the right needs not to fear." "To John A. McClernand (12 August 1863)," in *Collected Works*, 6: 383. Hebrews 12:1 refers to the saints of old as a "cloud of witnesses" who exhort Christians to a patient and steadfast life of faith.

100. Aristotle, *Rhetoric*, trans. W. Rhys Roberts and ed. Friedrich Solmsen (New York: Random House, Inc., 1954), bk. 1, chap. 2, 1356a1-1356a21, 24-25.

101. "Speech to Indians (27 March 1863)," in *Collected Works*, 6: 152. This followed the example of George Washington, who (through an interpreter) closed an address to the Cherokee nation with his best wishes and prayer that "the Great Spirit" preserve them. "Talk to the Cherokee Nation (29 August 1796)," in *George Washington: A Collection*, 648.

102. "Proclamation of Thanksgiving (3 October 1863)," in *Collected Works*, 6: 497. See Harold Holzer, ed., *Dear Mr. Lincoln: Letters to the President* (Reading, Mass.: Addison-Wesley Publishing Company, 1995), 57-58, for the letter Sarah Josepha Hale wrote to Lincoln (dated 28 September 1863) requesting "to have the *day of our annual Thanksgiving made a National and fixed Union Festival.*" William H. Seward, his secretary of state, drafted the proclamation, which Lincoln approved with minor changes. See John M. Taylor, *William Henry Seward: Lincoln's Right Hand* (Washington, D.C.: Brassey's, 1991), 224; Glyndon G. Van Deusen, *William Henry Seward* (New York: Oxford University Press, 1967), 401-402. The other proclamations contain similar appeals to the religious sentiments of the nation as follows: "I invite the People of the United States to assemble on that occasion in their customary places of worship, and in the forms approved by their own consciences, render the homage due to the Divine Majesty" in "Proclamation of Thanksgiving (15 July 1863)," in *Collected Works*, 6: 332; "I recommend that all patriots, at their homes, in their places of public worship, and wherever they may be, unite in common thanksgiving and prayer to Almighty God" in "To the Friends of Union and Liberty (9 May 1864)," in *Collected Works*, 7: 333; "all the other loyal and law-abiding People of the United States . . . [should]

assemble in their preferred places of public worship ... to render to the Almighty and Merciful Ruler of the Universe ... homages and ... confessions" in "Proclamation of a Day of Prayer (7 July 1864)," in *Collected Works*, 7: 432; "It is therefore requested that ... in all places of public worship in the United States, thanksgiving be offered to Him for His mercy" in "Proclamation of Thanksgiving and Prayer (3 September 1864)," in *Collected Works*, 7: 533; "to be observed by all my fellow-citizens wherever they may then be as a day of Thanksgiving and Praise to Almighty God the beneficent Creator and Ruler of the Universe" in "Proclamation for Thanksgiving (20 October 1864)," in *Collected Works*, 8: 55.

Chapter 4

The Political Vices of Religion:
An Interpretation of the Temperance Address

Abraham Lincoln made so many biblical references in his political speeches, one might wonder if he ever thought religion could pose a problem for a free society. One need look no further than the words of a contemporary of Lincoln's, the fiery abolitionist and former temperance newspaper editor William Lloyd Garrison, to find evidence of political rhetoric that employs religious language in a divisive manner. As editor of the *Liberator*, the abolitionist paper of record, Garrison declared the U.S. Constitution "a covenant with death and an agreement with hell"; asserted that "the kingdoms of this world are to become the kingdoms of our Lord and of his Christ"; and labeled all earthly governments as "anti-Christ."[1] This incendiary language left little room for discussion and mixed theological and political issues in a way that muddled public debate.

Moreover, it conveyed such condemnation that any merit in its argument would most likely be lost to anyone who dared to disagree. As a reflective, slave-owning Louisiana planter in *Uncle Tom's Cabin* shared with his pontificating cousin visiting from New England: "I make no manner of doubt that you threw a very diamond of truth at me, though you see it hit me so directly in the face that it was n't [*sic*] exactly appreciated, at first."[2] The well-intentioned slave-owner Augustine St. Clare acknowledges the truth of Cousin Ophelia's advice but points out that her abolitionist sentiments were conveyed with so little understanding of, or sympathy for, his situation that he felt the sting of her remarks more readily than their truth.

Throughout his public service, Lincoln disapproved of abolitionism for its tendency to exacerbate the evils of slavery rather than mitigate them. For example, in his second term as an Illinois state representative, Lincoln entered a protest with fellow Whig lawyer Dan Stone against the General Assembly's resolutions addressing "domestic slavery" memorials from other states. Lincoln and Stone argued that slavery "is founded on both injustice and bad policy," they concluded that as a political matter, "the promulgation of abolition doctrines tends rather to increase than to abate its evils."[3] Its religious aspect in particular led Lincoln to address its potential harm to American self-government in an 1842 speech before the Springfield Washington Temperance Society.

A week before Abraham Lincoln invited Stephen Douglas to a series of debates during their famous senatorial campaign of 1858, Lincoln remarked of Senator Douglas, "He says I have a proneness for quoting scripture."[4] Lincoln's frequent appeal to the religious sentiments of the citizenry fostered a lasting connection between their holy obligations and their political prosperity, aimed at minimum to train a people in the habits of self-government.[5] Self-government, however, implies limits or restrictions, and those of necessity must be placed by the very objects of that limitation. Therefore, Lincoln's expressions of public faith at times point toward a restriction of religious expression as it relates to the perpetuation of free government. Paradoxically, Abraham Lincoln's Temperance Address of 1842 frequently cites or alludes to the Bible while highlighting certain vices of religion that must be tempered if religion is to benefit republican life.

Next to his Gettysburg and Second Inaugural Addresses, one would be hard-pressed to imagine Lincoln sounding more like a preacher than in his Temperance Address.[6] This was all the more fitting, given that the venue for the speech and attendant festival was the Second Presbyterian Church of Springfield, Illinois. He spoke on the 110th anniversary of the birthday of George Washington at the behest of a society of reformed drunkards that took its namesake from the father of their country.[7] Senator-turned-historian Albert J. Beveridge records that the Springfield chapter of the Washington Temperance Society organized itself on December 20, 1841, just three months prior to Lincoln's address, and held their regular meetings at the church, despite a commitment not to be associated "with any political or religious agitation."[8]

The religious trappings of the address, however, should not be overstated. When the state capital moved from Vandalia to Springfield, the State House was still under construction, so the Illinois House of Representatives held its first session in December 1839 at the Second Presbyterian Church.[9] Moreover, churches commonly served as the venue for public meetings. To cite just one example, the Young Men's Lyceum of Springfield met regularly at the local Baptist church.[10] More to the point, Beveridge states that the speech angered the preachers, temperance speakers, and "reformers generally." An example he relates is the reaction of one listener that Lincoln's future law partner, William

Herndon, recorded: "'It's a shame,' I heard one man say, 'that he should be permitted to abuse us so in the house of the Lord.'"[11] Given the religious expression of Lincoln's thought, this response seems out of place. Lincoln, however, devotes most of his speech to criticisms of an older branch of the temperance movement given to religious fervor in their public utterances. In particular, he expounds against the errors of seeking to move people to reform by threats of damnation—a practice commonly ascribed to preachers. Lincoln's rhetorical intent in donning the frock of the preacher as he inquired into the reasons for the late success of the temperance movement remains quizzical unless seen in light of his understanding of the requirements of self-government.

In perhaps his most puzzling speech, Lincoln delivers his most direct criticism of the influence of religion on politics. Oddly enough, this comes in a speech rife with biblical rhetoric and addressed to a crowded church! The address was political, however, focusing implicitly on the effect of social reform movements on a republican regime, even as it celebrated the recent successes of the temperance movement. This was not the overt aim of the speech, for Lincoln introduces his topic as "the Temperance cause," and proposes to examine the "rational causes" that brought it "a degree of success, hitherto unparalleled."[12] Just two weeks earlier, Lincoln had delivered a eulogy for a departed member of the Washington Temperance Society.[13] One would expect that his temperance speech delivered on the birthday of George Washington would serve to praise the gains made by a society of reformed drunkards who took the name of the nation's most revered statesman. And this it did. Long associated with Protestant churches in America,[14] the temperance movement had gathered steam through the 1830s and 1840s. As a result, the annual consumption of alcohol dropped by more than half from 1800 to 1840.[15] Nevertheless, the manner with which Lincoln praised the Washingtonians suggests multiple aims, as well as a less than enthusiastic endorsement of temperance reform as a political movement.[16]

To prepare the way, recall Lincoln's famous statement from the first of the organized Lincoln-Douglas debates of 1858:

In this and like communities, public sentiment is everything. With public sentiment, nothing can fail; without it nothing can succeed. Consequently he who moulds public sentiment, goes deeper than he who enacts statutes or pronounces decisions. He makes statutes and decisions possible or impossible to be executed."[17]

As a lawmaker, he understands that laws would be binding in practice only if the general opinion of the community supported them.[18] Lincoln spoke to reform-minded folk with the locutions of the typical reform speaker, but subservient to his own understanding of the threat that such rhetoric could pose to public sentiment and the peace of the community.[19] Lincoln's criticism of the old temperance movement, especially as it embodied the religious expectations of a part of the community, focused on the factionalism and discord that would result if bombast and fanaticism instead of discourse and moderation were practiced and encouraged by those at the stump. This would also apply to those who would use such measures to enervate the growing immigrant population, which would fall especially hard on the wave of Irish and German Catholics then entering the country.[20] Completing his fourth term as a state legislator, Lincoln addressed the packed church in his local community with an eye toward educating public sentiment.

Herewith is an outline of Lincoln's temperance speech:

    I. underscore the recent success of the temperance movement;
    II. critique the early temperance reformers and their tactics;
    III. praise the Washingtonians and their tactics;
    IV. argue that non-drunkards should sign the temperance pledge;
    V. suggest the temperance movement promotes political freedom.

In short, Lincoln chooses to commemorate Washington's birthday before a society of reformed drunkards by praising the recent success of the temperance movement—in large part due to the Washington Temperance Society—and examining the causes of that success "if we would have it to continue."

Although the speech focuses ostensibly on temperance with regards to liquor, at bottom it is about temperance or moderation in speech—how citizens go about persuading one another on a given social or political issue. A close reading of the address reveals that the subtext about persuasion, and not the overt teaching about temperance advocacy, is the more serious objective of Lincoln. This becomes most evident when one looks at Lincoln's own rhetoric, which fluctuates between plain, unornamented prose and florid, grandiose phrasing. Curiously enough, his speech takes on its most flowery and exaggerated cast when he uses biblical language. Lincoln's Temperance Address, therefore, exhibits both temperance and intemperance in its argument and leads the attentive listener or reader to draw conclusions about Lincoln's opinion of the respective temperance reformers and the movement in general that are not obvious on a cursory hearing.

To cite just one example of Lincoln's concern that his speech not only be heard but also read with care, he saw to its publication (appearing one month later, March 25) in the *Sangamo Journal.* Moreover, in a letter to his close friend Joshua Speed, he expressed disappointment that few paid any attention to his speech. He thereupon asked Speed to read it with his wife "as an act of charity to me; for I can not learn that any body else has read it, or is likely to."[21] Lincoln even reminded him of this request in a letter he wrote to Speed over three months later.[22]

Near the beginning of the speech, Lincoln comments that the "new and splendid success" of the temperance cause "is doubtless owing to rational causes; and if we would have it to continue, we shall do well to enquire what those causes are."[23] He then spends more than half of his time on the evolution of the temperance movement (in nineteen of thirty paragraphs, of varying length), contrasting a "new class of champions" and a "*new* system of tactics" against "the old school champions" and "their system of tactics." Lincoln argues that the early temperance reformers lacked "*approachability*" due to their occupations; they consisted of preachers, lawyers, and "hired agents," each of whom could be too easily suspected of promoting their own agenda: "The *preacher*, it is said, advocates temperance because he is a fanatic, and desires a union of Church and State; the *lawyer*, from his pride and vanity of hearing himself speak; and the *hired agent*, for his salary."[24] The observation about lawyers (read: politicians) was not lost on his political rivals, as seen in an article published in the *Illinois State Register*, the Democratic newspaper of record: "They [temperance societies] are almost sure, in the end, to be turned from their original purpose, and made to promote the election of some political demagogue. Does any rational man believe for a moment that Abraham Lincoln, William L. May, B. S. Clements, and Edward D. Baker, have joined the Washington society from any other than political motives? Would they have joined it if it had been exceedingly unpopular?"[25] The Washingtonians, as a lodge for reformed drunkards who were drawn primarily from the artisan and unskilled laboring classes, did not carry these occupational hazards to the podium.[26]

As for the "tactics" of the early temperance guard, Lincoln terms them "impolitic and unjust." They pilloried the sellers and drinkers of alcohol in "thundering tones of anathema and denunciation," blaming them for "all the vice and misery and crime in the land."[27] Moreover, given the longstanding and widespread use of "intoxicating liquor," with its attendant sale as a "respectable article of manufacture," one could not fault the present use or sale of spirits without indicting the community at large that allowed it. As evidence of the intemperance of the early temperance movement, the American Temperance Society had begun its national campaign in 1826 by promoting abstinence among temperate drinkers and not targeting drunkards but soon cast their teetotaling net over all of society. Moreover, the society did not initially adopt a pledge against use of all "ardent spirits," but did so by 1831.[28] If any were injured by it, "none seemed to think the injury arose from *the* use of a *bad thing*, but from the *abuse* of a *very good thing*."[29] The old reformers also presumed "that all habitual drunkards were utterly incorrigible" and, therefore, without remedy. This, of course, belied their professed object of reforming those who most needed it. An approach so devoid of hope, in Lincoln's mind, "never did, nor ever can enlist the enthusiasm of a popular cause."[30] The Washingtonians, on the other hand, extend kindness and charity toward their erstwhile drinking buddies: "They know they are not demons, nor even the worst of men."[31] Foreshadowing the famous concluding sentence of his Second Inaugural Address, Lincoln says of the Washingtonians: "*They* teach *hope* to all—*despair* to none."[32]

Lincoln gives his clearest criticism of the vices of religious reform efforts when he evaluates temperance reformers who maintained "that all habitual drunkards were utterly incorrigible, and therefore, must be turned adrift, and damned without remedy, in order that the grace of temperance might abound to the temperate *then*, and to all mankind some hundred years *thereafter*."[33] Lincoln borrows from St. Paul: "What shall we say then? Shall we continue in sin, that grace may abound?" (Rom. 6:1). The context of the original verse suggests that the old school reformers' condemnation of habitual drunkards is analogous to the person who continues in a life of sin under the perverse reasoning that it will produce more of God's "grace," i.e., forgiveness. Verse two reads: "God forbid. How shall we, that are dead to sin, live any longer therein?" He goes on to fault these reformers for espousing a system of reformation whose benefits "were too remote in time, to warmly engage many in its behalf. Few can be induced to labor exclusively for posterity; and none will do it enthusiastically." He states that "there is something so ludicrous in *promises* of good, or *threats* of evil, a great way off, as to render the whole subject with which they are connected, easily turned into ridicule."[34]

To illustrate the absurdity of threatening men with divine judgment as a public means of changing their habits, Lincoln relates an exchange between an old-style reformer and a potential thief: "'Better lay down that spade you're stealing, Paddy,—if you don't you'll pay for it at the day of judgment." "By the powers, if ye'll credit me so long, I'll take another, jist."[35] Ever the jokester, Lincoln alludes to the issue of temperance by having the reformer address the potential thief by the Irish nickname Paddy. More to the point, invoking the wrath of God—at least when one attempts to reform the personal habits of another—appears futile to Lincoln. Inviting the scorn of the person to be reformed, it drives him away from reformation while leaving the old-style reformer mistakenly satisfied that he had done all he could for him. Lincoln believes this poses one of the greatest political dangers for a republic: the creation of a faction within the community that becomes entrenched in its claim to sole possession of the truth. Lincoln remarks that the failure of the old reformers came in part from using "the thundering tones of anathema and denunciation" instead of "the accents of entreaty and persuasion, diffidently addressed by erring man to an erring brother."[36]

The famed revivalist Charles Finney "advocated the reproving word as a weapon for moral reform: 'converting these abandoned people [e.g., prostitutes] to God by *preaching*.'"[37] Referred to as "the duty of rebuke" in abolition circles, denunciation of particular moral evils took priority over effecting reform of said evils, for through denunciation one fulfilled one's responsibility to God for the spiritual account of one's neighbor: for example, "'The question is not so much, how shall we abolish slavery, as how we shall best discharge our duty . . . to ourselves.'"[38] In this context, the vices of religion involve both a deficiency and excess: religious deficiency by showing a lack of charity towards one's audience, and religious excess by expressing an inordinate confidence in one's knowledge of the truth. Without moderation as one appeals to the judgment of one's neighbors and fellow citizens, without temperance in political discourse, the public dialogue essential to a republic becomes strident and fanatical rather than deliberate and accommodating in its pursuit of the common good.

Juxtaposing the new approach of the Washingtonians with the old school reformers serves not only to highlight the differences between the old and new schools—differences that flatter the new school—but to instruct the discerning listener on how to examine any attempt at moral or political reformation. This, of course, includes the methods of the Washingtonians. When Lincoln describes their methods and results in the same flowery prose he uses to denigrate the old reformers, he implies a similarity between the two that suggests a separate aim of Lincoln's speech. For example, commenting on the Washingtonians' success with habitual drunkards, Lincoln states: "On every hand we behold those, who but yesterday, were the chief of sinners, now the chief apostles of the cause. Drunken devils are cast out by ones, by sevens, and by legions; and their unfortunate victims, like the poor possessed, who was redeemed from his long and lonely wanderings in the tombs, are publishing to the ends of the earth, how great things have been done for them."[39] Moreover, that Lincoln fills his rhetoric with a biblical familiarity and tone unsurpassed by any of his other speeches and writings begs one to wonder about the significance or role of the Bible in public speaking. The old reformers adopted the preacher's text and manner, as was typical at the founding of these movements, inasmuch as Protestant churches spearheaded the moral reformation of the nation.[40] Lincoln imitates this, but with a craft and precision that questions its use in the hands of men who—for right or wrong—use religion in a way that confuses the public mind.

In contrast to the grandiose biblical language he uses to praise the current temperance movement, his own observations about the effectiveness of temperance advocacy new and old are the pictures of simplicity: "When the conduct of men is designed to be influenced, *persuasion*, kind, unassuming persuasion, should ever be adopted."[41] The clarity of his message follows from the lack of biblical ornamentation. Even the proverb he quotes to illustrate this point, "a drop of honey catches more flies than a gallon of gall," is called "an old and a true maxim" that noticeably does not derive from the Bible. Many biographers have observed that Lincoln was as comfortable employing the precepts of Aesop and other worldly writers (e.g., Shakespeare and Robert Burns) as the Bible. An 1843 campaign circular rallying Illinois Whigs to party unity shows Lincoln's concern to educate the public in a manner consistent with mere human reason as well as biblical revelation: "That 'union is strength' is a truth that has been known, illustrated and declared, in various ways and forms in all ages of the world. That great fabulist and philosopher, Aesop, illustrated it by his fable of the bundle of sticks; and he whose wisdom surpasses that of all philosophers [i.e., Jesus], has declared that 'a house divided against itself cannot stand.'"[42] By quoting Aesop alongside the Bible, Lincoln shows how an "important, and universally acknowledged truth," whether its source be mortal or divine, is difficult to resist in the political realm. He models the kind of moderation or temperance in speech he hopes to inspire within the temperance movement in precisely those parts of the address where he shares his true opinion.

He would adopt the same approach when he was visited at the White House by the Sons of Temperance. They delivered a lengthy temperance address, with recommendations for promoting temperance through "the organization of Divisions of our Order"[43] in the army. Lincoln began his response by informing them in no uncertain terms of his commitment to the cause:

> If I were better known than I am, you would not need to be told that in the advocacy of the cause of temperance you have a friend and sympathizer in me.
>
> When I was a young man, long ago, before the Sons of Temperance as an organization, had an existence, I in an humble way, made temperance speeches, and I think I may say that to this day I have never, by my example, belied what I then said.[44]

He then apprises them of existing policies on the subject: "To prevent intemperance in the army is even a part of the articles of war. It is part of the law of the land—and was so, I presume, long ago—to dismiss officers for drunkenness." After promising to submit their suggestions for consideration by the military, Lincoln makes a telling statement: "I think that the reasonable men of the world have long since agreed that intemperance is one of the greatest, if not the very greatest of all evils amongst mankind. That it is not a matter of dispute, I believe. That the disease exists, and that it is a very great one is agreed upon by all." That he cites "reasonable men" as a standard of opinion on the relative evil of intemperance makes one suspect that the intemperance referred to may mean intemperance generally—the root of all evils—and not specifically the evil of drunkenness. Lincoln reminds the Sons of Temperance, or at least any "reasonable" folk in his hearing, that intemperate drinking is but one of many societal evils that must be combated. A crusade, therefore, would not be in order as it would cloud one's thinking about the appropriate solutions to the problem. Although "the disease exists" and is "a very great one . . . agreed upon by all," the "mode of cure is one about which there may be differences of opinion." Lincoln's didactical manner, agreeing with their ends while suggesting that other means exist, follows the themes set forth in his original Temperance Address.

Lincoln's first depiction of the temperance movement as a religious people is a benign one: "The list of its friends is daily swelled by the additions of fifties, of hundreds, and of thousands."[45] This bears similarity with the Old Testament depictions (e.g., Ex. 18:21) of the Hebrew nation organized under officials presiding over "thousands, hundreds, fifties, and tens." However, he then goes on to describe the movement as "going forth 'conquering and to conquer.'" This alludes to the apocalyptic vision in the New Testament of the first of the four horsemen of judgment (Rev. 6:2b), an archer on a white horse: "And a crown was given unto him: and he went forth conquering and to conquer." Lincoln began the speech by observing that the temperance movement was just then "being *crowned* with a degree of success, hitherto unparalleled" (emphasis added). This militaristic image of the cause of temperance, although a seeming compliment for the recent successes of the cause, at minimum pictures a nation at war and not at peace. Furthermore, what is tolerated during wartime to prosecute the effort would be oppressive for a nation during peacetime. From the outset, Lincoln makes clear that temperance reform as a mass movement does not presage a kinder, gentler nation.

Instead, temperance reform as "a powerful chieftain" goes forth to conquer; what is more to the point, however, it goes forth to fight a mortal battle with spiritual repercussions: "The citadels of his great adversary are daily being stormed and dismantled; his temples and his altars, where the rites of his idolatrous worship have long been performed, and where human sacrifices have long been wont to be made, are daily desecrated and deserted. The trump of the conqueror's fame is sounding from hill to hill, from sea to sea, and from land to land, and calling millions to his standard at a blast." The temperance movement, "transformed from a cold abstract theory," becomes a modern-day crusade; the victorious cause, by right of its might, desecrates the temples and altars of the vanquished.[46]

By identifying the temperance movement with an ever-advancing army, Lincoln implicitly signals the danger this could pose for politics and, hence, tips the careful listener to an opposing message to that which appears on the surface. Curiously, the device he uses is biblical as well as militaristic, thereby implicating the prevailing political use of religion in the American republic. In his earlier Lyceum Address, Lincoln called on the faithful to support the government and the rule of law; he would eventually call on them to support the cause of Union during the Civil War. Does this association of temperance reform with war mongering of biblical proportions serve to condemn or applaud the methods of the new reformers?

For starters, Lincoln likens the new temperance reformers, led by the Washingtonians, to the Gadarene demoniac in the Book of Mark (5:2b-3a): "a man with an unclean spirit, who had his dwelling among the tombs," only to be made whole by Jesus casting out the many "devils" that once filled him. Just as a crowd witnessed the transformation of "him that was possessed with the devil, and had the legion, [now] sitting, and clothed, and in his right mind," so, too, the ex-drunkards that constitute the Washington Temperance Society have "long been known" to be "victim[s] of intemperance," but now each "appears before his neighbors 'clothed, and in his right mind.'" Each "stands up with tears of joy trembling in eyes, to tell of miseries, *once* endured, *now* to be endured no more forever . . ." Lincoln concludes that the ex-drunkard's testimony contains "a logic, and an eloquence in it, that few, with human feelings, can resist. They cannot say that he desires a union of church and state, for he is not a church member . . ." This makes the reformed drunkard a leader of a new school that accounts for the late successes of the temperance movement. At the very least, this new school promotes temperance in a manner that avoids the church-state controversy endemic to preachers who promote social or political reforms; for this, Lincoln gives them praise.[47]

Lincoln's reference to the early temperance reformers as "old school" champions is not a casual one. In 1838 the Presbyterian Church suffered a schism, presaged by heresy trials earlier that decade, that produced an "Old School" and a "New School" bloc.[48] As the split in the Presbyterian Church occurred only a few short years before Lincoln's temperance speech, his association of the early temperance reformers with the conservative wing of the Presbyterian Church begs discussion. C. Bruce Staiger writes that as the Presbyterian Church sought to minister to the western settlements under its 1801 "Plan of Union," the incorporation of Congregationalists in their endeavor brought in "the liberalizing Pelagian and Arminian ideas of Unitarianism." The result was "a bitter theological quarrel between the strictly orthodox Calvinists of the Old School and the New School group which embraced the 'radical' New Divinity representative of the Congregational influence."[49] The debate centered around the doctrine of original sin, that men are born into the sin of Adam with only a few foreordained for salvation and the rest destined for damnation.[50] Opposed to the strict Calvinism of old guard Presbyterians, the New School held that man possessed free will. Charles Finney, the New School revivalist par excellence, described a man's conversion as an act of his will: "'if the sinner ever has a new heart, he must . . . make it himself.'" Moreover, "'All sin consists in selfishness; and all holiness or virtue, in disinterested benevolence.'"[51] Here lies the connection between the Second Great Awakening and the social reform movements that would sweep across America from the late 1820s through the 1830s.[52]

In addition, Lincoln alludes to both the predestination and temperance controversies in his discussion of "persuasion," where he uses a more fitting and hopeful means of convincing a person of one's opinion: "On the contrary, assume to dictate to his judgment, or to command his action, or to mark him as one to be shunned and despised, and he will retreat within himself, close all the avenues to his head and his heart; and though your cause be naked truth itself, transformed to the heaviest lance, harder than steel, and sharper than steel can be made, and tho' you throw it with more than Herculean force and precision, you shall be no more able to pierce him, than to penetrate the hardshell of a tortoise with a rye straw." Not only does "hardshell" connote the old school understanding of original sin and predestination, held by so-called "hardshell" or "primitive Baptists" and the like,[53] but also "rye straw" alludes to the distilling cereal of rye whiskey, the frontiersman drink of choice. By alluding to the "hard doctrines" of old school, hardshell Calvinists along with frontier rye whiskey, he juxtaposes religious and drinking imagery as a not so subtle critique of old school rhetoric. To penetrate a "hardshell" with a "rye" straw was a roundabout way of saying that it would be as difficult to force a teetotaling (Old School) Calvinist to drink as it would be to persuade someone to give up drinking by condemning them.

Given the Old School Presbyterian connotation to "old school" temperance reform, Lincoln's use of the phrase could not have been missed by his audience—seated as they were in the Second Presbyterian Church of Springfield. He could not have picked a more coincidental (and controversial) pairing of religious doctrine and social reform. One understands his Temperance Address within a much more religious context, for his discussion of temperance as well as "human nature," "philanthropy," and "[b]enevolence and charity" takes place at a time of great spiritual revival, theological debate, and social and moral reform. For example, Gilbert Hobbs Barnes records that the American Temperance Society, "a product of the Great Revival," preached "the intimate connection of temperance with revivals."[54] Barnes also connects the "new measures" of Finney's religious revivals, including the aid of "a 'holy band' of new converts" in his ministry, with the cause of temperance and abolition (under Theodore Weld's leadership).[55] By the mid-1830s, the effort to prick the conscience of both North and South through pamphlets was deemed a failure. Nevertheless, as the spirit of revival still flourished, Weld turned to its methods for rejuvenating the antislavery movement: "The number of the expanded band [of antislavery speakers] was to be seventy, the number sent out in Bible times to convert the world to Christianity. Their name too was to be 'the Seventy,' and they were to be spread over the North to convert it to immediatism."[56] Lincoln's temperance lecture, with its religious tone, numerous references to the Bible as well as doctrinal disputes, and allusions to various reform causes that have been heretofore the preserve of church leaders, takes on the guise of precisely those religious reformers he seeks to reform—and this by way of informing public opinion about their relative inefficacy as compared to the more earthen approach of the Washingtonians.

Lincoln makes clear that the nature of man must be understood in order for speeches to be aimed with effect. He states early on that the temperance cause seeks to "convince and persuade." Unfortunately, the men and methods of the early movement did little to achieve that aim: "Too much denunciation against the dram sellers and dram-drinkers was indulged in." This Lincoln finds "impolitic," as "it is not much in the nature of man to be driven to any thing." He concludes: "To have expected them [i.e., dram sellers and drinkers] to do otherwise than as they did—to have expected them not to meet denunciation with denunciation . . . was to expect a reversal of human nature, which is God's decree, and never can be reversed."[57] Old School Presbyterians, strict adherents to the Westminster Confession of Faith, held that man's nature was "wholly defiled in all the faculties and parts of soul and body." A person could be saved by "God's free and special grace alone, not from any thing at all foreseen in man; who is altogether passive therein, until, being quickened and renewed by the Holy Spirit, he is thereby enabled to answer this call, and to embrace the grace offered and conveyed in it."[58] New School Presbyterians, spurred in part by the controversy over infant damnation for all but "[e]lect infants . . . regenerated and saved by Christ through the Spirit," deviated from their Old School brethren by preaching that repentance was volitional.[59] The problem of predestination, as stated by the famed Congregationalist and moderate New Schooler Lyman Beecher, was its inability "'to treat converts as reasonable beings.'"[60] Of course, this is precisely where the matter lay, in Lincoln's mind, with respect to the success of the late temperance movement: "If you would win a man to your cause, *first* convince him that you are his sincere friend. Therein is a drop of honey that catches his heart, which, say what he will, is the great high road to his reason . . ."[61]

At first glance, it appears too strong for Lincoln to say that human nature "is God's decree, and can never be reversed," for that is exactly what the church-goers in his audience believed would happen to those whom God saved. Remember the quintessential verse on the subject (2 Cor. 5:17): "Therefore if any man be in Christ he is a new creature: old things are passed away; behold, all things are become new."[62] The Bible recognizes the power of God to change man in such a radical way as to make him "born again," i.e., to take on a new nature. Lincoln knew his

Bible all too well not to know this doctrine. Hence, he must be implying something other than the immutability of man's nature. To begin, he criticizes the early temperance reformers for trying to change men through condemnation rather than entreaty, whereas the new temperance reformers persuaded primarily by their example. New School Presbyterian revivalists Finney and Weld began the practice by enlisting a "holy band" of new converts to spark their revival meetings. These reformed sinners offered an example for the Washington Temperance Society's reformed drunkards, who would hold "experience meetings" where a few ex-drunkards would give their testimony.[63] Instead of condemnation, potential temperance converts heard the soothing voice of experience beckoning them to a life free of the evils of drink. If drinking could not be driven from man, as man is not wont "to be driven to anything," the more successful alternative proved to be the New School's confidence in the sinner's testimony as showing the way to recovery for all similarly situated. The living proof of reformed drunkards shows that Lincoln did not mean to say that self-improvement was impossible.

Lincoln also says that the old reformers mistakenly believed "that all habitual drunkards were utterly incorrigible."[64] On the one hand they tried to change men's habits through tirades about the evils of drink, while on the other hand they "damned without remedy" those who would not respond to their calls to quit. Lincoln praises, in contrast, the Washingtonians for their adherence to a Christian doctrine reflected in a verse he cites from a hymn book: "While the lamp holds out to burn,/The vilest sinner may return."[65] Their hope in the reformation of man, a belief rejected by Old School Presbyterians, shared the optimism of New School Presbyterians. Lincoln the legislator implicitly takes sides in a religious quarrel, quarrels that history has shown undermine the peace and safety of the community. This illustrates his concern for sectarian strife that creates the possibility for public division, and, hence, his desire to prevent such a division from occurring. Lincoln observes what the New School observed: human beings are both "heart" and "mind." One's appeal must, therefore, take them both into account. This simple truth eluded the old reformers, as their attempts to reform society aim for man's soul and yet manage to miss both the heart and mind.

Nevertheless, the rhetoric Lincoln uses to compare the old school reformers with the new school testifiers led by the Washington Temperance Society makes his praise of the Washingtonians equivocal. Only a paragraph earlier Lincoln referred to drunkenness as "the demon of Intemperance." His next biblical allusion would liken Washingtonians to the Gadarene demoniac: once a "victim of intemperance," now "a redeemed specimen of long lost humanity." Lincoln makes clear that their success comes partly from the reformed character of the Washingtonians. Without the suspected hidden agenda of the preachers (or the suspected "vanity" and "salary" of the lawyer and hired speaker), this new society of reformers gains at least a hearing from those they would reform by virtue of their changed lives. Yet, Lincoln initially gives short shrift to the effort required to effect this conversion, saying "how easily it all is done, once it is resolved to be done." Then, later in the speech, he describes the addiction to alcohol as a "burning desire," "fixed habits," and "burning appetites."[66] Finally, he states, "For the man to suddenly, or in any other way, to break off from the use of drams, who has indulged in them for a long course of years, and until his appetite for them has become ten or a hundred fold stronger, and more craving, than any natural appetite can be, requires a most powerful moral effort." Therefore, the apparent praiseworthiness of the Washingtonians as a reform movement or "cause" is undercut by the conflicting assessment of the alcoholic's addiction, in addition to the heavy-handed biblical allusions that raise suspicions about the political legitimacy of any reform movement linking spiritual and political means.

Lincoln makes the clearest contrast of the good and bad uses of religion in his praise of the Washingtonians for not adhering to one Christian doctrine while practicing another: "As applying to *their* cause, *they* deny the doctrine of unpardonable sin." The doctrine of unpardonable sin comes from the New Testament:

> "Verily I [Jesus] say unto you, All sins shall be forgiven unto the sons of men, and blasphemies wherewith soever they shall blaspheme: But he that shall blaspheme against the Holy Ghost hath never forgiveness, but is in danger of eternal damnation": Because they [the scribes] said, "He hath an unclean spirit." (Mk. 3:28-30; also Lk. 12:10 and Mt. 12:31-32)

While the old school reformers maintained "that all habitual drunkards were utterly incorrigible, and therefore, must be turned adrift, and damned without remedy," the new school reformers "adopt a more enlarged philanthropy." When Lincoln says of the Washingtonians, "Benevolence and charity possess *their* hearts entirely,"[67] he again invites a comparison of the new temperance reformers with the New School Presbyterians responsible for much of the philanthropic and benevolent societies spawned by the Great Revival. Led by New School preachers and converts, for as Barnes notes, "Calvinists—Old-School Presbyterians—seldom appeared as officers in the benevolent societies," these societies extolled "'benevolence as a controlling preference of the mind.'" Accordingly, despite the societies' lack of formal ties with the established churches, "Jealous sectarians insisted that 'these great national societies should assume their proper denomination, and be declared Presbyterian, as they really are in effect.'"[68]

With respect to slavery, Staiger demonstrates "the coincidence between New School theology and an antislavery position," observing that "those Synods which had declared against the 'sin' of slaveholding had strong New School leanings." More to the author's point, "opposition to abolitionism was to become the strongest tie between the two groups [the conservative Philadelphia and moderate Princeton groups] . . . They stood as one in their opposition to the New School premise that slaveholding was *sin*."[69] Lincoln praises the Washingtonians for not condemning drunkards to the misery of drink but rather having hope that they, too, can overcome their vice. Their sympathy toward the present misfortune of those they seek to free from their vice resembles the hope Lincoln found essential to the reformation of Southern sentiment on the slavery controversy.[70] This takes on particular significance within the American regime of self-government, which necessitates a shared conviction that one's fellow citizens can be persuaded if they happen to disagree on a particular issue. From this common belief Lincoln would derive the spirit of compromise that averted for a time a civil war.[71]

Lincoln then observes that the successes of the Washingtonians rival those of the church, with conversions on both sides from the dregs of society. Lincoln reinforces his point with an allusion to St. Paul's conversion from a persecutor of Christians to a missionary of the early church: "On every hand we behold those, who but yesterday, were the chief of sinners, now the chief apostles of the cause."[72] Paul's First Letter to Timothy reads: "Paul, an apostle of Jesus Christ by the commandment of God our Saviour, and Lord Jesus Christ, which is our hope . . . This is a faithful saying, and worthy of all acceptation, that Christ Jesus came into the world to save sinners; of whom I am chief" (1 Tim. 1:1, 15). Lincoln continues with further references to the Bible that focus on the deliverance of men from unclean spirits or demons: "Drunken devils are cast out by ones, by sevens, and by legions; and their unfortunate victims, like the poor possessed, who was redeemed from his long and lonely wanderings in the tombs, are publishing to the ends of the earth, how great things have been done for them." Gleaning from two New Testament passages,[73] Lincoln returns to his original reference to the Gadarene demoniac possessed by a legion of demons. Lincoln dresses "these new champions" and their late successes, however, in no less biblical garb than the Bible-thumping, early reformers he criticizes. This suggests that for Lincoln, although the method of the Washingtonians—private, moral suasion through "experience" speeches—is above reproach, the temperance movement in general—a public reform effort open to demagoguery by self-interested parties, including religious leaders—subjects the community to potentially divisive forces inimical to self-government.

That Lincoln may not be the wholehearted advocate of temperance reform as a public movement can be seen in the turn his argument takes. After praising the Washingtonians, he now refutes the logical conclusion of his speech to this point: namely, that only a small portion of the public, reformed drunkards, should carry the banner of temperance reform. He states that if they constitute "the most powerful and efficient instruments to push the reformation to ultimate success, it does not follow, that those who have not suffered, have no part left them to perform."[74] He reports that the benefit to the world from a "total and final banishment . . . of all intoxicating drinks, seems to me not *now* to be an open question."[75] He then alludes to a New Testament passage about the method of salvation as a picture of that apparently universal belief: "Three-fourths of mankind confess the affirmative with their *tongues*, and, I believe, all the rest acknowledge it in their *hearts*."[76] Following the rhetorical math, if three-fourths of the world openly favor getting rid of liquor once and for all, and one-fourth (i.e., "all the rest") agree with this privately, together this makes for universal teetotalism. In short, if all favor temperance—most do so openly, and the rest privately—then all should contribute to its accomplishment.

Based on the apparent unanimity toward temperance reform as a community effort, Lincoln asks, "Shall he, who cannot do *much*, be, for that reason, excused if he do *nothing*?" He goes on to argue that those who "never drink even without signing" the temperance pledge can lend "moral support" to those who must exercise "a most powerful moral effort" to quit the drink. Otherwise, the drunkard struggling to reform would read nonparticipation as a sign that temperance is not the public necessity some make it out to be, and, hence, be tempted back "to his former miserable 'wallowing in the mire.'"[77] Here Lincoln quotes 2 Peter 2:22, a reference to religious backsliding, to support his claim that "every moral prop, should be taken *from* whatever argument might rise in his mind to lure him to his backsliding." Objecters counter that "*moral influence* is not the powerful engine contended for." Lincoln responds with an example to illustrate the power that mere "fashion" has on the actions of men: It keeps women's bonnets off their husbands' heads. He concludes, "[W]hat is the influence of fashion, but the influence that *other* people's actions have [on our own] actions, the strong inclination each of us feels to do as we see all our neighbors do? Nor is the influence of fashion confined to any particular thing or class of things. It is just as strong on one subject as another. Let us make it as unfashionable to withhold our names from the temperance pledge as for husbands to wear their wives bonnets to church, and instances will be just as rare in the one case as the other."

Curiously, Lincoln began by arguing for moral influence to support the reform of drunkards but concludes by calling for pledge signing to become fashionable. Equating moral influence with the influence of fashion, the conclusion should have been that overt teetotalism by the community—i.e., their pledge not to drink—would make it unfashionable for determined drunkards to continue drinking. However, even Lincoln admits in the previous paragraph that giving up habitual drinking requires "a most powerful moral effort" to overcome an appetite that "has become ten or a hundred fold stronger, and more craving than any natural appetite can be." Public teetotalism, while it would not undermine temperance by habitual drinkers, would offer little in comparison to the drunkard's own resolve to quit drinking. In his argument to support the reforming drunkard by example, Lincoln moves from making drinking unfashionable to making a refusal to sign the pledge unfashionable. This makes non-drinkers who refuse to sign, as opposed to drunkards, the object of public ostracism, thereby showing the discerning listener that Lincoln does not mean his suggestion to be taken too seriously. To date, no evidence has surfaced to show that Lincoln himself ever signed a temperance pledge or joined a temperance society, making his exhortation all the more suspect.

He goes on to answer the objection of those who fear their reputation would suffer by associating with ex-drunkards in a group like the Washington Temperance Society: "Surely no Christian will adhere to this objection." Addressing those of his listeners who upheld the proverb, "Bad company corrupts good character" (1 Cor. 15:33), Lincoln draws on their belief that the Creator "condescended to take on himself the form of sinful man, and, as such, to die an ignominious death for their sakes" to illustrate an alternative approach to keeping the faith.[78] By joining a reformed drunkards' society, they submit "to the infinitely lesser condescension, for the temporal, and perhaps eternal salvation, of a large, erring, and unfortunate class of their own fellow creatures."[79] However, this, too, proves to be a flawed reason for joining, as Lincoln concludes the paragraph, "Nor is their condescension very great." What he meant to be seen as high-minded sacrifice on behalf of Christians who stooped to associate with former drunkards turns out to be no sacrifice at all, for he now says that "such of us as have never fallen victims, have been spared more from the absence of appetite, than from any mental or moral superiority over those who have." Lincoln asserts that those who have avoided addiction to alcohol have done so not from any virtue in their soul but from lack of "appetite."

Of course, this too cannot be taken seriously because it would imply no praiseworthiness of pursuing virtue over vice. He makes his intent clear by following this argument with the now suspect imagery of the Bible (Ex. 11-12): He compares the "demon of intemperance" to "the Egyptian angel of death, commissioned to slay if not the first, the fairest born of every family." The paragraph culminates with yet another biblical reference, which compares the "victims" of intemperance with the valley of dry bones that the Old Testament prophet Ezekiel used to depict Israel's spiritual poverty in the eyes of God. Lincoln states: "Far around as human breath has ever blown, he [the demon of intemperance] keeps our fathers, our brothers, our sons, and our friends, prostrate in the chains of moral death. To all the living every where, we cry, 'come sound the moral resurrection trump, that these may rise and stand up, an exceeding great army'—'Come from the four winds, O breath! and breathe upon these slain, that they may live.'" Ezekiel 37:9-11 reads: "Then he said unto me, Prophesy unto the wind, prophesy, son of man, and say to the wind, thus saith the Lord God; Come from the four winds, O breath, and breathe upon these slain, that they may live. So I prophesied as he commanded me, and the breath came into them, and they lived, and stood up upon their feet, an exceeding great army. Then he said unto me, Son of man, these bones are the whole house of Israel: behold, they say, Our bones are dried, and our hope is lost: we are cut off for our parts." Again one sees the identification of temperance reform with war, its adherents with an army.

Moreover, Lincoln places the temperance advocates in the position of the prophet Ezekiel, their reform speeches imitating the prophesy of Ezekiel as he called down God's spirit to vivify the nation of Israel: "Again he said unto me, Prophesy upon these bones, and say unto them, O ye dry bones, hear the word of the Lord. Thus saith the Lord God unto these bones; Behold, I will cause breath to enter into you, and ye shall live" (Ezek. 37:4-5). Hence, to the mass of his audience, Lincoln proposes a moral solidarity with their more downtrodden brothers as cause for taking up the temperance crusade. Nevertheless, the underlying message, signaled by his exaggerated appeal to a biblical prophesy, continues to alert the discerning listener to the dangers of bringing a primarily theological understanding of a moral issue into the public arena.

Therefore, the temperance cause need only be promoted by the reformed drunks Lincoln praises and be directed toward those not yet reformed. In short, it seems that the rest of the community need concern themselves little with the movement precisely because the most recent cause of its success had nothing to do with them. Sure, their signing the pledge would do no harm and perhaps offer some sense of camaraderie, but it does not lend near the level of support that the drunkard's own resolve to quit does when encouraged by the example of a reformed drunkard. One might speculate that Lincoln's express charge for non-drunkards to sign the pledge was a goad to see if the old school reformers really sympathized with the plight of those to whom they directed their fiery speeches.

Lincoln closes his address with a comparison of "the temperance revolution" with "our political revolution of '76" and presents a supposition regarding their respective merits: "If the relative grandeur of revolutions shall be estimated by the great amount of human misery they alleviate, and the small amount they inflict, then, indeed, will this [the temperance cause] be the grandest the world shall ever have seen." With the first word, "If," Lincoln already qualifies what he is about to say about temperance in light of the American revolution. He is not willing to assume without qualification that revolutions should be compared by gains relative to losses. This should come as no surprise to those familiar with Lincoln's appreciation of the American Founders' achievement. Therefore, one must examine his assessment of the two revolutions in light of the certain appreciation he had for the American Revolution and the qualified appreciation he has shown for the temperance movement.

First, there is a clear distinction in the language he uses to describe the two revolutions in comparing both the gains achieved and losses incurred by the respective revolutions. He describes the gains of the political revolution of 1776 with little exaggeration and scant rhetorical flourish: "Of our political revolution of '76, we are justly proud. It has given us a degree of political freedom, far exceeding that of any other of the nations of the earth. In it the world has found a solution of that long mooted problem, as to the capability of man to govern himself. In it was the germ which has vegetated, and still is to grow and expand into the universal liberty of mankind." Lincoln's true opinions in this address have been seen in those sections where his rhetoric bore little if no affectation, flowery prose, or biblical hyperbole. In contrast, the following paragraph exaggerates the miseries inflicted by the American Revolution: "But with all these glorious results, past, present, and to come, it had its evils too. It breathed forth famine, swam in blood and rode on fire; and long, long after, the orphan's cry, and the widow's wail, continued to break the sad silence that ensued. These were the price, the inevitable price, paid for the blessings it bought." Note the personification of the Revolution, "It breathed . . . , swam . . . , and rode"; the poetically stressed accents in "breathed forth famine, swam in blood, and rode on fire" and the iambic meter in "the orphan's cry and the widow's wail"; and the alliteration and assonance in "past, present," "forth famine," "widow's wail," "sad silence that ensued," "blessings it bought," and "price, paid." Although the revolution did generate various losses, Lincoln notes that these "evils" were "the inevitable price" of a nation born amid the ruins of war. These misfortunes always accompany violent struggles, and although they are justly lamented for their immediate effect on the participants, it would be unjust to overstate their cost in light of the "blessings" to be won. In the case of the American Revolution, our forefathers pledged their lives, their fortunes, and their sacred honor to establish a regime of self-government—an eventual blessing that far outweighed the immediate cost to life, property, and self-respect.

"Turn now," Lincoln continues, "to the temperance revolution." He now evaluates the temperance cause in light of miseries incurred or avoided, all the while describing the movement with a rhetorical flourish that suggests a less than serious appreciation of its achievements: "In *it*, we shall find a stronger bondage broken; a viler slavery, manumitted; a greater tyrant deposed. In *it*, more of want supplied, more disease healed, more sorrow assuaged. By *it* no orphans starving, no widows weeping. By *it*, none wounded in feeling, none injured in interest. Even the dram-maker, and dram seller, will have glided into other occupations *so* gradually, as never to have felt the shock of change; and will stand ready to join all others in the universal song of gladness."[80] In highlighting the glories of the temperance revolution, Lincoln does not remind his audience that both the evils overcome (e.g., alcohol addiction) and evils avoided (e.g., starving orphans and weeping widows) are the result of merely returning the drunkard to the normal condition of men. Orphans starve and widows weep because of the habits of drunken relatives and not because of a pursuit of some noble end, as was the case for the American Revolutionaries. Of course, drunkards on the mend are a good thing, but the question of virtuous and noble pursuits—such as liberating a people from an oppressor—arises only among those self-controlled enough not to get hooked in the first place. Alleviating this suffering, while certainly a blessing, brings little glory to the drunkard who should not have caused the suffering in the first place.

One finds it difficult to praise a man, i.e., to call it virtue, for giving up drinking and restoring his family to health and peace when he was the original cause of those evils. We expect him to do no less and to receive no glory since we expect the same for ourselves and the rest of society. We reserve honors for those who rise above the normal expectations of the community to achieve greater goods for their fellow citizens. Lincoln, in setting the achievements of the temperance movement above those of the American Revolution, pays homage to a sympathetic audience but in a manner that does not bear up under closer scrutiny. His rhetoric gives notice to his true understanding of the glories of the American Revolution and the lesser credit due the successes of the temperance cause.

As if to accentuate these claims further, he states in the next paragraph that the temperance movement is "a noble ally . . . to the cause of political freedom."[81] This presents an opposing thesis to the one proposed in this chapter, which argues that temperance reform undermines public deliberation. Not to worry, for Lincoln reaches the peak of his purposeful, rhetorical excesses in this address in describing how political freedom shall find its consummation with the help of the temperance movement:

> With such an aid, its march cannot fail to be on and on, till every son of earth shall drink in rich fruition, the sorrow quenching draughts of perfect liberty. Happy day, when, all appetites controled, all passions subdued, all matters subjected, *mind*, all conquering *mind*, shall live and move the monarch of the world. Glorious consummation! Hail fall of Fury! Reign of Reason hail, all hail!

If one did not doubt Lincoln's sincerity in his appreciation of the temperance cause, his statement that "every son of earth shall *drink* in rich fruition, the sorrow quenching *draughts* of perfect liberty" (emphasis added) should prove persuasive. To depict all men drinking, albeit from the cup of "perfect liberty," in a speech about temperance illustrates the deliberate ambiguity Lincoln presents about the public hazards of drinking and especially the measures adopted to reform those who did.[82] Lincoln, moreover, would be the last man on earth to believe that reason could attain such control over men and governments that all appetites, passions, and matters would submit to its direction. His ode to the "Reign of Reason" comes at a time when some Americans were experimenting with communal living driven by perfectionist hopes of a new moral world. Examples include utopian socialist Robert Owen's Community of Equality at New Harmony, Indiana (1825), and transcendentalist George Ripley's Brook Farm at West Roxbury, Massachusetts (1841-47).

Lincoln's deliberately naive view of the future of the world is nothing less than apocalyptic, envisioning "the political and moral freedom of their species," offering yet another clue that Lincoln does not intend this reverie to be taken at face value.[83] Instead, coupled with previous admonitions against similar types of rhetorical excesses with the Bible, Lincoln teaches by example the temptation and, hence, the danger in applying heaven-sent visions to earth-bound problems. He reforms the reformers in an effort to restore the true meaning and exercise of temperance (or moderation) to the benefit of both society and government.

* * * * *

An indication of the spirit of temperance reform that Lincoln would endorse comes from an 1853 lecture, "A Discourse on the Bottle—Its Evils, and the Remedy," delivered by a close friend of the Lincoln family, the Reverend James Smith.[84] Lincoln heard this speech "with great satisfaction," and the very next day joined thirty-eight others in requesting a copy for publication, "believing, that, if published and circulated among the people, it would be productive of good . . ."[85] With the ironic subtitle "A Vindication of the Liquor-Seller, and the Liquor Drinker, from Certain Aspersions Cast upon Them by Many," the lecture focuses on the hypocrisy of those who castigate the liquor seller or drinker as "the only sinner in this matter."[86] Dr. Smith argues that consistency implicates the laws that permit their sale and consumption, and, thus, the lawmakers and therewith the public at large who empower them.

The epigram that prefaces the temperance address conveys Dr. Smith's argument in a nutshell: "Woe unto him that giveth his neighbor drink, that putteth thy bottle to him" (Hab. 2:15). Interpreted broadly, the Old Testament pronouncement applies to anyone who facilitates the drinking of liquor and not merely the direct seller of liquor. By offering a "vindication" or defense of the liquor-seller and drinker from "certain aspersions cast upon them by many," as the subtitle states, Dr. Smith tries to move the temperance campaign forward in a somewhat Swiftian manner. He modestly proposes that those who sell and drink liquor should escape public condemnation as long as the community refuses to acknowledge their own complicity in the liquor traffic: "I have shown you that however guilty he [the 'liquor-seller'] may be before God, he is not a violator of the law of the land; but he is an honest dealer . . ."[87] Lincoln certainly agreed with the charge of hypocrisy, insofar as his own temperance address highlights that "denunciations against dram-sellers and dram-drinkers, are *unjust* as well as impolitic."[88] Our earlier reading of Lincoln's Temperance Address, however, gives reason to think that his endorsement of Dr. Smith's address is not without reservation.

So where does Lincoln's sympathy with the Reverend James Smith's temperance advocacy lie? First and foremost, in the preacher's refusal to turn a blind eye to the culpability of those who are quick to assign all blame to the sellers and drinkers of liquor. In the Book of Matthew, Jesus warns, "Judge not, that ye be not judged," and tests the sincerity of the fault-finder by asking, "why beholdest thou the mote that is in thy brother's eye, but considerest not the beam that is in thine own eye?" (Matt. 7:1, 3). As one would expect from a preacher, the Reverend Smith applies these biblical principles to a public issue that too readily divides the community into blameless and blameworthy camps. He concludes that "it is the duty of all who have in any way contributed to place temptation before him [the 'inebriate'], as an act of justice to the wronged, to labor for his emancipation from his cruel thraldom. Until this be done, that aweful woe in the text [Hab. 2:15] must rest upon us as a people, for in the sight of God, we are all guilty."[89]

In similar fashion, Lincoln's political career reveals a concern that the citizenry not become factious in its pursuit of justice. Even after seven states had "seceded" from the Union, the newly inaugurated President Lincoln reminded a loyal Pennsylvania delegation to "act in such a way as to say nothing insulting or irritating. I would inculcate this idea, so that we may not, like the Pharisees, set ourselves up to be better than other people."[90] Of course, the foremost testimony of Lincoln's political humility is his magisterial Second Inaugural Address, with its biblical exhortation to "judge not that we be not judged," and concession of national responsibility for the enormity of slavery, for which God "gives to both North and South, this terrible war, as the woe due to those by whom the offence came . . ."[91]

Second, the Reverend Smith calls for "charity and forbearance" on the part of "all the friends of humanity," as he tries to unite disparate elements of the temperance movement. Members of the "old

Temperance," Washingtonians, and Sons of Temperance, former members of the aforementioned groups, and those who never joined a temperance society but worked toward the same end should stop their bickering and name-calling, and consider each other "a valuable fellow-laborer in the same great work, and heartily accept of his co-operation."[92] Of the Springfield Washingtonians, Lincoln observed, "Benevolence and charity possess *their* hearts entirely," noting that their sympathy and hope for the dram-drinker served as a most persuasive entreaty for their reform.[93] More generally, Lincoln recognized that the perpetuation of self-government required a citizenry that trusted one another and was able to compromise politically without gainsaying the motives or patriotism of others.

This comes to light most clearly in the conclusion of his First Inaugural Address, where Lincoln addresses what he calls "my dissatisfied fellow countrymen": "I am loth to close. We are not enemies, but friends. Though passion may have strained, it must not break our bonds of affection. The mystic chords of memory . . . will yet swell the chorus of the Union, when again touched, as surely they will be, by the better angels of our nature."[94] This hopeful, conciliatory plea demonstrates his desire to preserve the Union through peaceful cooperation and not military coercion. In his Second Inaugural Address four years hence, Lincoln would famously proclaim, "With malice toward none, with charity for all," in an attempt to heal the nation's wounds at the close of a devastating civil war.[95]

Finally, Dr. Smith closed with a benediction that Lincoln would repeat in one form or another throughout his presidential years: "Perseverance in the work, and a dependence upon the Divine blessing, will infallibly secure a final and glorious victory."[96] The Reverend Smith's hope was that "the people may be thoroughly informed on this great subject, and prepared to act as rational men, who are accountable to God for their use of the high privilege, which, as free men, they enjoy, of saying through the ballot-box, how they desire to be governed, and what laws must be enacted and enforced." Lincoln spent his adult life promoting an informed citizenry by delivering speeches as a private citizen as well as a state and federal officeholder. Moreover, his promotion and practice of civic virtue consistently called to the public mind their responsibility to act as a nation under divine providence. Witness his closing words in his first annual address to Congress: "With a reliance on Providence, all the more firm and earnest, let us proceed in the great task which events have devolved upon us."[97] He repeated this idea in the concluding paragraph of his Second Inaugural Address: "with firmness in the right, as God gives us to see the right, let us strive on to finish the work we are in . . ."[98] Lincoln, therefore, shares the Reverend Smith's conviction that human endeavors can and should be carried out with the hope of divine approbation and support.

As for their differences, the most significant would be that Lincoln would not agree with the Reverend Smith's ultimate remedy for intemperance—"a law altogether abolishing the liquor traffic, except for mechanical, chemical, medicinal and sacramental purposes."[99] Admittedly, Lincoln was an avowed teetotaler. Albert Beveridge relates a telling exchange on the subject between Lincoln and Stephen Douglas. At a reception hosting Douglas during the congressional campaigns of 1854, Lincoln declined a drink; whereupon Douglas exclaimed, "Why! are you a member of the Temperance Society?" Lincoln replied, "No! I am not a member of any Temperance Society . . . but I am temperate in this, that I don't drink anything."[100] Moreover, hearing that Lincoln only served "Adam's ale" (i.e., cold water) to the committee notifying him of his nomination as presidential candidate of the Republican Party, a journalist and temperance advocate inquired of Lincoln's temperance sentiments. In a letter explicitly marked confidential, Lincoln refused to comment on his temperance beliefs but stated, "Having kept house sixteen years, and having never held the 'cup' to the lips of my friends then, my judgment was that I should not, in my new position, change my habit in this respect."[101]

However, Lincoln never turned his personal habits regarding alcohol into a public campaign for the prohibition of the liquor traffic.[102] His Temperance Address, in fact, chastised the early temperance reformers for denouncing sellers and drinkers of liquor without considering their "pecuniary interest, or burning appetite": "it is not much in the nature of man to be driven to any thing; still less to be driven about that which is exclusively his own business . . ."[103] The Reverend Smith, needless to say, did not consider the sale or drinking of liquor as a private affair.

In addition, Lincoln's praise of the Washingtonians as the "new champions" to which "our late success is mainly owing" reflects a belief that moral suasion and not legal sanction provides the most effective means of promoting temperance among the population. As Ian R. Tyrrell explains in *Sobering Up* (1979), "the Washingtonians renounced all reliance on legal measures. Their pledge required abstinence from the use of liquor as a beverage, but unlike the ATU [American Temperance Union] pledge, it did not demand personal abstinence from the manufacture and traffic in liquor."[104] Does this imply duplicity on Lincoln's part? Not if one considers that even the Reverend Smith recognized that any law proposed for the abolition of the liquor traffic must be "so framed that no principle of the constitution of the State, or of the United States, be violated."[105] This raises the issue of personal freedom versus the public good and, hence, requires public debate over the extent to which personal intemperance constitutes a threat to the health, safety, welfare, and morals of the community.

Lincoln would agree with Dr. Smith's recommendation that if this law were to be presented for public approval, "the most vigorous exertions should be made to secure that end by spreading information on the subject, broadcast throughout the land." For example, a few years after his address before the Washington Temperance Society, Lincoln helped schedule a temperance speech by T. S. Fairchild—"a talented and eloquent young gentleman, eminently qualified to advance the cause of virtue and temperance & to promote the best interests of society"—at the Illinois Hall of Representatives.[106] Without agreeing with Dr. Smith on the outcome of this plebiscite on prohibition, Lincoln can fully endorse the idea that a proposal directly affecting the lives and fortunes of every citizen should receive a hearing at "the bar of public opinion."

Reading the temperance lecture of the Reverend James Smith in light of Lincoln's own temperance address teaches that religious reform efforts in the political arena can pose problems for a republic if not tethered to a principled understanding of the nature of personal and communal self-government. As Dr. Smith noted in his discourse on the bottle, bringing the salient issues of the day before "the bar of public opinion" was all-important for communities based on the consent of the governed. Or as Lincoln himself put it, "Our government rests in public opinion. Whoever can change public opinion, can change the government, practically just so much."[107] How Americans seek to change their government will determine what kind of government they preserve over the long haul. Abraham Lincoln's political *raison d'être*, the perpetuation of American self-government according to the principles of the Declaration of Independence, informed his understanding of the temperance movement of his day.

Notes

1. Cited in *William Lloyd Garrison, 1805-1879: The Story of His Life Told by His Children*, Wendell Phillips Garrison and Francis Jackson Garrison, eds., 4 vols. (Boston: Houghton, Mifflin and Company, 1889), 3: 100, and John L. Thomas, ed., *Slavery Attacked: The Abolitionist Crusade* (Englewood Cliffs, N.J.: Prentice-Hall, Inc., 1965), 77, 78. For an excellent description of

Garrison's "punitive style" of oratory against slaveowners as well as abolitionists who adopted a less vociferous rhetoric, see William E. Cain, ed., *William Lloyd Garrison and the Fight against Slavery* (Boston: Bedford Books of St. Martin's Press, 1995), 37-45, and Henry Mayer, *All on Fire: William Lloyd Garrison and the Abolition of Slavery* (New York: St. Martin's Press, 1998), 113-26.

2. Harriet Beecher Stowe, *Uncle Tom's Cabin* (New York: Signet Classic— Penguin USA Inc., 1966), 194.

3. "Protest in Illinois Legislature on Slavery (3 March 1837)," in *The Collected Works of Abraham Lincoln*, Roy P. Basler, ed., 9 vols. (New Brunswick: Rutgers University Press, 1955), 1: 75. Hereinafter cited as *Collected Works*; all emphases in original except where otherwise noted. Later that year, a mob threatened to storm a lecture by the Reverend Jeremiah Porter, who had announced he would be speaking on slavery that night at the First Presbyterian Church. He was allowed to speak but soon after was spirited away from town before riled citizens could get their hands on him. A resolution condemning abolitionism (i.e., "immediate emancipation" as opposed to colonization, which they favored) as divisive, unproductive, and un-Christian passed a few days after the speech. Abolitionist leaders received express contempt as "designing, ambitious men, and dangerous members of society" to be "shunned by all good citizens." Paul M. Angle, *"Here I Have Lived": The Story of Lincoln's Springfield, 1821-1865* (New Brunswick, N.J.: Rutgers University Press, 1935), 79-80.

4. "Speech at Springfield, Illinois (17 July 1858)," in *Collected Works*, 2: 510.

5. For an introduction to the supportive role Lincoln saw religion playing in the preservation of the American regime, see "Address before the Young Men's Lyceum of Springfield, Illinois (27 January 1838)," in *Collected Works*, 1: 108-115, and our examination of the address in Chapter 2.

6. Lincoln's "First Lecture on Discoveries and Inventions (6 April 1858)," in *Collected Works*, 2: 437-42, delivered before the Young Men's Association, surpasses his Temperance Address only in its number of biblical quotations. Nevertheless, as a lecture on the historical development of man's improvement of the earth and his condition, it bears little resemblance to a political speech— unlike the Temperance Address. See also his "Second Lecture on Discoveries and Inventions," delivered on February 11, 1859 and thereafter on at least two other occasions. *Collected Works*, 3: 356-363.

7. For a history of the Washingtonians and their connection to the larger temperance movement, see Ian R. Tyrrell, *Sobering Up: From Temperance to Prohibition in Antebellum America, 1800-1860* (Westport, Conn.: Greenwood Press, 1979), chaps. 7-8, "The Washingtonians: Artisans and Alcohol" and "Cooperation and Conflict in Temperance Agitation," 159-224. See also Robert H. Abzug, *Cosmos Crumbling: American Reform and the Religious Imagination* (New York: Oxford University Press, 1994), chap. 4, "The Temperance Reformation," 81-104; Jack S. Blocker, Jr., *American Temperance Movements:*

Cycles of Reform (Boston: Twayne Publishers, 1989), chap. 2, "Washingtonians, Fraternal Societies, and Maine Laws (1840-60)," in 30-60; and Mark A. Noll, *One Nation under God? Christian Faith and Political Action in America* (New York: Harper & Row, 1988), chap. 8, "The Promise and Peril of Reform II: Prohibition," 128-41.

8. Albert J. Beveridge, *Abraham Lincoln, 1809-1858*, 2 vols. (Cambridge, Mass.: The Riverside Press, 1928), 1: 325, n. 2. The founding officers of the Springfield chapter were close friends of Lincoln: William D. Herndon as president, James H. Matheny as corresponding secretary, and William W. Pease as secretary *pro tem*. The first Washington Temperance Society originated in Baltimore in 1840; Ian R. Tyrrell, *Sobering Up*, 159-60 and Clifton E. Olmstead, *History of Religion in the United States* (Englewood Cliffs, N.J.: Prentice-Hall, Inc., 1960), 355. Paul M. Angle records that the Springfield chapter reached seven hundred members only three months after Lincoln's address. See William H. Herndon and Jesse W. Weik, *Herndon's Life of Lincoln: The History and Personal Recollections of Abraham Lincoln*, with introduction and notes by Paul M. Angle and new introduction by Henry Steele Commager (Cleveland: World Pub. Co., 1942; reprint edition, New York: Da Capo Press, Inc., 1983), 206 n. 17.

9. *Lincoln Day by Day: A Chronology, 1809-1865*, Earl Schenck Miers, ed., 2 vols. (Washington: Lincoln Sesquicentennial Commission, 1960), William E. Baringer, vol. 1: *1809-1848*, 124, "December 9" entry; Angle, *"Here I Have Lived": The Story of Lincoln's Springfield*, 75, 83-84, 87.

10. Thomas F. Schwartz, "The Springfield Lyceums and Lincoln's 1838 Speech," *Illinois Historical Journal* 83 (Spring 1990): 48.

11. Beveridge, *Abraham Lincoln*, 1: 329, n. 2. See also, Joseph R. Gusfield, *Symbolic Crusade: Status Politics and the American Temperance Movement* (Urbana: University of Illinois Press, 1972), 48-49.

12. "Temperance Address (22 February 1842)," in *Collected Works*, 1: 271.

13. "Eulogy on Benjamin Ferguson (8 February 1842)," in *Collected Works*, 1: 268-69.

14. See Olmstead, *History of Religion in the United States*, 354-55, and note 8 above regarding the Washingtonians in particular. Anson Phelps Stokes cites Benjamin Rush in 1785 on the role of churches in promoting public temperance: "I am disposed to believe that the business [i.e., temperance] must be effected finally by religion alone. Human reason has been employed in vain . . . we have nothing to hope from the influence of *law* in making men wise and sober. Let these considerations lead us to address the heads of the governing bodies of all the Churches in America." *Church and State in the United States: Historical Development and Contemporary Problems of Religious Freedom under the Constitution*, Anson Phelps Stokes, ed., 2 vols. (New York: Harpers & Brothers, 1950), 1: 40.

15. John Niven, *The Coming of the Civil War, 1837-1861* (Arlington Heights, Ill.: Harlan Davidson, Inc., 1990), 42. Niven summarizes: "The

movement was so effective that that by the 1840s the temperance lobby became an important political force on the state and local level."

16. My interpretation of the Temperance Address owes much to Harry V. Jaffa, *Crisis of the House Divided: An Interpretation of the Issues in the Lincoln-Douglas Debates* (Seattle: University of Washington Press, 1973; reprint ed., Chicago: University of Chicago Press, 1982, © 1959), chap. 10, "The Teaching Concerning Political Moderation," 236-72.

17. "First Debate with Stephen A. Douglas at Ottawa, Illinois (21 August 1858)," in *Collected Works*, 3: 27.

18. See David Zarefsky, "'Public Sentiment Is Everything': Lincoln's View of Political Persuasion," *Journal of the Abraham Lincoln Association* 15, No. 2 (1994): 23-40, which argues that Lincoln understood that public sentiment was "not purely cognitive and rational" but "sprang from the nexus of religious and ethical conviction" and "cultural tradition and narrative."

19. Cf. John G. West, Jr., *The Politics of Revelation and Reason: Religion and Civic Life in the New Nation* (Lawrence: University Press of Kansas, 1996), which argues that in the formative years of the American republic, some reform movements were led by evangelicals who made political appeals "without making religious doctrines the focus of their efforts." West adds: "Even when they did tie their political discussions back to the Bible, however, the 'biblical' principles they cited most often coincided with the 'natural' principles accepted by free thinkers and deists" (*The Politics of Revelation and Reason*, 96 and 122, respectively).

20. See Richard H. Sewell, *A House Divided: Sectionalism and Civil War, 1848-1865* (Baltimore: Johns Hopkins University Press, 1988), 40-41; James M. McPherson, *Battle Cry of Freedom: The Civil War Era* (New York: Ballantine Books, 1989), 32-33; and Niven, *The Coming of the Civil War*, 69-70. Don E. Fehrenbacher notes that there was "a strong scent of nativism" to a prohibition law passed by the Illinois legislature in 1855 but rejected by popular referendum. *Prelude to Greatness: Lincoln in the 1850's* (Stanford: Stanford University Press, 1962), 13.

21. "To Joshua F. Speed (27 March 1842)," in *Collected Works*, 1: 283. "Fortunately, it is not very long and I shall deem it a sufficient compliance with my request, if one of you listens while the other reads it."

22. "To Joshua F. Speed (4 July 1842)," in *Collected Works*, 1: 290. "I have made you a subscriber to the [Sangamo] Journal; and also sent the number containing the temperance speech."

23. "Temperance Address (22 February 1842)," in *Collected Works*, 1: 271.

24. *Collected Works*, 1: 272.

25. "The Washington Society," *Illinois State Register*, 11 March 1842, 2; Angle, *"Here I Have Lived": The Story of Lincoln's Springfield*, 65. Contrary to the claim of the *Illinois State Register*, there is no record that Lincoln actually signed the pledge or officially joined the Washington Temperance Society.

26. Blocker, *American Temperance Movements*, 41-42; David S. Reynolds, "Black Cats and Delirium Tremens: Temperance and the American

Renaissance," in *The Serpent in the Cup: Temperance in American Literature,* Davis S. Reynolds and Debra J. Rosenthal, eds. (Amherst: University of Massachusetts Press, 1997), 26-27.

27. "Temperance Address (22 February 1842)," in *Collected Works,* 1: 273.

28. Blocker, *American Temperance Movements,* 12; Abzug, *Cosmos Crumbling,* 98.

29. "Temperance Address (22 February 1842)," in *Collected Works,* 1: 274. For a history of the evolution in thinking about alcohol consumption from the American colonial period through the twentieth century, see Paul Aaron and David Musto, "Temperance and Prohibition in America: A Historical Review," in *Alcohol and Public Policy: Beyond the Shadow of Prohibition,* Mark H. Moore and Dean R. Gerstein, eds. (Washington, D.C.: National Academy Press, 1981), 121-81.

30. "Temperance Address (22 February 1842)," in *Collected Works,* 1: 275.

31. *Collected Works,* 1: 273.

32. *Collected Works,* 1: 276.

33. *Collected Works,* 1: 275.

34. *Collected Works,* 1: 275-76.

35. *Collected Works,* 1: 276.

36. *Collected Works,* 1: 273.

37. Cited by Gilbert Hobbs Barnes in *The Antislavery Impulse, 1830-1844* (New York: D. Appleton-Century Company, 1933), 25.

38. Barnes, *The Antislavery Impulse,* 25, 101, 210, n. 19. To his credit, Finney recognized the excess to which public rebuke could be taken: only if exercised in a spirit of love and not hate, and especially within the context of a revival of religious devotion, could denunciation be of good effect. For example, "If abolition can be made an appendage of a general revival of religion, all is well. . . . I fear no other form of carrying this question will save our country." Relating temperance reform and religious revival, Finney stated: "We made temperance an appendage of the revival in Rochester. . . . I was almost alone in the field as an Evangelist. Then 100,000 were converted in one year, everyone of which was a temperance man." Barnes, *The Antislavery Impulse,* 162, 275, n. 4.

39. "Temperance Address (22 February 1842)," in *Collected Works,* 1: 276.

40. "For the older temperance regulars, temperance and religion had to go hand in hand through the leadership of religious temperance men." Moreover, "They would direct the benevolent work to the ultimate task of saving souls." Tyrrell, *Sobering Up,* 198, 199.

41. "Temperance Address (22 February 1842)," in *Collected Works,* 1: 273.

42. "Campaign Circular from Whig Committee (4 March 1843)," in *Collected Works,* 1: 315. In his last official debate with Stephen Douglas, Lincoln remarked: "The Bible says somewhere that we are desperately selfish. I think we would have discovered that fact without the Bible." "Seventh and Last Debate with Stephen A. Douglas at Alton, Illinois (15 October 1858)," in *Collected Works,* 3: 310.

43. "To Edwin M. Stanton (30 September 1863)," in *Collected Works*, 6: 489, n. 1. Lincoln sent Stanton a copy of the address by the Sons of Temperance in order that "the suggestions therein, as to the Army, may be considered, and adopted if thought to be expedient." Two years earlier, he had written Secretary of War Simon Cameron to determine if he had "legal authority" to appoint men to promote temperance in the military. "To Simon Cameron (17 July 1861)," in *Collected Works*, 4: 451. This was prompted by a memorial sent to him by the governor of Connecticut requesting a military commission for James B. Merwin to do temperance work in the army. According to his own testimony, Merwin received his appointment "as an *ordained* chaplain" (emphasis in original) the following September. Roy P. Basler notes that it came in June of 1862. See "To Benjamin F. Larned (1 July 1862)," in *Collected Works*, 5: 297 and "To Simon Cameron (17 July 1861)," *Collected Works*, 4: 451 n. 1.

44. "Reply to Sons of Temperance (29 September 1863)," in *Collected Works*, 6: 487.

45. "Temperance Address (22 February 1842)," in *Collected Works*, 1: 271.

46. "If a city was conquered, the gods were supposed to have been vanquished with it." Numa Denis Fustel de Coulanges, *The Ancient City: A Study on the Religion, Laws, and Institutions of Greece and Rome* (Baltimore: Johns Hopkins University Press, 1980), 144. Exodus 34:12-14 reads:

> Take heed to thyself, lest thou make a covenant with the inhabitants of the land whither thou goest, lest it be for a snare in the midst of thee: But ye shall destroy their altars, break their images, and cut down their groves: For thou shalt worship no other god: for the Lord, whose name is Jealous, is a jealous God . . . (See also Deut. 7:5, 12:1-3; 2 Kgs. 11:18; and 2 Chr. 23:17.)

47. Cf. Lincoln as he repeats the position of professed anti-slavery men who nevertheless side with the Democratic Party in holding to the policy of "indifference" with respect to slavery:

> [W]e must not call it wrong in politics because that is bringing morality into politics, and we must not call it wrong in the pulpit because that is bringing politics into religion; we must not bring it into the Tract Society or the other societies, because those are such unsuitable places, and there is no single place, according to you, where this wrong thing can properly be called wrong!

"Speech at New Haven, Connecticut (6 March 1860)," in *Collected Works*, 4: 21.

48. For an examination of this split as it related to the political tensions of the times (slavery, in particular), see C. Bruce Staiger, "Abolitionism and the Presbyterian Schism of 1837-1838," *The Mississippi Valley Historical Review* 36 (December 1949): 391-414. See also Mitchell Snay, *Gospel of Disunion: Religion and Separatism in the Antebellum South* (Chapel Hill: University of North Carolina Press, 1997; orig. publ., Cambridge University Press, 1993), chap. 4, "Harbingers of Disunion: The Denominational Schisms," 113-50; *Dictionary of Christianity in America*, Daniel G. Reid with Robert D. Linder, Bruce L. Shelley, and Harry S. Stout, eds. (Downers Grove, Ill.: InterVarsity Press, 1990), s.v. "New School Presbyterians," 819-20; and *Encyclopedia of the*

American Religious Experience: Studies of Traditions and Movements, Charles H. Lippy and Peter W. Williams, eds., 3 vols. (New York: Charles Scribner's Sons, 1988), s.v. "Presbyterianism," by Louis Weeks, 1: 502-503. The Methodists and Baptists would split in 1843 and 1845, respectively, over the issue of slavery. See Edwin S. Gaustad, ed., *A Documentary History of Religion in America: To the Civil War* (Grand Rapids, Mich.: William B. Eerdmans Publishing Company, 1982), 491-97.

49. Staiger, "Abolitionism and the Presbyterian Schism of 1837-1838," 393.

50. For a brief history of this doctrinal development within the Presbyterian Church, see Barnes, *The Antislavery Impulse*, 3-12. See also Olmstead, *History of Religion in the United States*, 311-14, and 189-90, for discussion of the preceding generation's dispute over the doctrine of original sin and the free will of man.

51. Cited in Barnes, *The Antislavery Impulse*, 11.

52. Barnes lists several of the early aims of "the Great Eight" societies that would take shape under the leadership of the Great Revivalists like Charles Grandison Finney and protégé Theodore Dwight Weld: promoting home and foreign missions, distributing Bibles and tracts, funding Sunday schools, promoting temperance, and converting sailors. He notes, "the benevolent empire was dominated by 'New-School' Presbyterians, liberals of the Great Revival." Barnes, *The Antislavery Impulse*, 17, 18. See also Staiger, "Abolitionism and the Presbyterian Schism," 397: "Although Finney devoted himself almost exclusively to revivalism, his doctrines lent themselves to a great interest in social reform. Theodore Dwight Weld, a convert of Finney's, shaped this interest into another revival, one in which slaveholding was identical with sin." Weld would go on to become the great temperance speaker of frontier America, as well as write *Slavery as It Is*, an 1839 book from which Harriet Beecher Stowe mined details for her 1852 literary bombshell, *Uncle Tom's Cabin*. Joan D. Hedrick, *Harriet Beecher Stowe: A Life* (New York: Oxford University Press, 1994), 230.

53. For derivation of the "hard shell" label and its theological import, see "Baptist Churches in U.S.A." and "Primitive Baptists" descriptions in the *Dictionary of Christianity in America*, 110-11 and 940, respectively, and "Primitive Baptist" in Frank S. Mead, ed., Samuel S. Hill, rev. ed., *Handbook of Denominations in the United States*, 9th ed. (Nashville: Abingdon Press, 1985), 51-52.

54. Barnes, *The Antislavery Impulse*, 17-18.

55. Barnes, *The Antislavery Impulse*, 7-8, 18, 80: "Sanguine hope pervaded the [temperance] movement. 'The intimate connection of temperance with revivals' made the downfall of liquor and the conversion of the nation a single object, to be obtained within a decade or so, and to be followed by the conquest of the world"; "Weld's methods were the 'New Measures' of Finney in the Great Revival, the form and spirit of a protracted meeting."

56. Barnes, *The Antislavery Impulse*, 100-101, 104-108. See also Abzug, *Cosmos Crumbling*, chap. 4, "The Temperance Reformation," 81-104.

57. "Temperance Address (22 February 1842)," in *Collected Works*, 1: 272-73.

58. G. I. Williamson, *The Westminster Confession of Faith for Study Classes* (Philadelphia: Presbyterian and Reformed Publishing Co., 1964), 53, 88.

59. Williamson, *The Westminster Confession*, 91.

60. Barnes, *The Antislavery Impulse*, 5.

61. "Temperance Address (22 February 1842)," in *Collected Works*, 1: 273.

62. 2 Cor. 4:18 reads: "But we all, with open face beholding as in a glass the glory of the Lord, are changed into the same image from glory to glory, even as by the Spirit of the Lord." See also Jn. 1:12-13; 3:3-6.

63. Blocker, *American Temperance Movements*, 43; Olmstead, *History of Religion in the United States*, 355.

64. Temperance Address (22 February 1842)," in *Collected Works*, 1: 275.

65. Isaac Watts, *Hymns and Spiritual Songs* (1707), book I, hymn 88, cited in *Abraham Lincoln: Speeches and Writings*, Don E. Fehrenbacher, ed., 2 vols. (New York: Library of America, 1989), 1: 860, n. 86.20-21. The actual source may have been the *Missouri Harmony*, published by Morgan and Sanxay in Cincinnati, as described by Carl Sandburg: "It was a collection of psalm and hymn tunes, and anthems, from eminent authors . . ." *Abraham Lincoln*, Sangamon ed., 6 vols. (New York: Charles Scribner's Sons, 1950), vol. 1: *The Prairie Years*, 181.

66. "Temperance Address (22 February 1842)," in *Collected Works*, 1: 272, 275.

67. *Collected Works*, 1: 275, 276, and 274. As "practical philanthropists" (*Collected Works*, 1: 274), the Washingtonians personify that "sympathy with the suffering, and of devotion to the progress of the whole human race" that typified the great reform movements of the 1830s. Barnes, *The Antislavery Impulse*, 3.

68. Barnes, *The Antislavery Impulse*, 11-19, 208, n. 5.

69. Staiger, "Abolition and the Presbyterian Schism," 391, 395, and 398.

70. It was this hope that, surprisingly, New School Presbyterians did not hold out in their crusade to free American slaves. Although originally striving for "immediate abolition, gradually accomplished" through appeals to northerners and southerners alike, the movement soon embraced immediate abolition, simply; this involved a redirection of their appeal to the North primarily and through petitioning Congress. Barnes, *The Antislavery Impulse*, 48-49, 79, 104, and chaps. 11-13.

71. In his famous Peoria Address of 1854, Lincoln castigated Stephen Douglas for sponsoring the Kansas-Nebraska Act, which repealed the anti-slavery clause of the Missouri Compromise of 1820. Lincoln explained how "the spirit of compromise" helped unify the American states and upheld the promise of self-government: "But restore the [Missouri] compromise, and what

then? We thereby restore the national faith, the national confidence, the national feeling of brotherhood. We thereby reinstate the spirit of concession and compromise—that spirit which has never failed us in past perils, and which may be safely trusted for all the future." "Speech at Peoria, Illinois (16 October 1854)," in *Collected Works*, 2: 272.

72. "Temperance Address (22 February 1842)," in *Collected Works*, 1: 276.

73. The first is Mark 5:18-20: "And when he [Jesus] was come into the ship, he that had been possessed with the devil prayed him that he might be with him. Howbeit Jesus suffered him not, but saith unto him, 'Go home to thy friends, and tell them how great things the Lord hath done for thee, and hath had compassion on thee.' And he departed, and began to publish in Decapolis how great things Jesus had done for him: and all men did marvel." The second is Luke 11:14, 24-26:

> And he [Jesus] was casting out a devil, and it was dumb. And it came to pass, when the devil was gone out, the dumb spake; and the people wondered. . . . [Jesus said,] "When the unclean spirit is gone out of a man, he walketh through dry places, seeking rest; and finding none, he saith, 'I will return unto my house whence I came out.' And when he cometh, he findeth it swept and garnished. Then goeth he, and taketh to him seven other spirits more wicked than himself; and they enter in, and dwell there: and the last state of that man is worse than the first."

74. "Temperance Address (22 February 1842)," in *Collected Works*, 1: 276.

75. As president, Lincoln would give the same assessment when he agreed to add his name to a "Presidential Temperance Declaration" signed by ten other American presidents. Its author, Edward C. Delavan (a former wine merchant, now temperance reformer), had been collecting presidential signatures for the declaration since 1833. It states:

> Being satisfied from observation and experience, as well as from medical testimony, that ardent spirits, as a drink, is not only needless, but hurtful and that the entire disuse of it would tend to promote the health, the virtue and happiness of the community: we hereby express our conviction, that should the citizens of the United States, and especially all young men, discountenance entirely the use of it, they would not only promote their own personal benefit, but the good of the country and of the world.

"Temperance Declaration [c. 4 July 1861)," in *Collected Works*, 4: 420.

76. "Temperance Address (22 February 1842)," in *Collected Works*, 1: 276-77.

77. *Collected Works*, 1: 277. The biblical verse 2 Peter 2:22 reads: "But it is happened unto them according to the true proverb, The dog is turned to his own vomit again; and the sow that was washed to her wallowing in the mire."

78. The relevant Bible passage reads:

> Let nothing be done through strife or vainglory; but in lowliness of mind let each esteem other better than themselves. Look not every man on his own things, but every man also on the things of others. Let this mind be in you, which was also in Christ Jesus: Who, being in the form of God, thought it not robbery to be equal with God: But made himself of no reputation, and took

upon him the form of a servant, and was made in the likeness of men. And being in found in fashion as a man, he humbled himself, and became obedient unto death, even the death of the cross. (Phil. 2:3-8)

79. "Temperance Address (22 February 1842)," in *Collected Works*, 1: 278.

80. *Collected Works*, 1: 278-79.

81. *Collected Works*, 1: 279.

82. Cf. the namesake of the Washingtonian Society in his "General Orders" (18 April 1783), which called for a cessation of hostilities between the United States and Great Britain. George Washington's order concluded with a call to toast the successful termination of the Revolutionary War: "An extra ration of liquor to be issued to *every* man tomorrow, to drink Perpetual Peace, Independence and Happiness to the United States of America." *George Washington: A Collection*, W. B. Allen, ed. (Indianapolis: Liberty Fund, Inc., 1988), 238.

83. A recent study of temperance literature misses the irony in the flamboyant rhetoric of Lincoln's Temperance Address. John W. Crowley cites Lincoln's association of temperance reform with the political revolution of 1776 as an expression of "Lincoln's triumphant moral vision." "Slaves to the Bottle: Gough's *Autobiography* and Douglass's *Narrative*," *The Serpent in the Cup: Temperance in American Literature*, David S. Reynolds and Debra J. Rosenthal, eds. (Amherst: University of Massachusetts Press, 1997), 123.

84. James Smith, "A Discourse on the Bottle—Its Evils, and the Remedy" (Springfield, Ill.; privately printed, 1853, 1892), 1-9 (unnumbered pages). The Lincoln family began renting a pew in the Reverend Smith's First Presbyterian Church of Springfield the previous year. Wayne C. Temple, *Abraham Lincoln: From Skeptic to Prophet* (Mahomet, Ill.: Mayhaven Publishing, 1995), 47-48. In 1850 the Reverend Smith had conducted the funeral service for the Lincolns' second child, Edward; as president, Lincoln would appoint the Scotsman to the U.S. Consulate in Dundee, Scotland. Edgar DeWitt Jones, *Lincoln and the Preachers* (New York: Harper & Brothers Publishers, 1948), 30-34, 178; "To William H. Seward (14 January 1863)," in *Collected Works*, 6: 58 and n. 1; "To William H. Seward (9 January 1863)," in *Collected Works*, 6: 51-52 and n. 1.

85. "To James Smith (24 January 1853)," in *Collected Works*, 2: 188 and n. 1.

86. Smith, "A Discourse on the Bottle—Its Evils, and the Remedy," 5.

87. Smith, "A Discourse on the Bottle—Its Evils, and the Remedy," 5.

88. "Temperance Address (22 February 1842)," in *Collected Works*, 1: 274.

89. Smith, "A Discourse on the Bottle—Its Evils, and the Remedy," 7.

90. "Reply to Pennsylvania Delegation (5 March 1861)," in *Collected Works*, 4: 274.

91. "Second Inaugural Address (4 March 1865)," in *Collected Works*, 8: 333.

92. Smith, "A Discourse on the Bottle—Its Evils, and the Remedy," 8.

93. "Temperance Address (22 February 1842)," in *Collected Works*, 1: 274.

94. "First Inaugural Address—Final Text (4 March 1861)," in *Collected Works*, 4: 271.

95. "Second Inaugural Address (4 March 1865)," in *Collected Works*, 8: 333.

96. Smith, "A Discourse on the Bottle—Its Evils, and the Remedy," 9.

97. "Annual Message to Congress (3 December 1861)" *Collected Works*, 5: 53.

98. "Second Inaugural Address (4 March 1865)," in *Collected Works*, 8: 333.

99. Smith, "A Discourse on the Bottle—Its Evils, and the Remedy," 7.

100. Beveridge, *Abraham Lincoln*, 2: 241-2.

101. "To J. Mason Haight (11 June 1860)," in *Collected Works*, 4: 75. For the fullest examination of Lincoln's teetotalism, see William H. Townsend, *Lincoln and Liquor* (New York: Press of the Pioneers, Inc., 1934).

102. Merrill D. Petersen, *Lincoln in American Memory* (New York: Oxford University Press, 1994), 247-51. See Beveridge, *Abraham Lincoln, 1809-1858*, 1: 249-50, 268-69, 288-89, and 2: 293-96 for an account of Lincoln's role in 1838 in presenting a petition of Sangamon County "praying the repeal of all laws authorizing the retailing of intoxicating liquors"; his subsequent votes on the subject as a state legislator the following year; and his abstaining from the issue as a public figure in 1855. Benjamin P. Thomas writes: "Except for three temperance speeches, Lincoln took no part in the manifold social and reform movements that swept the country in the forties." *Abraham Lincoln: A Biography* (New York: Random House, Inc.—First Modern Library Edition, 1968), 111. In addition to his 1842 address to the Springfield Washingtonians, the other two documented times Lincoln made temperance speeches occurred on August 31, 1846 (to the Springfield Juvenile Society), and June 20, 1847 (to the Langston's Settlement Temperance Society). See Leonard U. Blumberg with William L. Pittman, *Beware the First Drink: The Washington Temperance Movement and Alcoholics Anonymous* (Seattle: Glen Abbey Books, 1991), 103; Miers, *Lincoln Day by Day*, 1: 275, 290. Cf. the contrary testimony of his junior law partner at that time, William Herndon: "But, nothing daunted, Lincoln kept on and labored zealously in the interest of the temperance movement. He spoke often again in Springfield, and also in other places over the country, displaying the same courage and adherence to principle that characterized his every undertaking." Herndon and Weik, *Herndon's Life of Lincoln*, 206. See also the dubious claims made by James B. Merwin, among which was that Lincoln and he campaigned together for prohibition during their canvass for Richard Yates's congressional re-election bid in the fall of 1854: "Mr. Lincoln's political friends were alarmed for him because of his radicalism on the temperance question, and made a combined effort to silence him, but he continued in the fight." "Lincoln as Prohibitionist," in J. T. Hobson, *Footprints of Abraham Lincoln* (Dayton: The Otterbein Press, 1909), 59, and 57-67, generally. No speech by Lincoln even alluding to temperance reform exists from that very busy period of Lincoln's public life, while his stump speeches and newspaper editorials from August 26

to November 1 focus exclusively on the Kansas-Nebraska Act and its repeal of the Missouri Compromise—*the* issue that led Lincoln to run for Illinois State Representative in 1854 to support Yates and the anti-Nebraska effort in general. Even newspaper and diary accounts of his speeches fail to record a single reference to temperance. *Lincoln Day by Day*, 2: 126-31. For the context of the Yates campaign as it related to Lincoln's alleged temperance advocacy, see David Herbert Donald, *Lincoln* (New York: Simon & Schuster, 1995), 169-73. Lincoln later described his activities of 1854 in a presidential campaign autobiography:

> In 1854, his profession had almost superseded the thought of politics in his mind, when the repeal of the Missouri compromise aroused him as he had never been before.
>
> In the autumn of that year he took the stump with no broader practical aim or object that [than?] to secure, if possible, the reelection of Hon Richard Yates to congress. His speeches at once attracted a more marked attention than they had ever before done. As the canvass proceeded, he was drawn to different parts of the state, outside of Mr. Yates' district. He did not abandon the law, but gave his attention, by turns, to that and politics.

"Autobiography Written for John L. Scripps [c. June, 1860)," in *Collected Works*, 4: 67. It should come as no surprise that Lincoln made no reference to the contentious issue of temperance in the campaign of 1854, for it would have distracted his audience from his examination of the Kansas-Nebraska Act—a measure he thought should be "rebuked and condemned every where." "To John M. Palmer (7 September 1854)," in *Collected Works*, 2: 228.

103. "Temperance Address (22 February 1842)," in *Collected Works*, 1: 272.

104. Tyrrell, *Sobering Up*, 199. The Springfield pledge read as follows. "The undersigned, being desirous of carrying out the principles of temperance, *do pledge our honor* that we will abstain from all intoxicating drinks" (emphasis in original). *Historical Encyclopedia of Illinois and History of Sangamon County*, Newton Bateman and Paul Selby, eds., 2 vols. (Chicago: Munsell Publishing Company, 1912), 2: 993 (Part One). The original Washingtonian pledge read as follows: "We, whose names are annexed, desirous of forming a society for our mutual benefit, and to guard against a pernicious practice which is injurious to our health, standing, and families, do pledge ourselves as gentlemen that we will not drink any spirituous or malt liquors, wine or cider." Blocker, *American Temperance Movements*, 43.

105. Smith, "A Discourse on the Bottle—Its Evils, and the Remedy," 7.

106. "Request for Use of Hall of Representatives for a Temperance Lecture (25 January 1845)," in *Collected Works*, 1: 343.

107. "Speech at a Republican Banquet, Chicago, Illinois (10 December 1856)," in *Collected Works*, 2: 385.

Chapter 5

The Political Limits of Reason and Religion: An Interpretation of the Second Inaugural Address

At a White House reception following his second inauguration as president, Abraham Lincoln spotted Frederick Douglass among a throng of visitors making their way through the receiving line. "Here comes my friend Douglass," Lincoln announced, as he hailed the first black citizen permitted to attend an inaugural reception. Lincoln then asked Douglass's opinion of the Second Inaugural Address: "there is no man in the country whose opinion I value more than yours. I want to know what you think of it?" To which Douglass replied, "Mr. Lincoln, that was a sacred effort."[1] These two protagonists of antebellum politics had differed in their approaches to resolving the crisis over slavery. Now, as the constitutional head of the national government, Lincoln asked the opinion of a former slave! The greater irony of Douglass's answer is that Lincoln's Second Inaugural Address used religious language to demonstrate the insufficiency of religion to hasten the end of the Civil War.

In his Temperance Address of 1842, Lincoln offered a guarded explanation of the potential dangers of religion to a republic, while his Lyceum Address of 1838 invited religion to play a supporting role in the political arena. But these and other speeches and writings of his consistently present reason as the star of the political stage. Nevertheless, this is too ready a conclusion without an examination of his most profound statement regarding reason and religion in politics—the Second Inaugural Address of 1865. In it he offers a startling interpretation of the Civil War that highlights America's failure to resolve the conflict using reason *or* religion.

Lincoln had already expressed misgivings about certain religiously inspired social movements bent on remaking the world into their own image. He never explored, however, the efficacy of reason as the only guide to public opinion. To be sure, he closes the Lyceum and Temperance Addresses with tributes to reason as all-powerful to solve political problems. But these statements suggest more in the way of rhetorical flourish than serious reflection on the power of reason to check or curb the public passions.[2] Crises may yet arise that frustrate both the reason and religion of the national community. The evolving crisis for the United States was the attempt at secession by southern states, the ensuing Civil War, and the future of slavery. Lincoln appealed to the reason of the "seceding states" in his First Inaugural Address, but to no avail.[3] Five months later, at the behest of Congress, he added religion to the mix by proclaiming a national fast-day. Again, there was no resolution of the conflict. Not until Lincoln's second presidential inauguration do we find his answer for dealing with these crises.

The Second Inaugural Address shows Abraham Lincoln at the peak of his rhetorical expression, with his more famous speech at Gettysburg as its only rival in argument and eloquence. The Sunday before the inauguration, Lincoln commented on his upcoming speech: "Lots of wisdom in that document, I suspect . . ."[4] He would later write that he expected the Second Inaugural Address "to wear as well as—perhaps better than—any thing I have produced; but I believe it is not immediately popular."[5] What elevates this speech above the Gettysburg Address is its focus on the will of God in discussing the fate of the Union. Where the original draft of the Gettysburg Address contains no direct reference to God or providence,[6] the Second Inaugural Address rests on an exposition of God's will in the American Civil War. Lincoln interprets how the war had progressed under divine and human guidance, and where the Almighty may yet direct its consummation—especially in the third paragraph of the four-paragraph speech. The address shows the extent to which Lincoln sees both reason and religion fall short in their attempts to direct the course of the nation before and during the Civil War. In a telling demonstration of republican statesmanship under the providence of God, Lincoln uses both reason and religion to deliver the lesson.

Paragraph One: "Little That Is New Could Be Presented."

Lincoln begins by saying that a lengthy speech is not needed because the nation has watched the progress of events closely since the first inauguration. Compared with the First Inaugural Address, written to address issues of "special anxiety" and "excitement" in the public eye, the Second Inaugural Address could offer little that would be new in the way of national policy. The first inauguration welcomed a new presidential administration, the first under the Republican banner, and witnessed seven states already separated from the Union and organized as the Confederate States of America. "Then, a statement, somewhat in detail, of a course to be pursued, seemed fitting and proper."[7] The purpose of the First Inaugural Address was to present the new Administration's plan for upholding the Constitution—in all its parts—in an effort to preserve the Union. The need, then, was to assure the South that the entering Republican president, whom they viewed as representing a sectional party,[8] would uphold the entire Constitution of the United States without infringing upon any of the existing rights of the citizenry. As this remained Lincoln's objective throughout the national crisis, "during which public declarations have been constantly called forth on every point and phase of the great contest," he concludes, "little that is new could be presented."

Moving from past events to the present, Lincoln draws special attention to the "progress of our arms, upon which all else chiefly depends." He rarely missed an occasion to highlight the efforts and accomplishments of the Union military in his public addresses—a habit that provided our country with its most famous eulogy, the 1863 dedication of the Gettysburg National Cemetery. Lincoln followed his Gettysburg Address one month later with his third Annual Message to Congress, which concludes with a verbal salute to the men in the field: "And it may be esteemed fortunate that in giving the greatest efficiency to these indispensable arms, we do also honorably recognize the gallant men . . . who compose them, and to whom, more than others, the world must stand indebted for the home of freedom disenthralled, regenerated, enlarged, and perpetuated."[9]

Lincoln received two letters within a week of his second inauguration that reflected his own resolve to call attention to the "progress of our arms" as the principal means of victory in the closing days of the war. One was written by the famed abolitionist and pastor, Henry Ward Beecher:

> You have brought the most dangerous and extraordinary rebellion in history, not only to a successful end, but, have done it without sacrificing *republican government* even in its forms. It is wonderful, and a sign of Divine help, that democratic institutions & feelings, are stronger today—after four years of War, . . . than when you began. . . .

> Would it not be well if the country could be told, deffinitely [*sic*]
> how the case stands? An address to the army, or to the nation,
> declaring that *peace can come only by arms*, if in your judgement the
> fact is so, would end these feverish uncertainties & give the spring
> campaign renewed vigor.[10] (Emphasis in original.)

Received only eight days before giving his Second Inaugural Address,
the letter could not have been more encouraging to Lincoln. The second
correspondence came from General Ulysses S. Grant, notifying the
president of General Robert E. Lee's desire to meet with Grant to discuss
"the possibility of arriving at a satisfactory adjustment of the present
unhappy difficulties."[11] Lincoln responded to Lee's suggestion for "an
interchange of views" in a telegram sent by Secretary of War Edwin M.
Stanton to Grant the day before the inauguration: "The President directs
me to say to you that he wishes you to have no conference with General
Lee unless it be for the capitulation of Gen. Lee's army, or on some
minor, and purely, military matter. . . . Meantime you are to press to the
utmost, your military advantages."[12] Lincoln's response reflected his
long-standing position that the Union would stop fighting as soon as the
states in rebellion ceased their efforts to dissolve the Union and
submitted to the federal authority under the Constitution.

Chief Justice Samuel P. Chase, Lincoln's former secretary of the
treasury, noted a telling example of the president's resolve to end the
war. When Chase administered the presidential oath of office, Lincoln
kissed a Bible opened to Isaiah 5:27-28: "None shall be weary nor
stumble among them; none shall slumber nor sleep; neither shall the
girdle of their loins be loosed, nor the latchet of their shoes be broken:
Whose arrows are sharp, and all their bows bent, their horses' hoofs shall
be counted like flint, and their wheels like a whirlwind."[13] This passage
refers to the remnant of Israel that will return to Jerusalem from exile to
reaffirm their covenant relationship with the living God. Accordingly,
Lincoln may have viewed the survivors of the Civil War as modern
counterparts of the Jewish remnant.[14] Just as the children of Israel
returned to the land of their fathers and once more revered and obeyed
the laws of Moses, so, too, would the descendants of the American
founding generation return to their homeland by honoring and preserving
the principles of republican government established by their forefathers.
Slavery was a departure from the principle of human equality upon
which the nation was founded. The return to this a principle required a
battle with those who had ceased to be faithful to the Founders' intention
of placing slavery on the course of ultimate extinction. As Israel's exile

and eventual return represented the chastening of a righteous and merciful God, so might America's Civil War signify the judgment of the "Living God" in whom both the North and South believe.

Lincoln closes the first paragraph by expressing "high hope for the future," aware that the surrender of the Confederate army was imminent. One month earlier, the failed peace conference at Hampton Roads, Virginia, convinced the president of the desperate position of the rebellious states. With Sherman and Grant closing in on Lee's Army of Northern Virginia, the end of the war was in sight. Thus, Lincoln sees no need to change course. The First Inaugural Address charted the national government's course of action; the Second Inaugural Address looks to its approaching consummation.

Yet Lincoln does not end the speech after the first paragraph. He continues for three more paragraphs to explain the Civil War, using a specific time reference for each paragraph as foreshadowed in the first paragraph. The first paragraph referred to the past, present, and future contexts of the Civil War period, introduced by the words "Then," "Now," and "future." The next three paragraphs focus distinctly on these time frames, chronologically elaborating on the first paragraph's overview of the Civil War era. The second paragraph addresses the past: specifically, the occasion of the First Inaugural Address and the impending Civil War. The third and most profound paragraph discusses the present, not simply focusing on the events surrounding the Second Inaugural but viewing the Civil War in its entirety from its actual beginning through its anticipated close. Finally, the fourth paragraph presents a national agenda for ending the war and maintaining a lasting peace.

Paragraph Two: "And the War Came."

As paragraphs two, three, and four represent the core of Lincoln's thoughts on the Civil War, paragraph two refers the listener back to the occasion of the First Inaugural Address. Seven states had "seceded" from the Union, organized a Confederate Congress, and installed Mississippi Senator Jefferson Davis as its provisional president. In January of 1861, South Carolina had fired upon the "Star of the West," an unarmed merchant ship (albeit garrisoned with two hundred soldiers) that was sent to reinforce Fort Sumter.[15] An attempt by the border slave state of Virginia to avert war through a peace conference had failed, leaving no doubt in the public mind that a genuine split of the nation was occurring only one month before the inauguration of its first Republican president.

"On the occasion corresponding to this four years ago," Lincoln states, "all thoughts were anxiously directed to an impending civil war. All dreaded it—all sought to avert it." At Lincoln's first inauguration, all citizens, including those who now fought against the Union, feared a civil war. By repeating the word "all" three times in the first two sentences of paragraph two, Lincoln impresses upon his listeners that the entire nation was attempting, in one way or another, to avoid a war.

So far, Lincoln has not mentioned the two-sided nature of the crisis. He maintains the unity of his audience rhetorically with the words "nation," "our arms," "the public," and "to all" in paragraph one and the thrice-repeated "all" at the start of paragraph two. Only when he explains the opposing means adopted to avert the war does he divide the country into two camps:

> While the inaugeral address was being delivered from this place, devoted altogether to *saving* the Union without war, insurgent agents were in the city seeking to *destroy* it without war—seeking to dissol[v]e the Union, and divide effects, by negotiation. Both parties deprecated war; but one of them would *make* war rather than let the nation survive; and the other would *accept* war rather than let it perish.

Lincoln now refers to the two sides of the conflict: the federal government, represented by the new Lincoln administration, and the insurgency.

One readily infers that the war would not have come about if there had been no "insurgent" effort. In the months leading up to Lincoln's first inauguration, the Confederacy took possession of federal property (for example, forts and customs houses) and sent delegations to Washington to negotiate the transfer of forts and arsenals into Confederate hands.[16] In addition, with local city government and law enforcement headed by secessionists, and a militia of mixed loyalties, the Buchanan administration spent its remaining days before Lincoln's inauguration reluctantly—for fear of inciting southern reaction—reinforcing the capitol with additional federal troops and militia companies.[17] Lincoln is careful to refer to the aggressors by their character—"insurgent agents"—and not their location—the South or southern states. Focusing on location would only entrench the idea that America was evidently not meant for one people under one national government. Moreover, with significant if not extensive Unionist support among southern residents, especially in the border slave states of

Kentucky, Maryland, and Missouri, Lincoln could not categorically refer to that region of the country as "the South" without conceding to it a secessionist political sentiment that was not as uniform as the name would imply.[18] With the reference to the "insurgent agents" and "Both parties," Lincoln begins an evaluation of the opposing sides in the war that will continue for the rest of the speech until he takes up the question of God's role in the contest.

After establishing that "all sought to avert" the war, Lincoln examines this seemingly united effort in light of the opposing methods chosen to achieve it. He shows that the ultimate aim of each side was not simply to avoid war, for "insurgent agents" sought to "destroy" the Union while the new administration pledged to save the Union. Rather, "Both parties deprecated war; but one of them would *make* war rather than let the nation survive; and the other would *accept* war rather than let it perish." Only in this light can the objective viewer of the ensuing events discern the cause of the Civil War. That is to say, the occurrence of the Civil War implicated neither the federal government nor the rebelling states as wholly desirous and, hence, guilty of starting the war. This is especially significant as Lincoln reiterates for the fourth time in this paragraph that both sides wanted to avoid a war. Lincoln suggests that knowledge of either side's *intention*—in this case, the common intent to avoid war—is not sufficient to assign blame for the war.

This brings one back to the main question of the address: If "all" the nation dreaded the possibility of war and was intent on avoiding it, why was it not averted? Lincoln makes clear in this paragraph that the insurgency (the rebelling southern states) was more desirous of leaving the Union than of avoiding war. Although he began the paragraph by mentioning the initial desire of both sides to attain their goal "without war," he concludes that the insurgency would "*make* war" while the federal government would "*accept* war," showing the insurgency to be the aggressor. Lincoln once commented, "I would consent to any GREAT evil, to avoid a GREATER one."[19] In 1854, the "great evil" Lincoln lamented was the extension of slavery into the federal territory through the Kansas-Nebraska Act, an extension he thought bore no relation to saving the Union. The "greater" evil was the dissolution of the Union, and with it, the hope for the eventual union of all the states abiding by the principle of human equality. Now at his second inauguration, Lincoln shows how the great evil of war is accepted by the federal government in order to avoid the greater evil of disunion from occurring. The government, in short, acted out of self-defense, as he explained in a private letter before his reelection:

> The preservation of our Union was *not* the sole avowed object for
> which the war was commenced. It was commenced for precisely the
> reverse object—*to destroy our Union*. The insurgents commenced it by
> firing upon the Star of the West, and on Fort Sumter, and by other
> similar acts. It is true, however, that the administration accepted the
> war thus commenced, for the sole avowed object of preserving our
> Union.[20]

Lincoln always understood the rebellious southerners as the
instigators of the conflict, thus making insurgent aggression the context
for federal government action. In his famous 1860 speech at the Cooper
Institute in New York City, which brought him national recognition as a
potential presidential candidate, Lincoln took time to address "the
Southern people" and their animosity toward the Republican Party:
"Your purpose, then, plainly stated, is, that you will destroy the
Government, unless you be allowed to construe and enforce the
Constitution as you please, on all points in dispute between you and us.
You will rule or ruin in all events."[21] The Civil War having not yet begun
in early 1860, Lincoln felt safe enough to speak boldly of southern
pretensions regarding any conflict resulting from the upcoming
presidential election.

Lincoln made the same point repeatedly to Congress when he called
them into special session on July 4, 1861. A few examples will suffice:

> They knew that this Government desired to keep the garrison in the
> Fort [Sumter], not to assail them, but merely to maintain visible
> possession, and thus to preserve the Union from actual, and immediate
> dissolution—trusting, as here-in before stated, to time, discussion, and
> the ballot-box, for final adjustment; and they assailed, and reduced the
> Fort, for precisely the reverse object—to drive out the visible authority
> of the Federal Union, and thus force it to immediate dissolution.

Also, "So viewing the issue, no choice was left but to call out the war
power of the Government; and so to resist force, employed for its
destruction, by force, for its preservation." Finally, "It was with deepest
regret that the Executive found the duty of employing the war-power, in
defence of the government, forced upon him. He could but perform this
duty, or surrender the existence of the government."[22] Better still,
Lincoln made the case succinctly at the close of his last annual message
to Congress: "In stating a single condition of peace, I mean simply to say
that the war will cease on the part of the government, whenever it shall

have ceased on the part of those who began it."[23] One understands, therefore, the cause of the Civil War as an insurgency bent on dissolving the Union without war, but which resorted to violence to speed its destruction.

Lincoln ends the second paragraph with the observation: "And the war came." Although Lincoln saw the federal government's participation in the war as an act of self-defense, he does not explicitly state that the insurgents started the war. He mentions that they "would" make war while the government "would" accept war, leaving it to his listeners to come to their own conclusion as to who instigated the conflict. Unlike the private letter excerpted above, Lincoln's public address at his second inauguration as president makes no mention of the attack on Fort Sumter on April 12, 1861. Instead he concludes, "And the war came." This expresses, in part, his desire that the nation not dwell on the past errors of one section of the country, which would only hinder efforts toward reconstruction. As he will go on to implicate both sides, Lincoln lets his previous examination of each side's interests suffice as an explanation of how "the war came."

Perhaps more important, the personification of the war in this closing sentence gives the appearance that the war had a will of its own, or at least was directed by something or someone apart from the opposing sides of the conflict. Supported by Lincoln's previous reticence to assign blame for the conflict expressly to the rebellious states, this closing sentence provides an apt transition into the heart of the address—the third paragraph. Lincoln uses paragraph two as a brief explanation of each side's role in bringing on the Civil War in order to explore God's role in the war more fully in paragraph three. This is especially true as he omits any judgment of the South in paragraph two, foreshadowing God's judgment of both the North and the South in paragraph three.

Lincoln will refer to the human cause of the Civil War only twice in the third and longest paragraph of the address: one is a restatement of the goals of the opposing sides, and the other is an aside that comments on the presumption of the insurgents' pleas for divine help. At this point, one is left with the suspicion that forces external to those laid out in paragraph two may be influencing the course of events in America. The efforts of mere mortals on both sides of the ensuing conflict have failed. Once more one asks: If all sought to avert the war, why did it still happen? Is there a greater hand at work?

Paragraph Three: "The Almighty Has His Own Purposes."

In the first paragraph, Lincoln stated that four years after his first inauguration, "little that is new could be presented" about the Civil War. The country had followed the war with great interest and was now witnessing the demise of the southern rebellion. With the end of the war at hand and having outlined the human cause of the war in the second paragraph, Lincoln seems to have little more to say to the country. Nevertheless, he goes on in the third paragraph to suggest an ultimate cause of the unexpectedly long and devastating Civil War. In the longest paragraph of the address, Lincoln presents all of the dramatis personae of the Civil War and elucidates their essential though somewhat enigmatic roles. Lincoln will propose that the progress of the war lies not merely with the actions of men on either side of the conflict but with the intentions of "the Almighty Ruler of Nations."

In the first sentence of paragraph three, Lincoln introduces two terms crucial to understanding the American Civil War but curiously missing from his earlier explanation of the conflict in his address: "colored slaves" and "the Southern part of it [the Union]." Lincoln did not mention slavery earlier in his discussion of the cause of the war because he was contrasting the immediate actions and aims of the opposing sides. It now takes center stage, serving as the fulcrum of a more extensive discussion of the Civil War's cause, progress to date, and ultimate meaning. He is careful to preface "slaves" with the adjective "colored" to highlight its peculiar manifestation in the United States: that being, the enslavement of human beings solely on account of their skin color. Lincoln counts the slaves as an "eighth of the whole population," affirming their humanity and implying that such enslavement is grounded on a dubious criterion.[24]

The second phrase Lincoln introduces, "the Southern part," is the first mention of any specific region of the Union. He uses the phrase here, though, only to note the isolated location of slaves and not to designate the enemy of the Union. In fact, Lincoln does not refer anywhere in the speech to the South or southern states as the enemy of the Union. Lincoln was unwilling to grant even a rhetorical status to a supposedly unified South as the federal government's enemy. By referring to the secession adherents as "insurgents," he relegates them to the role of a mere political faction, such as that described in *Federalist* No. 10.[25] Such a faction has interests that are contrary to the rights of the American people as a whole, explicitly affirmed in the Declaration of

Independence and secured by the U.S. Constitution. The insurgency labored against the Declaration of Independence, the U.S. Constitution, and the Union, as Lincoln pointed out to the special July 4th, 1861, session of Congress: "Our adversaries have adopted some Declarations of Independence; in which, unlike the good old one, penned by Jefferson, they omit the words 'all men are created equal.' Why?" He continues,

> They have adopted a temporary national constitution, in the preamble of which, unlike our good old one, signed by Washington, they omit 'We, the People,' and substitute 'We, the deputies of the sovereign and independent States.' Why? Why this deliberate pressing out of view, the rights of men, and the authority of the people?[26]

Lincoln rightly concluded that their aims were erroneous, unlawful, and contrary to the common good, especially as they made war on the United States in order to achieve them.

Because the slaves "constituted a peculiar and powerful interest" and were "localized in the Southern part" of the Union, this interest was beholden not to the national public welfare but to a mistaken and "disloyal portion of the American people."[27] Thus, throughout the Civil War, and not only in the Second Inaugural Address, Lincoln refrains from identifying a monolithic South as the instigator of the conflict. Instead, he refers to the "disloyal portion" of the "American people," contrasting a minority faction with a unified nation. Moreover, whenever he characterized the South as a whole, he spoke in terms that were as favorable as those describing the North. In his Cooper Institute Address of 1860, Lincoln said to southern citizens, "You consider yourselves a reasonable and a just people; and I consider that in the general qualities of reason and justice you are not inferior to any other people."[28] Similarly in his Peoria Address of 1854, Lincoln spoke even more candidly:

> I think I have no prejudice against the Southern people. They are just what we would be in their situation. . . . When southern people tell us they are no more responsible for the origin of slavery, than we; I acknowledge the fact. . . . It does seem to me that systems of gradual emancipation might be adopted; but for their tardiness in this, I will not undertake to judge our brethren of the south.[29]

Returning to the Second Inaugural Address, Lincoln's only other mention of the South occurs toward the end of the third paragraph, where he accedes to his listeners' premise that the two sides of the war are the North and the South. Lincoln adopts their understanding rhetorically at that point only as he describes "both North and South" as the objects of God's wrath. But when speaking of the opposing sides of the war, his most explicit designations are "the government" and "the insurgents"; the majority of the time he uses words such as "Neither," "Each," and "Both." Mindful of the approaching close of the nation's most destructive and debilitating war, Lincoln seeks to establish throughout the address a uniformity of public sentiment that would be essential for the successful administration of national self-government after the war. He recognizes that even the long-awaited end of a costly civil war would not be sufficient to unite a nation divided in sentiment and spirit.

The original manuscript of the Second Inaugural Address shows that Lincoln chose his words carefully in an effort to express his principles and convictions with both integrity and persuasiveness. Lincoln deleted "half" and inserted "part" in the first sentence of paragraph three to read "the Southern part" of the Union instead of "the Southern half" of it.[30] His initial writing of "half," had it remained, would have been a rhetorical misstep, for he wanted to help the citizens of all the states to think as one people and not to believe that the country was naturally separated into two distinct halves. Lincoln is for the Union and against disunion or secession, and thus he scrupulously avoids addressing the nation as a defender of one geographical section against another, the North against the South. Consequently, the rhetoric of the Second Inaugural Address invites the audience to do the same.

Only a few months into the Civil War, Lincoln called attention to proper terminology when describing the various parties in the conflict. Discussing the reluctance of Maryland, Kentucky, and Missouri to join wholeheartedly in defense of the Union, he observes:

> In the border States, so called—in fact, the middle states—there are those who favor a policy which they call "armed neutrality" . . . This would be disunion completed. . . . It recognizes no fidelity to the Constitution, no obligation to maintain the Union; and while very many who have favored it are, doubtless, loyal citizens, it is, nevertheless, treason.[31]

His clarification that the so-called "border States" should more accurately be termed "middle states" follows logically from his constitutional philosophy, which views the American empire as having *national* borders but not regional or sectional ones. To be sure, the U.S. Constitution recognizes individual states, but not any constitutional boundary or "border" separating distinct regions of the American nation as "the South" or "the border states." Therefore, states that try to assume a neutral stance in the Civil War and happen to reside geographically in the "middle" of the United States should be referred to as "middle states," and not as "border states." The latter presumes that a border separates "the North" and "the South," which in Lincoln's mind forfeits the constitutional principle of national sovereignty he has sworn as president to uphold.

Lincoln had always believed that the nation could not be divided into two halves. In his 1862 Annual Message to Congress, the surveyor-turned-president states:

> There is no line, straight or crooked, suitable for a national boundary, upon which to divide. Trace through, from east to west, upon the line between the free and slave country, and we shall find a little more than one-third of its length are rivers, easy to be crossed, and populated, or soon to be populated, thickly upon both sides; while nearly all its remaining length are merely surveyor's lines, over which people may walk back and forth without any consciousness of their presence. No part of this line can be made any more difficult to pass, by writing it down on paper, or parchment, as a national boundary. . . .

> Our national strife springs not from our permanent part; not from the land we inhabit; not from our national homestead. There is no possible severing of this, but would multiply, and not mitigate, evils among us. In all its adaptations and aptitudes, it demands union, and abhors separation.[32]

His First Inaugural Address also sounds this note:

> Physically speaking, we cannot separate. We cannot remove our respective sections from each other, nor build an impassable wall between them. A husband and wife may be divorced, and go out of the presence, and beyond the reach of each other; but the different parts of our country cannot do this. They cannot but remain face to face; and intercourse, either amicable or hostile, must continue between them. Is it possible then to make that intercourse more advantageous, or more satisfactory, *after* separation than *before*? Can aliens make treaties easier than friends can make laws? Can treaties be more faithfully enforced between aliens, than laws can among friends?[33]

Lincoln was convinced that there was no distinguishable southern "half" of the Union. Hence, there ought not to be a "Southern half of it" in the minds of the American people.

He now presents the crux of the Civil War controversy:

> These slaves constituted a peculiar and powerful interest. All knew that

this interest was, somehow, the cause of the war. To strengthen, perpetuate, and extend this interest was the object for which the insurgents would rend the Union, even by war; while the government claimed no right to do more than to restrict the territorial enlargement of it.[34]

Lincoln elaborates on his earlier statement about the cause of the war. Only now does he reveal the purpose for which the insurgents sought to destroy the Union: to fortify slavery. Where paragraph two focused on the immediate cause of the war—the destruction or the preservation of the American union—paragraph three reveals that the ultimate cause of the war was the divergent opinions about the future course of slavery and, therewith, the American republic.

Lincoln calls the slaves of the South a "peculiar" interest, borrowing a locution of the day to highlight the irregularity of an institution that sanctioned ownership of human beings in a nation founded on the belief that "all men are created equal." This classification of a specific race of people as chattel gradually led a portion of the citizenry to grow accustomed to "the peculiar institution." Spurred by a mounting abolitionist campaign in the North, which culminated in the mid-1830s in scores of thousands of petitions to Congress, southerners grew to defend slavery. "The relation now existing in the slave-holding States between the two [races], is," Senator John C. Calhoun of South Carolina declared, "instead of an evil, a good—a positive good."[35] Moreover, as slavery became a "powerful" interest, those holding the institution to be legitimate adamantly refused to give it up. Eleven states eventually fought against the federal government to protect it.

Thomas Jefferson described the impact of slavery in the Revolutionary era in his famous "Query XVIII" of the *Notes on the State of Virginia* (1787):

> There must doubtless be an unhappy influence on the manners of our people produced by the existence of slavery among us. . . . The man must be a prodigy who can retain his manners and morals undepraved by such circumstances. And with what execration should the statesman be loaded, who permitting one half the citizens thus to trample on the rights of the other, transforms those into despots, and these into enemies, destroys the morals of the one part, and the *amor patriae* of the other.[36]

Lincoln understands the corrupting effect that slavery's presence and recent promotion had on the public mind. He even charged Senator Stephen A. Douglas with perverting "public sentiment" regarding slavery by advocating unquestioning acceptance of any and all Supreme Court rulings, chief among them being the 1857 *Dred Scott v. Sandford* decision.[37]

And so, "All knew that this interest was, somehow, the cause of the war. To strengthen, perpetuate, and extend this interest was the object for which the insurgents would rend the Union, even by war . . ." Lincoln's precise wording conveys the insurgents' desire to go beyond the original intentions of the Founding Fathers regarding slavery: secessionist slaveowners wished to "strengthen, perpetuate, and extend" slavery. While the Constitution's fugitive slave clause only provides for the return of persons "held to service or labor in one state, under the laws thereof, escaping into another,"[38] the insurgents had concluded that the Constitution must be interpreted to protect the alleged right of slaveowners to carry their slaves as property into the federal territories. In response to a speech by Senator Douglas in July of 1858, Lincoln summarized the historical understanding of slavery's existence in the United States:

> [T]he great mass of the nation have rested in the belief that slavery was in course of ultimate extinction. . . . It may be argued that there are certain conditions that make necessities and impose them on us, and to the extent that a necessity is imposed upon a man, he must submit to it. I think that was the condition in which we found ourselves when we established this government. We had slavery among us, we could not get our Constitution unless we permitted them to remain in slavery, we could not secure the good we did secure if we grasped for more, and having by necessity submitted to that much, it does not destroy the principle that is the charter of our liberties. Let that *charter stand as our standard.*[39]

Lincoln surmises that to "strengthen, perpetuate, and extend" slavery violates the fundamental objectives of the Founding generation and the majority of the American people of his day.[40]

Mindful that the existence of slavery in America undermines the moral basis of the rights of free individuals, to say nothing of its influence abroad, Lincoln follows his explanation of the insurgents' interest in slavery with that of the federal government: "to restrict the territorial enlargement of it." Lincoln sees that curbing and not immediately abolishing slavery can help preserve the American republic in the near term, while signaling to the world its ultimate incompatibility with self-government. In a speech criticizing the Kansas-Nebraska Act of 1854, he commented on its "covert *real* zeal for the spread of slavery":

I hate it because of the monstrous injustice of slavery itself. I hate it because it deprives our republican example of its just influence in the world—enables the enemies of free institutions, with plausibility, to taunt us as hypocrites—causes the real friends of freedom to doubt our sincerity, and especially because it forces so many really good men amongst ourselves into an open war with the very fundamental principles of civil liberty—criticising the Declaration of Independence, and insisting that there is no right principle of action but *self-interest*.[41]

Lincoln, along with Thomas Jefferson,[42] envisioned an America that would best export the principles of human freedom and equality not by military conquest but by simply maintaining her own democratic institutions for all the world to see and emulate. As John Quincy Adams said of America: "Wherever the standard of freedom and Independence, has or shall be unfurled, there will her heart, her benedictions, and her prayers be. But she goes not abroad, in search of monsters to destroy. She is the well-wisher to the freedom and independence of all. She is the vindicator only of her own."[43]

What Lincoln foreshadowed at the end of paragraph two, he now makes explicit: "Neither party expected for the war, the magnitude, or the duration, which it has already attained. Neither anticipated that the *cause* of the conflict might cease with, or even before, the conflict itself should cease."[44] Lincoln states that neither the federal government nor the insurgency had envisioned the abolition of slavery as a result of the war. Reflecting on paragraph two, one remembers that the goal of neither side necessitated an immediate change in the status of slavery. Lincoln had stated many times that his duty as president—to "preserve, protect and defend the Constitution of the United States"[45]—prevented him from interfering with the domestic institutions of any state, even in the case of slavery. But what if slavery helped a domestic insurrection to subvert the U.S. Constitution and therewith the union of the several states? Does war provide a different context for the exercise of presidential power affecting slavery?

In his first Annual Message to Congress, Lincoln explained the main objective of the federal government's war effort: "I have, therefore, in every case, thought it proper to keep the integrity of the Union prominent as the primary object of the contest on our part . . ."[46] He summed up his grand strategy with respect to the Union and slavery, in the context of a Civil War, in a letter to the renowned editor of the New York *Tribune*, Horace Greeley. On August 19, 1862, Greeley had published an editorial, "The Prayer of Twenty Millions," that criticized Lincoln for not fully supporting emancipation.[47] Lincoln replied with a letter to Greeley three days later:

> My paramount object in this struggle *is* to save the Union, and is *not* either to save or to destroy slavery. If I could save the Union without freeing *any* slave I would do it, and if I could save it by freeing *all* the slaves, I would do it; and if I could save it by freeing some and leaving others alone I would also do that.[48]

Exactly one month prior to this letter, Lincoln had submitted a draft of an emancipation proclamation to his cabinet, which was later issued in preliminary form on September 22, 1862, to take effect on January 1, 1863.

By the war's end, Lincoln had progressed through all three of the union-saving scenarios cited in his letter to Greeley. His initial course of action, as presented in his First Inaugural Address of 1861, was to uphold the Constitution and not "to interfere with the institution of slavery in the States where it exists." Lincoln stated, "I believe I have no lawful right to do so, and I have no inclination to do so."[49] This was the same course announced in the 1860 Republican platform, which read:

> That the maintenance inviolate of the rights of the States, and especially the right of each State to order and control its own domestic institutions according to its own judgment exclusively, is essential to that balance of powers on which the perfection and endurance of our political fabric depends; and we denounce the lawless invasion by armed force of the soil of any State or Territory, no matter under what pretext, as among the gravest of crimes.[50]

He would try to save the Union without freeing any slaves because he believed he had no authority to touch slavery where it already existed under the protection of the U.S. Constitution and the laws and constitution of the slaveholding states.[51]

As the fighting progressed, however, he used his power as commander-in-chief, "warranted by the Constitution, upon military necessity,"[52] to proclaim emancipation for all slaves residing in states still in rebellion at the time, and to enlist all able-bodied, emancipated slaves into armed service. As of January 1, 1863, slaves held in Delaware, Maryland, Kentucky and Missouri were not declared free because these states remained loyal to the Union. As such, their domestic institutions received the same constitutional protection during the war as before the war. Thus, Lincoln tried to save the Union by freeing some slaves and leaving others alone. Finally on February 1, 1865, Congress submitted the Thirteenth Amendment—which Lincoln signed (to the chagrin of the Senate[53]), as he did all resolutions of Congress—for state ratification to abolish slavery in the United States. Although the amendment was ratified on December 6, 1865, months after the end of the war, the slaves saw their freedom secured by an official act of the federal government.

This being the case, why was the war still being fought? With the federal abolition of slavery all but certain, the primary cause for which the rebelling states had fought had disappeared. Here, Lincoln sets up the plausible conclusion that another hand is at work in continuing the war— that of Almighty God. That Lincoln saw providence at work prior to the total abolition of slavery is evident in his reply to a "Petition of the Children of the United States; that the President will free all slave children." "Please tell these little people," Lincoln wrote, "I am very glad their young hearts are so full of just and generous sympathy, and that, while I have not the power to grant all they ask, I trust they will remember that God has, and that, as it seems, He wills to do it."[54] Compare this to a similar statement he made later that year:

> I trust it is not too early for us to rejoice together over the promise of the speedy removal of that blot upon our civilization, always heretofore a standing menace to our peace and liberties, whose destruction, so long desired by all friends of impartial freedom, has at last been rendered possible by the crimes of its own reckless friends.[55]

So it seemed to Lincoln that the progress of the war would eventually result in freedom for southern slaves. Yet, with the Thirteenth Amendment undergoing ratification, the war still continued. Lincoln then saw the possibility of an even greater divine purpose than abolition behind the war, which he sought to convey in his Second Inaugural Address: to purge the nation not only of the evil of slavery but perhaps even its unjust gains made by both the North and the South as a means of divine punishment.

Lincoln foreshadowed this theme in a letter almost a year before his second inauguration:

> In telling this tale I attempt no compliment to my own sagacity. I claim not to have controlled events, but confess plainly that events have controlled me. Now, at the end of three years struggle the nation's condition is not what either party, or any man devised or expected. God alone can claim it. Whither it is tending seems plain. If God now wills the removal of a great wrong, and wills also that we of the North as well as you of the South, shall pay fairly for our complicity in that

wrong, impartial history will find therein new cause to attest and revere the justice and goodness of God.[56]

He would repeat the sentiment two weeks later in a speech to a sanitary fair in Baltimore:

> When the war began, three years ago, neither party, nor any man, expected it would last till now. Each looked for the end, in some way, long ere to-day. Neither did any anticipate that domestic slavery would be much affected by the war. But here we are; the war has not ended, and slavery has been much affected—how much needs not now to be recounted. So true is it that man proposes, and God disposes.
>
> But we can see the past, though we may not claim to have directed it.[57]

Lincoln discusses the supposition of divine intervention in the Civil War later in paragraph three of the Second Inaugural Address. In saying, "Neither anticipated that the cause of the conflict might cease with, or even before, the conflict itself should cease," he restates the goal of the federal government as simply to preserve the Union. With the *de facto* abolition of slavery and the war's end in sight, Lincoln feared that this would give rise to northern self-righteousness: a North that would see the Union victory as a vindication of their cause. Hence, Lincoln saw that focusing on a greater design behind the Civil War could help to unite the country. By offering a reason other than the abolition of slavery for the war, it could also deflate the vengeful hopes of the Radical Republicans for a postwar reconstruction of their own design.

Lincoln concludes, "Each looked for an easier triumph, and a result less fundamental and astounding."[58] Comparing the federal government's original goal of saving the Union with the imminent passing of American slavery as the great outcome of the war, Lincoln confesses that a Union victory aiming merely to restrict the territorial enlargement of slavery while enforcing the Fugitive Slave Act of 1850 pales in significance. Lincoln admits his own limited understanding of the war and the immediate purpose for which he fought it, exhibiting the kind of humility that he hopes to engender in his audience—especially in the North.

This admission was not the first. Lincoln confided the same more than two years earlier in an interview he gave to Eliza P. Gurney and fellow visiting Quakers: "If I had had my way, this war would never have been commenced; If I had been allowed my way this war would have been ended before this, but we find it still continues; and we must believe that He permits it for some wise purpose of his own, mysterious and unknown to us; and though with our limited understandings we may not be able to comprehend it, yet we cannot but believe that, he who made the world still governs it."[59] A Union or insurgent "triumph" would be "less fundamental" since either triumph would still leave slavery intact. Obviously, if the insurgents won, the institution of slavery would continue as a "positive good" in the eleven Confederate States of America, with hopes of extension into any territories acquired by the Confederate States and regulated by their Congress.[60] If the federal government won, slavery would still exist in at least the border states despite the hope that it would again be placed in the course of ultimate extinction. Lincoln raises doubts as to the nobility or righteousness of either side's aims, and thus prepares his audience for a theological look the war.

While the preservation of a self-governing regime should stand as a noble enough aim for any freedom-loving people, the unexpected abolition of slavery casts the American Civil War in a new light. Given that the perpetuation of the American republic was Lincoln's political lodestar, his admission that even the federal government "looked for an easier triumph, and a result less fundamental and astounding" gives a candid appraisal of his own progress to date as president of the United States. He commented as much in a letter written soon after his second inauguration, stating that "whatever of humiliation there is in it [his speech], falls most directly on myself..."[61] Reason has had its turn at explaining the war, and as questions remain, one must turn to a higher source for insight.

Turning to religion for the first time in his address, Lincoln prefaces his appeal to a divine purpose in the war by pointing out the insufficiency of even holy writ to solve a political dispute, especially over an institution as blatantly unjust as slavery: "Both read the same Bible, and pray to the same God; and each invokes His aid against the other." Although both sides read the Bible, they reached opposing conclusions about the justice of holding slaves. Northern abolitionists, along with less strident Christian movements against slavery, concluded that ownership of human beings was contrary to the Scriptures' declaration that man was made in the image of God and, therefore, was not to be treated like the beasts of the field. Many southern ministers, on the other hand, interpreted the Bible to condone slavery.[62] This fact was not lost on those who happened to witness the piety of the South during the war, as Lincoln recounts:

Why, the rebel soldiers are praying with a great deal more earnestness,

I fear, than our own troops, and expecting God to favor their side; for one of our soldiers, who had been taken prisoner, told Senator Wilson, a few days since, that he met with nothing so discouraging as the evident sincerity of those he was among in their prayers.[63]

Even before the Civil War, Lincoln noted the increasing appeal to "the Bible-right of slavery" among southerners: "In Kentucky, perhaps, in many of the Slave States certainly, you are trying to establish the rightfulness of Slavery by reference to the Bible. You are trying to show that slavery existed in the Bible times by Divine ordinance."[64] Historian Jack P. Maddox writes:

> In their controversy with the Northern abolitionists, Southern Presbyterian theologians insisted that the Bible recognized slavery as a legitimate system without hinting that it was bad or transient. . . . That argument did not serve only to rebut the abolitionist belief that holding slaves was a sin. It also enabled Southern Presbyterians to discard the Northern conservatives' axiom that slavery was a temporary and undesirable system.[65]

Aware of the danger religious fanaticism posed for democratic government, Lincoln highlights this dispute among citizens of a republic who disagree about slavery on religious grounds.

In 1858, he explored this conundrum in a fragment on slavery:

> Certainly there is no contending against the Will of God; but still there is some difficulty in ascertaining, and applying it, to particular cases. For instance we will suppose the Rev. Dr. Ross has a slave named Sambo, and the question is "Is it the Will of God that Sambo shall remain a slave, or be set free?" The Almighty gives no audable answer to the question, and his revelation—the Bible—gives none—or, at most, none but such as admits of a squabble, as to it's [*sic*] meaning.[66]

The minister referred to was the Reverend Frederick A. Ross, pastor of the Presbyterian Church in Huntsville, Alabama, and author of *Slavery Ordained of God* (1857). The book comprises speeches and letters of Dr. Ross that defend slavery as biblical, American slavery as a beneficent institution, and the slavery agitation by abolitionists as a spur to public discussion—especially regarding its merits on biblical grounds.

Ross takes particular umbrage at abolitionists who argue the sin of slavery on the basis of the second paragraph of the Declaration of Independence, which contains "false affirmations" as to the natural equality of man: to wit, "But I disagree with you as to their truth, and I say that not one of said affirmations is a self-evident truth, or a truth at all. On the contrary, that each one is contrary to the Bible . . ." Dr. Ross views the Declaration's reference to the natural equality of man, inalienable rights, and government by the consent of the governed as "the liberty and equality claimed by infidelity."[67] In his mind, "atheism" consists in believing that "right and wrong are eternal facts; that they exist *per se* in the nature of things; that they are ultimate truths above God . . ." He contends that true biblical epistemology teaches that "right and wrong are results brought into being, mere contingencies, means to good, made to exist solely by the will of God, expressed through his word; or, when his will is not thus known, he shows it in the human reason by which he rules the natural heart."[68] Lincoln's fragment on slavery, especially when read in light of the good Dr. Ross's sentiments—which were shared by other southern divines[69]—thus illustrates the inherent difficulty in appealing to religious texts to resolve political issues.

Lincoln took other opportunities to explore the difficulty of using the Bible to form public policy. To a Christian delegation pressing him for national emancipation in the fall of 1862, he replied: "I am approached with the most opposite opinions and advice, and that by religious men, who are equally certain that they represent the Divine will. I am sure that either the one or the other is mistaken in that belief, and perhaps in some respects both." He adds:

> I hope it will not be irreverent for me to say that if it is probable that God would reveal his will to others, on a point so connected with my duty, it might be supposed he would reveal it directly to me; for, unless I am more deceived in myself than I often am, it is my earnest desire to know the will of Providence in this matter. *And if I can learn what it is I will do it!*

Lincoln averred that "the days of direct revelation" were over, and so he had no choice but to "study the plain physical facts of the case, ascertain what is possible and learn what appears to be wise and right. The subject is difficult, and good men do not agree." Lincoln concludes his meeting with the religious leaders by saying, "And I can assure you that the subject is on my mind, by day and night, more than any other. Whatever shall appear to be God's will I will do."[70]

His decision regarding emancipation, in other words, does not resolve itself into a simple question of what the Bible or any other religious text, doctrine, or dogma mandates. He conveyed a similar sentiment to Eliza P. Gurney:

> In the very responsible position in which I happen to be placed, being
> an humble instrument in the hands of our Heavenly Father, as I am,
> and as we all are, to work out his great purposes, I have desired that all
> my works and acts may be according to his will, and that it might be
> so, I have sought his aid . . .[71]

As earnestly as Lincoln sought "God's will," he was never as sure that he
knew it as were most of his contemporaries—reverend or otherwise.
Historian Mark A. Noll called this "the great theological puzzle of the
Civil War." Lincoln "propounded a thick, complex view of God's rule
over the world and a morally nuanced picture of America's destiny,"
while the nation's "best theologians, by contrast, presented a thin, simple
view of God's providence and a morally juvenile view of the nation and
its fate."[72]

In his First Inaugural Address, Lincoln states, "Intelligence,
patriotism, Christianity, and a firm reliance on Him who has never yet
forsaken this favored land, are still competent to adjust, in the best way,
all our present difficulty."[73] Although he lists intelligence and patriotism
ahead of Christianity and faith, both reason and religion support a just
and ordered society. Lincoln knows, however, that the successful
preservation of democracy depends more on citizen deliberation and
choice than on adherence to certain religious doctrines. In an 1848
speech given before delegates to a Whig presidential convention in
Massachusetts, Lincoln expressed his consternation over the rise of the
"Free Soil" Party and what he believed to be a miscarriage of religious
devotion in the political arena:

> In declaring that they ["Free Soil" men] would "do their duty and leave
> the consequences to God," merely gave an excuse for taking a course
> that they were not able to maintain by a fair and full argument. To
> make this declaration did not show what their duty was. If it did we
> should have no use for judgment, we might as well be made without
> intellect, and when divine or human law does not clearly point out what
> *is* our duty, we have no means of finding out what it is by using our
> most intelligent judgment of the consequences. If there were divine
> law, or human law for voting for Martin Van Buren, or if a fair
> examination of the consequences and first reasoning would show that
> voting for him would bring about the ends they pretended to wish—
> then he would give up the argument.[74]

Lincoln thought the Free Soilers would achieve the opposite of their
intentions by organizing themselves in opposition to other Whigs without
regard for its impact on candidates more likely to defeat pro-slavery

opponents: for example, the election of Michigan Senator Lewis Cass, who championed "popular sovereignty" as the territorial answer to the slavery question, instead of Martin Van Buren, a former pro-slavery Democrat now beloved of Conscience Whigs. Lincoln understood that in the political arena, actions taken to "leave the consequences to God" were more than likely not actions that could bear the scrutiny of reason. A republic could not survive long by jettisoning deliberative politics.

Since deliberation is always for the sake of some action, for Lincoln the actions one took as the result of deliberation would always mark the clearest expression of one's convictions. When the Reverend William Nast sent Lincoln resolutions of the Central German Conference of the Methodist Episcopal Church, Lincoln replied:

> I have not been unprepared for this definite and unequivocal statement of the continued loyalty and devotion of the Church you represent, to the free institutions of the country of your adoption. The *conduct* of your people since the outbreak of this desolating rebellion, has been the best proof of the sincerity of your present *professions*.[75] (Emphasis added.)

Compare this to Lincoln's assessment of his close friend Joshua Speed, regarding his professed Christian sentiment toward slavery: "You say if Kansas fairly votes herself a free state, as a christian you will rather rejoice at it. All decent slave-holders *talk* that way; and I do not doubt their candor. But they never *vote* that way."[76] Though one can effectively appeal to both reason and religion for the preservation of a democratic regime, as Lincoln attempts in his Second Inaugural Address, reliance on the citizens' ability to reason is less tenuous than reliance on their piety to ensure sound government.

At this point in his elucidation of the pitfalls of religion applied to politics, Lincoln interjects a personal comment on the audacity of appealing to a just God for help in a manifestly unjust cause: "It may seem strange that any men should dare to ask a just God's assistance in wringing their bread from the sweat of other men's faces; but let us judge not that we be not judged." In his sole comment on the South's unambiguous defense of slavery, he alludes to Genesis 3:19, where God curses the ground as a lasting punishment of Adam for eating from the tree of the knowledge of good and evil: "In the sweat of thy face shalt thou eat bread, till thou return unto the ground; for out of it wast thou taken: for dust thou art, and unto dust shalt thou return." As southern slaveowners wring "their bread from the sweat of other men's faces," this biblical allusion implies that they were evading the curse of God and forcing other men to be the twofold recipients of God's punishment. Lincoln connected his explication of the Genesis passage to the problem of slavery several years earlier in a note to himself:

> As Labor is the common *burthen* of our race, so the effort of *some* to shift their share of the burthen on to the shoulders of *others*, is the great, durable, curse of the race. Originally a curse for transgression upon the whole race, when, as by slavery, it is concentrated on a part only, it becomes the double-refined curse of God upon his creatures.[77]

Thus in the Second Inaugural Address, Lincoln suggests that the South makes a mockery not only of human justice but of God's wrath.

He makes known his judgment about the Civil War and how God should intervene with this aside regarding the South's prayer that God help them win the war so that they could continue enslaving men. He had voiced a similar opinion in a Washington newspaper article, which he entitled, "The President's Last, Shortest, and Best Speech":

> On thursday of last week two ladies from Tennessee came before the President asking the release of their husbands held as prisoners of war at Johnson's Island. They were put off till friday, when they came again; and were again put off to saturday. At each of the interviews one of the ladies urged that her husband was a religious man. On saturday the President ordered the release of the prisoners, and then said to this lady "You say your husband is a religious man; tell him when you meet him, that I say I am not much of a judge of religion, but that, in my opinion, the religion that sets men to rebel and fight against their government, because, as they think, that government does not sufficiently help *some* men to eat their bread in the sweat of *other* men's faces, is not the sort of religion upon which people can get to heaven!"[78]

Lincoln uses reason to determine the merits of a religion, which, if true, would sanction inequality among a seemingly equal creation of God—human beings. He sees God as one who does not contradict a rational understanding of human equality and justice. But far be it from Lincoln to presume the judge's role in the case of American slavery. Note the peculiar parallel of this short story with the parable of the unjust (and impious) judge and the persistent widow found in Luke 18:1-8. Here, Lincoln likens himself to the *unjust* judge who gave in to the persistent widow's plea for justice, implying a similar attitude toward pious but insouciant slaveholders. Professing he is "not much of a judge of religion," and might even be an unjust and impious one, Lincoln argues that the God of heaven could scarcely approve of men who rebel against their earthly government in order to enslave others.

Lincoln saw the desire for justice and goodness as one placed in man by his Creator, as he noted in an 1858 speech: "Our reliance is in the *love of liberty* which God has placed in our bosoms. Our defense is in the preservation of the spirit which prizes liberty as the heritage of all men, in all lands, every where."[79] Lincoln appeals to his audience's belief in a Creator and exhorts them to nurture their God-given ability to pursue liberty. This presupposes a recognition of the fundamental rights and freedoms of all men. As Lincoln showed the limits of both sides' reason in preventing the war in paragraph two, he now shows the faults of turning the war into a purely religious crusade. Religion has joined reason in its failure to achieve its political goal.

Nevertheless, his disdain for the South's appeal to "a just God's assistance" also reflects Lincoln's belief in a righteous God. Lincoln seeks to inspire in the citizenry reverent fear of a God who exacts punishment. A year following his famous debates with Senator Stephen A. Douglas, Lincoln continued to correct Douglas's bowdlerization of Thomas Jefferson's intent in the Declaration of Independence and used the occasion to comment on God's justice as it applied to American slavery:

> There was danger to this country—danger of the avenging justice of God in that little unimportant popular sovereignty question of Judge Douglas. He [Jefferson] supposed there was a question of God's eternal justice wrapped up in the enslaving of any race of men, or any man, and that those who did so braved the arm of Jehovah—that when a nation thus dared the Almighty every friend of that nation had cause to dread His wrath.[80]

Moreover, in a letter commemorating Thomas Jefferson's birthday, Lincoln declares that "Those who deny freedom to others, deserve it not for themselves; and, under a just God, can not long retain it."[81] This sentiment alludes to Thomas Jefferson's reflections on slavery from his *Notes on the State of Virginia* (1787):

> And can the liberties of a nation be thought secure when we have removed their only firm basis, a conviction in the minds of the people that these liberties are of the gift of God? That they are not to be violated but with his wrath? Indeed I tremble for my country when I reflect that God is just: that his justice cannot sleep forever: that considering numbers, nature and natural means only, a revolution of the wheel of fortune, an exchange of situation, is among possible events: that it may become probable by supernatural interference! The

Almighty has no attribute which can side with us in such a contest.[82]

This statement by Jefferson would prove prophetic, considering that Lincoln suggests in his Second Inaugural Address that the nation view the Civil War as an execution of God's wrath for the very offense discussed by Jefferson. Lincoln shares Jefferson's belief in a just God who is not oblivious to the injustices committed by those created in His image and who will eventually mete out His wrath on the offenders.

With this in mind, Lincoln appends his comment on southern appeals to God with a paraphrase of Matthew 7:1: "But let us judge not that we be not judged." Although he condemned Douglas's professed neutral stance toward slavery because it would lead to the expansion of an institution that offended God, he now cautions against human judgment. He implies that those most likely to condemn, Unionists and especially the Radical Republicans in Congress, should balk at condemning southern slaveowners. With the South ravaged by a war fought mostly on its own soil, he fears that God may exact a similar judgment against the North for their own sins, especially regarding their complicity in the institution of slavery. One finds in the antebellum government as well as the northern population a compliance with and encouragement of slavery: examples include the Kansas-Nebraska Act (1854), the *Dred Scott* decision (1857), and President Buchanan's support of both of these as well as the Lecompton Constitution (1857) and the idea of "popular sovereignty."

For the culpability of the northern population for the slavery system, hear the words of the ill-famed Dr. Frederick A. Ross:

> Sir, why do your Northern church-members and philanthropists buy Southern products at all? You know you are purchasing cotton, rice, sugar, sprinkled with blood, literally, you say, from the lash of the driver! Why do you buy? What's the difference between my filching this bloodstained cotton from the outraged negro, and your standing by, taking it from me? . . . You hate the traitor, but you love the treason.[83]

Back to the Book of Matthew—chapter 7, verse 2 reads: "For with what judgment ye judge, ye shall be judged: and with what measure ye mete, it shall be measured to you again." This does not mean that one should never judge, but that one should judge others only with the caution that follows upon self-examination. "Thou hypocrite, first cast out the beam out of thine own eye; and then shalt thou see clearly to cast out the mote out of thy brother's eye" (Matt. 7:5). This was a frame of mind quite different from the self-righteousness of the abolitionists and Radical Republicans. Lincoln hopes that the North would temper its judgment of the South by remembering its own complicity in the peculiar institution.

After his parenthetical questioning of the audacious piety of the slaveowners, Lincoln returns to illuminate the tension between reason and religion: "The prayers of both could not be answered; that of neither has been answered fully. The Almighty has His own purposes." Human reason or logic recognizes the impossibility of both the North's and South's goals being achieved, even with divine help, hence the conclusion: "The prayers of both could not be answered." Lincoln makes this plain in a note he wrote at the time of the Union defeat at the Second Battle of Manassas (or Bull Run): "The will of God prevails. In great contests each party claims to act in accordance with the will of God. Both *may* be, and one *must* be wrong. God can not be *for*, and *against* the same thing at the same time."[84]

But to say that neither side's prayers "has been answered fully" invites the following question: To what extent were either side's prayers answered? By the time of Lincoln's second inauguration, the war was almost over, with General Robert E. Lee's surrender at the Appomattox Courthouse following just five weeks later. Lincoln surely realizes that his listeners believe that the prayers of the North were more successful than those of the South. In addition, such a victory would certainly take place on terms set by the federal government, whose prayers would then seem to have been finally answered.

God's will, however, is not the same as either the North's or the South's because the war still drags on after almost four years. Remember, "Neither party expected for the war, the magnitude, or the duration, which it has already attained.... Each looked for an easier triumph, and a result less fundamental and astounding." Therefore, Lincoln chooses to end this part of the address by attributing the prolonged duration of the war to a divine purpose. In other words, an eventual Union victory may not be due primarily to the righteousness of their cause or the strength of their men, but to some higher purpose of the Almighty. Reason may not calm the impassioned will of the North, so Lincoln appeals to the authority of God. This represents a rhetorical shift from the rational dialectic of paragraph two and the first half of paragraph three to the discussion of divine will in the second half of paragraph three. It seems the zealous North will have the will of God to contend with if they are slow to receive their rebellious countrymen of the South.

As a precursor for God's ultimate role in the conflict, Lincoln initially envisioned divine providence working through the law-abidingness of men and, hence, the successful functioning of their democratic political system. As stated in his First Inaugural Address:

> Why should there not be a patient confidence in the ultimate justice of the people? Is there any better, or equal hope, in the world? In our present differences, is either party without faith of being in the right? If the Almighty Ruler of nations, with his eternal truth and justice, be on your side of the North, or on yours of the South, that truth, and that justice, will surely prevail, by the judgment of this great tribunal, the American people.[85]

As long as the people maintained their "virtue and vigilance," God's justice would prevail. At that time, Lincoln was pleading with his "dissatisfied fellow countrymen" to work out their complaints through the existing framework of government, appealing to the sovereignty of God as a guarantor of the plans of the righteous. As it turned out, the insurgents did not welcome his message and proceeded to take matters into their own hands.

After nearly four years of civil war, Lincoln finds a different scenario in which to interpret the will of God. Apparently, God's truth and justice had not prevailed through the "great tribunal, the American people." They came to a point where they could not resolve the controversy over slavery through the peaceful medium of representative democracy. They took to war, and by March 4, 1865, the providential workings of the American republic had still not wrought a conclusion to the nation's strife. With slavery practically defunct, the war still continued. It now appeared that a higher end was being worked out: "The Almighty has His own purposes."

Back in 1855, Lincoln had grown less sanguine about the prospects for a "peaceful extinction of slavery." He believed that the foremost national problem was the country's continuance half-slave and half-free and concluded, "The problem is too mighty for me. May God, in his mercy, superintend the solution."[86] In his Second Inaugural Address, the problem appears too mighty even for the country. Lincoln turns to the Gospel of Matthew for guidance: "Woe unto the world because of offences! for it must needs be that offences come; but woe to that man by whom the offence cometh!" (Matt. 18:7). Because he has already observed, "Both read the same Bible, and pray to the same God," he can therefore use a verse from that "same Bible" to explain what that "same God" might be doing through the American crisis: "If we shall suppose that American Slavery is one of those offences which, in the providence of God, must needs come, but which, having continued through His appointed time, He now wills to remove, and that He gives to both North and South, this terrible war, as the woe due to those by whom the offence came, shall we discern therein any departure from those divine attributes which the believers in a Living God always ascribe to Him?"[87] The verse now reads: "Woe unto the United States because of the things that cause it to stumble! For such stumbling blocks will always arise; but a ravaging war will befall the United States (both North and South) by whom slavery and its concomitant evils came and were preserved!" Herein Lincoln suggests a reason for the severity and longevity of the Civil War: the nation's failure to resolve the Founding compromise on slavery in favor of freedom.

The people of the United States acquiesced in its continuance out of necessity. The union of the states, and their political prosperity, hinged on the inclusion of the southern states. Although they originally put slavery on the course of ultimate extinction, northerners and southerners alike were sidetracked by slavery's profitability subsequent to the invention of the cotton gin—an event that led to its entrenchment in the agrarian South. As a point of comparison, the United States exported 138,328 pounds of cotton in 1792, the year before Eli Whitney invented the cotton gin. By 1794, cotton exports rose over ten-fold to 1,601,000 million pounds of cotton—a figure that would grow to thirty-five million pounds by 1820. This reflected the growing demand for slaves and the increasing profitability of the slave trade.[88] As the American people were unable to wean themselves from slavery under a government of their own choosing and operation, the entire nation would suffer punishment in the form of a war that would produce devastating losses in lives and property.

Lincoln publicly intimated the guilt of the nation in two proclamations for a national fast day. In the first he called as president in 1861, Lincoln states that "it is peculiarly fit for us to recognize the hand of God in this terrible visitation, and in sorrowful remembrance of our own faults and crimes as a nation and as individuals, to humble ourselves before Him, and to pray for His mercy . . ."[89] In the second fast-day proclamation, Lincoln presents a Judaeo-Christian view of God's punishment of the entire nation: "[B]y His divine law, nations like individuals are subjected to punishments and chastisements in this world, may we not justly fear that the awful calamity of Civil War, which now desolates the land, may be but a punishment, inflicted upon us, for our presumptuous sins, to the needful end of our national reformation as a whole People?"[90] In contrast to these examples, Lincoln's last thanksgiving proclamation of his presidency forgoes any mention of the war as God's punishment. Instead, he states that the Civil War came "by our adherence as a nation to the cause of Freedom and Humanity." The purpose of the proclamation, a day of thanksgiving as opposed to fasting, suggests the reason for the different emphasis: a focus on blessings to be appreciated rather than woes to lament and sins for which to ask forgiveness. Yet, Lincoln is not altogether oblivious to the need for national humility, for he "recommend[s] to my fellow-citizens aforesaid that on that occasion they do reverently humble themselves in the dust and from thence offer up penitent and fervent prayers and supplications to the Great Disposer of events . . ."[91]

Lincoln's earliest hope for the war was a return of peaceful submission by the seceding states to the authority of the entire U.S. Constitution for the sake of union. (See his First Inaugural Address for a discussion of the errors of extremists on both sides who denied the authority of certain sections of the Constitution.) Nevertheless, he valued the American union not as an end in itself but as a means to the progressive liberation of all men. As seen in his response to a presentation of resolutions by the Evangelical Lutheran Church in 1861, Lincoln places this hope within the context of divine intention:

> You all may recollect that in taking up the sword thus forced into our hands this Government appealed to the prayers of the pious and the good, and declared that it placed its whole dependence upon the favor of God. I now humbly and reverently, in your presence, reiterate the acknowledgment of that dependence, not doubting that, if it shall please the Divine Being who determines the destinies of nations that this shall remain a united people, *they will, humbly seeking the Divine guidance, make their prolonged national existence a source of new benefits to themselves and their successors, and to all classes and conditions of mankind.*[92] (Emphasis added.)

Lincoln comments that if providence grants them victory, their responsibility as a nation remains that of their forebears: namely, to make the constitutional union a source of "new benefits" to themselves and their posterity, as well as "to all classes and conditions of mankind." Similarly, Lincoln responded "with pleasure and gratitude" to a letter from the secretaries of a Quaker society, who expressed appreciation for Lincoln's issuance of the Emancipation Proclamation:

It is most cheering and encouraging for me to know that in the efforts which have made and am making for the restoration of a righteous peace to our country, I am upheld and sustained by the good wishes and prayers of God's people. No one is more deeply than myself aware that without His favor our highest wisdom is but as foolishness and that our most strenuous efforts would avail nothing in the shadow of His displeasure. I am conscious of no desire for my country's welfare, that is not in consonance with His will, and of no plan upon which we may not ask His blessing. It seems to me that if there be one subject upon which all good men may unitedly agree, it is imploring the gracious favor of the God of Nations upon the struggles our people are making for the preservation of their precious birthright of civil and religious liberty.[93]

For America to become "the source of new benefits," renewed efforts on behalf of liberty could very well include emancipation measures consistent with state control over domestic institutions. While the initiative remains under state authority, the federal government should do all it can to promote the eventual abolition of that peculiar institution.

Earlier in the Second Inaugural Address, Lincoln chose the phrase "colored slaves," as opposed to "slaves," simply, to emphasize the peculiarity of an institution that used skin color as the basis for its despicable practice. He now prefaces slavery with the adjective, "American": "If we shall suppose that American Slavery is one of those offences which, in the providence of God, must needs come . . ." He implies that it is uniquely different than slavery anywhere else in the world. Here, he focuses on its peculiarity as an institution existing in a regime whose central idea is freedom—the natural endowment of all human beings. He distinguishes it from mere slavery because other countries that practice slavery do not even pretend to justify it as a necessary evil. Lincoln said as much in a letter to his friend Joshua F. Speed, where he comments on the bigotry of the Know-Nothing party:

As a nation, we began by declaring that "*all men are created equal.*" We now practically read it "all men are created equal, *except negroes.*" When the Know-Nothings get control, it will read "all men are created equal, except negroes, *and foreigners, and catholics.* When it comes to this I should prefer emigrating to some country where they make no pretence of loving liberty—to Russia, for instance, where despotism can be taken pure, and without the base alloy of hypocracy.[94]

As "the almost chosen people," the American citizenry had seen itself on a divine mission to stand as an exemplar of self-government to all nations. However, they were unable to rid their nation of its most pernicious institution and, hence, reneged on a founding compromise that allowed them to form the Union in the first place. In view of this, Lincoln offers the supposition that where man had failed, God chose to succeed. The Almighty allowed the war as the instrument of both their chastening and redemption.

Lincoln asks, "Shall we discern therein any departure from those divine attributes which the believers in a Living God always ascribe to Him?" Lincoln again echoes Thomas Jefferson's "Query XVIII" from his *Notes on the State of Virginia*:

> Indeed I tremble for my country when I reflect that God is just: that his justice cannot sleep for ever: that considering number, nature and natural means only, a revolution of the wheel of fortune, an exchange of situation, is among possible events: that it may become probable by supernatural interference! The Almighty has no attribute which can side with us in such a contest.[95]

In the only question posed in the address, Lincoln manages to depict both God and the American people as judge and judged. On the one hand, America stands as "the world" of Matthew 18:7, receiving the "woe" that follows from its own "offences." America stands in the dock of God's judgment, wherein "He gives to both North and South, this terrible war." On the other hand, Lincoln puts a rhetorical question before the judgment of the accused. The American people must acknowledge the justice of God's judgment.

The standard for this judgment, given that both sides of the conflict "read the same Bible, and pray to the same God," is found in Galatians 6:7: "Be not deceived; God is not mocked: for whatsoever a man soweth, that he shall also reap." In the American scenario, God "gives to both North and South, this terrible war, as the woe due to those by whom the offence came." As Glen Thurow explains:

> Lincoln uses the more easily known truth, the horror of the war, to reveal the less obvious but more decisive truth, the sin of slavery. To believe that God sent the war as punishment causes one to believe that slavery is unjust. Lincoln thus attempts to share something of the more difficult truth by means of the more easily understood truth.[96]

Instead of belaboring the South's culpability for the war (or the North's complicity in the slave economy, or the abolitionists' stoking the fires of disunion), Lincoln seeks to have the country see itself before the eternal throne of justice. Both North and South stand guilty of the sin of slavery *if* both can be led to agree in judgment that God's direction of the war was a fitting national chastisement.

The logical and paramount conclusion Lincoln implies by this line of rhetorical reasoning is the injustice of slavery. Thurow states:

> Lincoln must make men aware that their purposes are not God's, but they do not see this by their reason. Lincoln attempts to point it out to them by using the more easily perceived truth, the horror of the war, to reveal the harder truth, the sin of slavery and hence the limits of their intentions. To do this, it must be supposed that God is governing the world and that he gives the war as punishment.[97]

The role reversal of judge and judged works to the extent that the American people fail to understand the devastation of a war all sought to avoid. With both North and South perplexed as to the war's meaning, Lincoln offers a theological interpretation for the assent of all.

Although his interpretation of the Civil War would fail to succeed with southern minds despite the Union victory over their armies, it should be understood in the same context as his First Inaugural Address. Both speeches proposed an understanding of the American regime counter to that of a significant portion of the American public, but neither side granted a concession in principle that might have won over more opponents to the detriment of preserving the United States as a free, self-governing nation.

"Fondly do we hope," Lincoln continues, "fervently do we pray—that this mighty scourge of war may speedily pass away." Lincoln previously observed that though both sides prayed to God, neither side's prayers were answered completely. Followed with the declaration, "The Almighty has His own purposes," he suggested that God had a different plan than either side and would prevail in spite of their petitions. Why, then, does Lincoln continue to pray and exhort the nation to do so as well? Although God did not answer either side's prayers fully, the progress of the war showed that the intentions of the North fit more closely within God's designs than those of the South. The North had finished a successful winter campaign in 1864, and Lincoln had left the Hampton Roads Peace Conference on February 3, 1865, convinced that the rebellious states could not persevere for long. Thus, his suggestion that all should continue to pray aligns closely with the prospects of a Union (or Northern) victory, albeit one that would secure a result not intended at the outset—the demise of slavery.

Lincoln builds upon the idea of a divided though praying nation with a reminder that it is God's plan that would prevail:

Yet, if God wills that it continue, until all the wealth piled by the bond-man's two hundred and fifty years of unrequited toil shall be sunk, and until every drop of blood drawn with the lash, shall be paid by another drawn with the sword, as was said three thousand years ago, so still it must be said "the judgments of the Lord, are true and righteous altogether[.]"

The phrase, "Yet, if God wills that it [the war] continue," follows the previous acknowledgment, "The Almighty has His own purposes." Lincoln also elaborates his supposition that God's purposes include more than just the abolition of slavery: the Almighty might seek justice in the form of lost lives and wealth. In this light, Lincoln uses "bond-man" instead of "slave" to tie the slaves' years of "unrequited toil" to the need for a debt to be paid off. This constitutes the judgment of God, that "all the wealth piled by the bond-man's . . . unrequited toil . . . be sunk" and "every drop of blood drawn with the lash . . . be paid by another drawn with the sword." As a bond-man was held bound for service until his debt was paid off, God forced payment in American lives and property through a costly civil war to free those held in American bondage. Lincoln proposes that the debt in this case is not the slaves' but the nation's for profiting from slavery, and that the nation may not be released from its debt until it pays off the debt in full. Lincoln intimated this in his revision of an 1861 letter that Secretary of State William H. Seward sent to Charles Francis Adams, the minister to Britain. Responding to the Queen's May 13th declaration of neutrality toward the American conflict, he compares the condition of Europe to Israel's wandering in the desert: "A war not unlike it between the same parties [Great Britain and the United States] occurred at the close of the last century. Europe atoned by forty years of suffering for the error that Great Britain committed in provoking that contest."[98]

Although Lincoln offers an interpretation of the Civil War as punishment for slavery, he does not claim that he knows this is what God is doing. He does not even claim to know the will of God. "The Almighty has *His own* purposes" (emphasis added), so Lincoln cannot declare for certain what those purposes are. Instead, after quoting Matthew 18:7 verbatim, Lincoln begins, "*If* we shall suppose . . ." (Emphasis added.) He does not state what God's designs are but simply offers a supposition for the audience's consideration.[99] As the second and third paragraphs of the Second Inaugural Address demonstrate, the purposes of God remain veiled to Americans: how else does one explain the nation's inability to avert a civil war (the argument of the second paragraph), as well as their inability to direct God's will decisively through prayer (the argument of the first part of the third paragraph).

"And the war came," despite efforts by both sides to avert it; "Neither party expected" the severity of the civil war, let alone the emancipation of slaves before the war ended; and neither side's prayers have been "answered fully." From these observations Lincoln concludes, "The Almighty has His own purposes." Therefore, he can only go on to "suppose" and not "declare" that American slavery has come and gone according to some divine plan that is still being worked out—a plan that *could* involve punishment without contradicting what "the believers in a Living God always ascribe to Him." Lincoln's interpretation of "this terrible war" as "the woe due to those by whom the offence [of slavery] came" is a plausible conclusion, given that the nation does not know for sure what God's will is, but they do know the Bible (Ps. 19:9) reveals "the judgments of the Lord" to be "true and righteous altogether."[100]

Every indication shows that God "now wills to remove" slavery from the United States, but this does not imply that the Almighty had to do so by violent means.[101] Lincoln's First Inaugural Address appealed to the "better angels of our nature" in hopes of forestalling any escalation of the sectional crisis. He believed, then, that human beings working in concert with divine providence could resolve the conflict through peaceful measures. The failure of that appeal eventually led to a national crisis that would require force to secure right, which to the surprise of many led to the eradication of slavery. Because both North and South interpreted the war theologically,[102] Lincoln used the religious conviction in his listeners as a rhetorical premise to offer a biblical interpretation for the prolonged nature of the war.

He closes the supposition by asking, "shall we discern therein any departure from those divine attributes which *the believers* in a Living God always ascribe to Him?" (Emphasis added.) Describing the religious convictions of the nation from a third-person perspective is consistent with an interpretation that Lincoln intends to be tentative in the face of the inscrutable ways of Providence. Lincoln does not say that *he* ascribes these attributes to God.[103] The burden of his rhetoric remains the inculcation of a common understanding of the war from which the citizens of all the states can move forward to a lasting peace. As most Americans considered themselves "believers in a Living God," Lincoln suggests that they interpret the war in a manner that unites their judgment of God's hand in the Civil War as well as their guilt before that same God's judgment.

Placed in a syllogism of sorts, Lincoln's argument before he brings God's purposes into the picture reads as follows:

  I. Both sides tried to avoid the war, but it came anyway;
  II. neither side expected the severity of the war;
  III. neither side expected slavery to end with or before the war's close;
  IV. both sides tried to get God on their side;
  V. neither side's prayers were answered fully;
  VI. therefore, God must be doing something else!

After he announces, "The Almighty has His own purposes," his argument reads:

  I. God's ways are not our ways;
  II. we don't know His ways for certain, so we can only speculate;
  III. speculation should follow an authority both sides trust—the Bible;
  IV. the biblical God in His providence allowed slavery for a season;
  V. slavery is evil;
  VI. both sides profited from slavery;
  VII. the biblical God punishes evil;
  VIII. therefore, we can view the war as God's punishment for slavery.

Lincoln asks both sides to concede something: the North must admit they benefited from the goods produced by slave labor, and the South must admit that slavery is wrong. Of course, Lincoln does not come out and say that slavery is wrong. This would undermine his attempt to persuade southern citizens to rejoin the Union in spirit as well as in body and would also stir up self-righteousness in the North. Given that he will soon ask the country to bear "malice toward none," but instead extend "charity for all," Lincoln practices here what he preaches by not explicitly condemning the South for defending slavery.[104] Nevertheless, he intimates the evil of slavery every way he can. More important, if he can get both sides to agree that slavery is wrong *and* that both sides profited from it and therefore deserve punishment, then the nation can reunite based on the common suffering of both sides in the Civil War. What remains is getting both sides to move toward the goal of healing, the theme of the final paragraph of the Second Inaugural Address. The third paragraph required a change of mind and heart for both sides of the conflict, in order to prepare them for a common course of action in the fourth paragraph—a work of reconstruction fraught with "onerous and perplexing duties and responsibilities" for the president.[105]

Following his second inauguration as president, Lincoln answered a congratulatory letter from New York's Republican Party boss, Thurlow

Weed: "Men are not flattered by being shown that there has been a difference of purpose between the Almighty and them. To deny it, however, in this case, is to deny that there is a God governing the world. It is a truth which I thought needed to be told . . ."[106] A few years earlier, he had expressed the same sentiment to the Quaker widow Eliza P. Gurney:

> If I had had my way, this war would never have been commenced; If I had been allowed my way this war would have been ended before this, but we find it still continues; and we must believe that He permits it for some wise purpose of his own, mysterious and unknown to us; and though with our limited understandings we may not be able to comprehend it, yet we cannot but believe that, he who made the world still governs it.[107]

He presents an interpretation of the war from a disinterested viewpoint, "the believers in a Living God," and assumes a non-religious perspective to "discern" the validity of a biblical interpretation of the Civil War as God's just vengeance. Lincoln does not say that this biblical understanding is the only way to understand the continuing conflict, only that it makes sense of both the chronology of the war and the "divine attributes which the believers in a Living God always ascribe to Him." Given that "all sought to avert" the war, "[n]either party expected for the war, the magnitude, or the duration, which it has already attained," and the prayer "of neither has been answered fully," one would be hard-pressed to arrive at a more cogent explanation of the conflict.

Paragraph Four: "Let Us Strive on to Finish the Work We Are in."

The brevity of the fourth and final paragraph of the Second Inaugural Address contrasted with the lengthy third paragraph reflects their different objectives. The third paragraph, seeking to explain, requires a more lengthy discourse than the fourth paragraph, which simply offers a course of action to be pursued. The now familiar words that open the final paragraph, "With malice toward none; with charity for all,"[108] can only be understood and applied given the groundwork laid by the previous paragraphs. In his speeches and writings leading up to his second inauguration, Lincoln anticipates the theme of charity that testifies to his highest public concern: to unite the American people, during its most pressing conflict, behind right principles of self-government.

In an 1862 letter to a New Orleans Unionist, Lincoln defends the military's presence in Louisiana but exhorts him and his fellow citizens to "reinaugurate the national authority" to eliminate the need for federal occupation of the state. Almost overshadowed by the strident tone of the letter is his sympathy expressed at the close of the letter: "I shall do *all* I can to save the government, which is my sworn duty as well as my personal inclination. I shall do nothing in malice. What I deal with is too vast for malicious dealing." Louisianians loyal to the federal cause had complained about Union General John W. Phelps, an abolitionist who provided refuge to southern slaves escaping to his army camp in New Orleans. But because Louisiana loyalists did little to help the Union cause in their own right, thereby necessitating the presence of General Phelps and federal troops in general, Lincoln vented his frustration: "What would you do in my position? Would you drop the war where it is? Or, would you prosecute it in future, with elder-stalk squirts, charged with rose water?" Lincoln points out that his "vast" responsibility of reuniting a divided nation necessitates a military presence in Louisiana notwithstanding indications that Louisiana's secession ordinance "was adopted against the will of a majority of the people."[109] Two days earlier, he wrote a similar letter to Maryland Senator Reverdy Johnson, whom he sent to New Orleans to investigate British complaints against General Benjamin F. Butler's occupation of the region. It closed with a reference to the Christian practice of forgiveness: "I am a patient man—always willing to forgive on the Christian terms of repentance; and also to give ample *time* for repentance. Still I must save this government if possible."[110] Even in these private letters, Lincoln tries to convince loyal, but worried, southern citizens that the actions of the federal administration stem from duty to the Union and not vengeance toward southerners—loyalist or not. Lincoln's duty to defend the United States is one he believes all should emulate, but not with an impure motive like malice—especially when one's opponents are fellow citizens.

This he made clear in his last thanksgiving proclamation, wherein he alluded to Matthew 10:36 as he thanked God for "defending us with his guardian care against unfriendly designs from abroad, and vouchsafing to us in His mercy many and signal victories over *the enemy, who is of our own household.*"[111] (Emphasis added.) The biblical context happens as well to be a belligerent one: "Think not that I [Jesus] am come to send peace on earth: I came not to send peace, but a sword. . . . And a man's foes shall be they of his own household" (Matthew 10:34, 36). Lincoln always considered southern rebels as American citizens, which meant that federal action must balance efforts to punish with charity.

A few weeks after he announced a preliminary Emancipation Proclamation, Lincoln included a similar message in his state of the union address of December 1862. In it he proposed a constitutional amendment for the emancipation of all slaves and compensation for all cooperating states and loyal owners. He prefaced this resolution with the remark: "Our strife pertains to ourselves—to the passing generations of men; and it can, without convulsion, be hushed forever with the passing of one generation." Here he quotes Ecclesiastes 1:4 in this context: "One generation passeth away, and another generation cometh, but the earth abideth forever." Lincoln hopes the nation will move beyond the war and to the perpetuation of a self-governing union. By eliminating slavery, he believes Americans can put the great conflict behind them, and in the process promote the longevity of their self-government to match that of the nation's territory: "the only part which is of certain durability."[112] An amendment to emancipate the slaves would be a giant step forward in the national task of preserving and promoting self-government.

When serenaders came to the White House to celebrate his reelection, Lincoln touted the theme of charity: "Let us, therefore, study the incidents of this [election], as philosophy to learn wisdom from, and none of them as wrongs to be revenged." He continues one paragraph later:

> But the rebellion continues; and now that the election is over, may not all, having a common interest, re-unite in a common effort, to save our common country? For my own part I have striven, and shall strive to avoid placing any obstacle in the way. So long as I have been here I have not willingly planted a thorn in any man's bosom.
>
> While I am deeply sensible to the high compliment of a reelection; and duly grateful, as I trust, to Almighty God for having directed my countrymen, to a right conclusion, as I think, for their own good, it adds nothing to my satisfaction that any other man may be disappointed or pained by the result.
>
> May I ask those who have not differed with me, to join with me, in this same spirit towards those who have?[113]

With the phrase "planting a thorn in any man's bosom," Lincoln borrows an Old Testament reference to alien nations whom the Israelites allowed to remain in the promised land: "But if ye will not drive out the inhabitants of the land from before you; then it shall come to pass, that those which ye let remain of them shall be pricks in your eyes, and thorns in your sides, and shall vex you in the land wherein ye dwell" (Num. 33:55; see also Josh. 23:13, Judg. 2:3, and 2 Cor. 12:7). He also exhibits a gracious demeanor, gleaned from Proverbs 24:17-18: "Rejoice not when thine enemy falleth, and let not thine heart be glad when he stumbleth: lest the Lord see it, and it displease him, and he turn away his wrath from him." Here Lincoln summarizes the teaching he had given in the previous paragraphs of the address: "With malice toward none; with charity for all; with firmness in the right, as God gives us to see the right . . ." Lincoln contrasts bearing no malice toward any single individual with giving charity to all individuals, encouraging the extremes of both cases because of the severity of the crisis that must be overcome.

He also acknowledges that truth comes from God, or at least can be known only with His assistance. In a letter to Mrs. Eliza P. Gurney, he states: "We hoped for a happy termination of this terrible war long before this; but God knows best, and has ruled otherwise. We shall yet acknowledge His wisdom and our own error therein. Meanwhile we must work earnestly in the best light He gives us, trusting that so working still conduces to the great end He ordains."[114] This is similar to his closing words in his first state of the union address: "With a reliance on Providence, all the more firm and earnest, let us proceed in the great task which events have devolved upon us."[115] Thus, Lincoln sees reason and revelation cooperating in a self-governing society, an idea he expressed in the Second Inaugural Address with the exhortation, "with firmness in the right, as God gives us to see the right, let us strive on to finish the work we are in . . ."

Lincoln then describes the national agenda to follow the end of the war: "to bind up the nation's wounds; to care for him who shall have borne the battle, and for his widow, and his orphan." This involves the efforts of the American people as well as the will of God. This accounts for the two biblical allusions in this sentence. The phrase "to bind up the nation's wounds" recalls Hosea 6:1, which reads, "Come, and let us return unto the Lord: for he hath torn, and he will heal us; he hath smitten, and he will bind us up."[116] In a February 1862 letter to Queen Victoria lamenting the death of Prince Albert, Lincoln commends the royal family "to the tender mercies of God." He then states his belief "that the Divine hand that has wounded, is the only one that can heal . . ."[117] This was no perfunctory condolence; he had already suffered the death of one son, Edward (not yet four years old), on February 1, 1850, and the deaths of two personal friends during the first months of the war. Lincoln's eleven-year-old son Willie would soon take ill and pass away on February 20.

The second phrase, "to care for him who shall have borne the battle, and for his widow, and his orphan," alludes to James 1:27: "Pure religion and undefiled before God and the Father is this, To visit the fatherless and widows in their affliction . . ." Taken together, the two phrases remind the listener of the roles both man and God played in the Civil War, as suggested by Lincoln in the third paragraph of the Second Inaugural Address and previously stated in his Thanksgiving Proclamation of 1863:

> And I recommend to them that while offering up the ascriptions justly due to Him for such singular deliverances and blessings, they do also, with humble penitence for our national perverseness and disobedience, commend to His tender care all those who have become widows, orphans, mourners or sufferers in the lamentable civil strife in which we are unavoidably engaged, and fervently implore the interposition of the Almighty Hand to heal the wounds of the nation and to restore it as soon as may be consistent with the Divine purposes to the full enjoyment of peace, harmony, tranquility and Union.[118]

The verses alluded to also illustrate that human beings, made in the image of God, must assume a certain role in order for peace and harmony to return. As Lincoln did not know for certain what God's purposes were, he states what he believes he knows a little more about—man's duty in the eyes of a watchful God. The role Lincoln saw for the people was that of a patriotic defense and care of one's country and fellow citizens. He recognized that the success of a self-governing regime depends mostly on the character of its citizens, embracing both right reason and belief in God. Lincoln confessed this on his way to the White House in 1861: "[T]here has fallen upon me a task such as did not rest even upon the Father of his country, and so feeling I cannot but turn and look for the support without which it will be impossible for me to perform that great task. I turn, then, and look to the American people and to that God who has never forsaken them."[119] This would constitute the chief refrain of Lincoln's rhetoric: the statesman's reliance on both popular deliberation and divine providence.

Not to be forgotten among those who "have borne the battle" were the emancipated slaves, who now had the task of building a life for themselves in a nation that had robbed them of that birthright. On the eve of Lincoln's second inauguration, the president and members of his cabinet went to the capitol to review last-minute bills of the adjourning

Thirty-eighth Congress. Included was an act establishing the Bureau for the Relief of Freedmen and Refugees, as well as one to charter the Freedmen's Savings and Trust Company. In signing these and other bills into law, Lincoln bolstered a general reconstruction program that sought to reconcile the constitutional rights and privileges of all American citizens with the "new birth of freedom" anticipated by a Union victory in the Civil War.

Lincoln closes his Second Inaugural Address with a call "to do all which may achieve and cherish a just, and a lasting peace, among ourselves, and with all nations." He exhorts the nation not only to "achieve" an end to the costly war, but to do "all" or everything in their power to end the war so as to produce "a lasting peace." In other words, peace will not follow from the mere conclusion of the war; it must be prepared for, nurtured, and maintained. In a war, one side wins and the other side loses, which gives rise to the unique problem in the case of a civil war where the combatants must once again live as one people, one United States of America. In short, civil peace must replace civil war. As if "the nation's wounds"—which include the wounds of those who fought as well as their widows and orphans—stand as too faint a reminder of the perils of war, Lincoln counsels the citizenry to "cherish" or revere the peace that would follow the end of the war.

Lincoln spoke of peace in his Thanksgiving Proclamation of October 20, 1864:

> And I do farther recommend to my fellow-citizens . . . [that] they do reverently humble themselves in the dust and from thence offer up penitent and fervent prayers and supplications to the Great Disposer of events for a return of the inestimable blessings of Peace, Union and Harmony throughout the land, which it has pleased him to assign as a dwelling place for ourselves and for our posterity throughout all generations.[120]

Here Lincoln gleans from Acts 17:24-31, especially verse 26: "And [God] hath made of one blood all nations of men for to dwell on all the face of the earth, and hath determined the times before appointed, and the bounds of their habitation . . ." The Proclamation lends sacredness to "Peace, Union and Harmony throughout the land" as it depicts "the Great Disposer of events" as its author. Thus, one ought to revere the peaceful conclusion of the Union even more, given its divine origin. While "Man proposes, but God disposes" is certainly a Lincolnian sentiment, he is mindful of man's partnership with the Almighty in carrying out His purposes.[121] This necessarily involves every citizen's desire and effort to preserve the peace, which represents the will of many to join together as one people committed to a common way of life.

Replying to an invitation to attend a Buffalo, New York, rally for the National Union Party—the Republican Party re-christened as a broader coalition party for the portentous 1864 elections—Lincoln reflects on the prospect of peace in the fall of 1864: "Much is being said about peace; and no man desires peace more ardently than I. Still I am yet unprepared to give up the Union for a peace which, so achieved, could not be of much duration." A premature peace with the rebellious states, Lincoln states, "insures the success of the rebellion. An armistice—a cessation of hostilities—is the end of the struggle, and the insurgents would be in peaceable possession of all that has been struggled for."[122] Lincoln, even in the closing sentence of his Second Inaugural Address, teaches Americans about the kind of peace that a democratic nation must foster and for which the federal government had fought the war—"a lasting peace."

Yet, a peace that is merely "lasting" says nothing about the kind of peace it is. It is probably not a peace most men would be willing to die for. More important, only a good or just peace would be worthy of the enjoyment of a free people. Only if they see an end as good or honorable will they risk all that they have and are to achieve it. Speaking of peace in the summer of 1863, Lincoln wrote that he hoped "it will come soon, and *come to stay*; and so come as to *be worth the keeping* in all future time."[123] (Emphasis added.) Similarly, Lincoln's Second Inaugural Address exhorts the nation to achieve and cherish a peace that is not only "lasting" but "just." In his famous Peoria Address of 1854, Lincoln declared, "Let north and south—let all Americans—let all lovers of liberty everywhere—join in the great and great work. If we do this, we shall not only have saved the Union; but we shall have so saved it, as to make, and to keep it, forever worthy of saving."[124] He is convinced that an end to the war that left the southern states to secede and form a new nation would not be just. A just and lasting peace requires a Union victory, as the federal government had done little to provoke the southern slave states into rebelling against the new administration, which represented the will of the constitutional majority of the American people in 1860.[125] In Lincoln's mind, the example of states seceding from the Union would only serve as a precedent for anarchy in the long run. Having expounded on the justice of the federal government's efforts throughout the course of the war, Lincoln now closes the Second Inaugural Address with a call to "achieve and cherish a just, and a lasting peace" that would secure self-government at home and stand as an example to "all nations."

With the close of the war at hand, Lincoln focused almost all of his attention in the Second Inaugural Address on explaining the prolonged duration of the war. In order to have "malice toward none" and "charity for all," the citizenry (especially in the North) needed to see the war as divine in its mission and not solely attributable to human frailties on either side. Only as the people both North and South understand the Civil War as part of God's intention for them could they be persuaded to look beyond the faults of their brothers and aspire to the noble aim of America—"government of the people, by the people, for the people." Lincoln wanted the nation to see the war as punishment for failing to resolve their differences through sober reflection and choice and not irregular passion or force.[126] In his Lyceum Address of 1838, Lincoln said that "Passion has helped us; but can do so no more. It will in future be our enemy."[127] A quarter century later, Lincoln contemplated the peace that he hoped would follow from an eventual Union victory: "It will then have been proved that, among free men, there can be no successful appeal from the ballot to the bullet; and that they who take such appeal are sure to lose their case, and pay the cost."[128] Through the Second Inaugural Address, Lincoln sought to curb the vengeful passions of the North while assuaging the fears of the South and thus bring the entire nation back to its providential mission as a country devoted to the equal rights of all human beings.

*   *   *   *   *

So what does the Second Inaugural Address say about the political relevance of religion? While not censuring religious excess *per se*, Lincoln wonders aloud at the audacity of southern pleas to God for "assistance in wringing their bread from the sweat of other men's faces." This was too much malice and not enough charity! He commented on this more openly in an 1864 letter to a Baptist committee that had presented Lincoln with resolutions supporting his administration:

> When, a year or two ago, those *professedly* holy men of the South, met in the *semblance* of prayer and devotion, and, *in the name* of Him who said "As ye would all men should do unto you, do ye even so unto them" appealed to the christian world to aid them in doing to a whole race of men, as they would have no man do unto themselves, to my thinking, they contemned and insulted God and His church, far more

than did Satan when he tempted the Saviour with the Kingdoms of the
earth. The devils [*sic*] attempt was no more false, and far less
hypocritical.[129] (Emphasis added.)

Lincoln consistently addressed slavery as an enormity for, to put it
lightly, its excess in rule. He stated it famously in his 1854 Peoria
Address, coming as close as anyone ever has to expressing the heart of
the equality principle of the Declaration of Independence: "When the
white man governs himself that is self-government; but when he governs
himself, and also governs *another* man, that is *more* than self-
government—that is despotism. . . . What I do say is, that no man is good
enough to govern another man, *without that other's consent*."[130] In a
letter written a year later, he feared the passing of the equality principle:

> When we were the political slaves of King George, and wanted to be
> free, we called the maxim that "all men are created equal" a self
> evident truth; but now when we have grown fat, and have lost all dread
> of being slaves ourselves, we have become so greedy to be *masters* that
> we call the same maxim "a self-evident lie."[131]

Lincoln found the Golden Rule at the core of the equality principle: "As I
would not be a *slave*, so I would not be a *master*."[132]

But these words were to no avail against southern appeals to the
Bible in defense of slavery, which countered northern appeals
condemning slavery on the same religious basis. Lincoln lamented the
extreme reliance on biblical "proof-texting" for (and to a degree against)
slavery that could not be refuted, whether by religion or reason, because
of its tie to a sacred text. Interpreting the Holy Scriptures dogmatically
on slavery would spell the end of the discussion and, therefore, the end
of political dialogue about the issue. This intransigence left little hope for
the perpetuation of a regime founded upon the capacity of a people to
rule by majority but for the sake of all the governed. In the words of
Thomas Jefferson's First Inaugural Address, "All, too, will bear in mind
this sacred principle, that though the will of the majority is in all cases to
prevail, that will, to be rightful, must be reasonable; that the minority
possess their equal rights, which equal laws must protect, and to violate
which would be oppression."[133] Lincoln's Second Inaugural Address
suggests that political humility, or as the current Pledge of Allegiance
states it, "one nation under God," should inform the civic participation of
every American.[134]

Does the Second Inaugural Address support revealed religion's claim
to the adherence of men, or does it promote reason as the principal virtue

of republics? Lincoln depends on revealed religion—in particular, he alludes to and quotes the Bible—in the process of forging a governmental resolution of the war. While Lincoln refers to the sacred text of most Americans of his day, his reason interprets biblical truths for the good of the country. This does not argue for reason solely, nor religion for religion's sake. Instead, both reason and religion were weighed and found wanting. The Civil War progressed beyond what both sides initially expected and had undertaken in light of what each defended as rational and godly. Lincoln both criticizes and affirms reason and revelation in his address.

In so doing, he demonstrates the necessity of a statesman to guide a republic to its legitimate ends. Professor Thurow makes this his concluding statement on Lincoln's political religion:

> The political religion can ultimately be held in proper tension only by a statesman, a man such as Lincoln.
> Men must participate in God's order by acknowledging the justice of God. But they cannot transcend the nation in this sense unassisted. They need someone who will point out to them what God's judgment is. . . . The need of democratic citizens to transcend the nation can be fulfilled only if they have a guide who stands between God and man.[135]

However, Thurow does not account for the political accommodation Lincoln makes for revealed religion. The most obvious characteristic of the Second Inaugural Address is its reliance on a revealed religion, Christianity, to reconcile North and South. Lincoln, though, does not content himself with a civil religion—an explanation of "the relation of God to the nation" by a public official[136]—as the sole avenue for religion *qua* religion to influence the American regime. Thurow interprets Lincoln's "political religion" more expansively than was intended by Lincoln's only use of the phrase in the Lyceum Address of 1838. To be sure, Lincoln promotes a civil religion in many of his other speeches and writings. In his efforts to perpetuate the constitutional union of the states, he appeals to Christianity as the predominant religion of America.

Nevertheless, Lincoln saw the need for government to facilitate the expression of religious faith at minimum out of a responsibility to protect this fundamental right of the people. In the case of the Civil War, he needed American citizens to practice the Christianity they preached: namely, to withhold what they perceived as just punishment and instead bestow mercy and forgive their enemies. This was religion being put to a secular political end, but Lincoln saw that the Christian understanding of the moral requirements of a free society was consistent with the worldly aim of American government. Thus, no infringement of individual conscience took place. While careful to moderate religion's vices as an expressly political institution or movement, the statesmanship of Abraham Lincoln reflects a conviction that the happiness of a people cannot be pursued without a due protection and encouragement of their religion.

As the Second Inaugural Address shows, Lincoln did not respond to the apparent failure of both reason and religion to prevent the crisis of Union with an implicit appeal merely to his own prudence. The grand case in point, the prudence displayed in his First Inaugural Address, however rational and eloquent, failed to avert the Civil War. In his Second Inaugural Address, despite pointing out the inefficacy of religion to speed the war to a close, Lincoln appeals to religion to establish a consensus for postwar national policy. Reason or prudence remains the ruling principle of the republic, guiding deliberation among the citizens and their government, but it must allow the rightful exercise and, hence, influence of religion. The statesman's art lies in the ability to inform public discourse along both rational and religious lines while tempering the excesses following from either rational self-sufficiency or religious fanaticism. Abraham Lincoln augmented the national political religion with a consistent protection of the nation's revealed religions, thereby perpetuating American self-government as well as guarding that personal attention to spiritual needs that holds the possibility for man's greatest happiness and fulfillment.

"The address sounded more like a sermon than like a state paper." So observed Frederick Douglass of Lincoln's Second Inaugural Address.[137] In so doing, Douglass notes what is hard to miss in the Lincoln corpus of speeches and writings: the judicious use of the Bible in private and public writings. Understanding the relevance of religion, especially Christianity, to Lincoln's politics helps us better understand his political project: namely, the defense of the American constitutional union as an expression of his faith in God's purposes for him and his country.

Notes

1. Cited from *Life and Times of Frederick Douglass* in *Frederick Douglass: Autobiographies* (New York: Library of America, 1994), 804. Hereinafter cited as *Life and Times of Frederick Douglass*.

2. "Reason, cold, calculating, unimpassioned reason, must furnish all the materials for our future support and defence." "Address before the Young

Men's Lyceum of Springfield, Illinois (27 January 1838)," in *The Collected Works of Abraham Lincoln*, Roy P. Basler, ed., 9 vols. (New Brunswick, N.J.: Rutgers University Press, 1955), 1: 115. Hereinafter cited as *Collected Works*; all emphases in original except where otherwise noted. "Happy day, when, all appetites controled, all passions subdued, all matters subjected, *mind*, all conquering *mind*, shall live and move the monarch of the world. Glorious consummation! Hail fall of Fury! Reign of Reason, all hail!" "Temperance Address (22 February 1842)," in *Collected Works*, 1: 279.

3. "My countrymen, one and all, think calmly and *well*, upon this whole subject. Nothing valuable can be lost by taking time. If there be an object to *hurry* any of you, in hot haste, to a step which you would never take *deliberately*, that object will be frustrated by taking time; but no good object can be frustrated by it." "First Inaugural Address—Final Text (4 March 1861)," in *Collected Works*, 4: 270-71.

4. F. B. Carpenter, *The Inner Life of Abraham Lincoln* (Lincoln: University of Nebraska Press, 1995; originally published in 1866 as *Six Months at the White House with Abraham Lincoln* by Hurd and Houghton, New York), 234.

5. "To Thurlow Weed (15 March 1865)," in *Collected Works*, 8: 356.

6. Lincoln probably added the phrase "under God" on the platform as he listened to Edward Everett's oration. Lincoln's famous last line reads: "that this nation, under God, shall have a new birth of freedom—and that government of the people, by the people, for the people, shall not perish from the earth." "Address Delivered at the Dedication of the Cemetery at Gettysburg (19 November 1863)," in *Collected Works*, 7: 23 and 7: 20, n. 19. Cf. Garry Wills, *Lincoln at Gettysburg: The Words That Remade America* (New York: Simon & Schuster, 1992), 194, 198, and 261: "that the nation shall, under God, have a new birth of freedom, and that the government of the people, by the people, and for the people, shall not perish from the earth."

7. "Second Inaugural Address (4 March 1865)," in *Collected Works*, 8: 332. His first inauguration also necessitated a lengthy speech inasmuch as Lincoln, though anxiously beset by many for any personal indication of where he would take the country, kept with tradition in not giving public statements for the duration of the presidential campaign. For example, when asked his opinion on the fugitive slave law, he replied, "I consider it would be both imprudent, and contrary to the reasonable expectation of friends for me to write, or speak anything upon doctrinal points now. Besides this, my published speeches contain nearly all I could willingly say. Justice and fairness to all, is the utmost I have said, or will say." "To T. Apolion Cheney (14 August 1860)," in *Collected Works*, 4: 93. Lincoln quotes Luke 16:31 in response to another inquirer: "Those who will not read, or heed, what I have already publicly said, would not read, or heed, a repetition of it. 'If they hear not Moses and the prophets, neither will they be persuaded though one rose from the dead.'" "To William S. Speer (23 October 1860)," in *Collected Works*, 4: 130. After the election he would quote Luke 11:29 on the same subject: "This is just as I expected, and just what

would happen with any declaration I could make. . . . 'Party malice' and not 'public good' possesses them entirely. 'They seek a sign, and no sign shall be given them.'" "To Henry J. Raymond (28 November 1860)," in *Collected Works*, 4: 146.

8. An excerpt from a speech of Alabama Congressman Jabez Lamar Monroe Curry is representative of southern sentiment: "The Republican Party . . . exists only in the northern States, and for the first time in our history a partisan organization, exclusively and intensely sectional, has obtained ascendancy in our Government." "The Perils and Duty of the South, . . . Speech Delivered in Talladega, Alabama (26 November 1860)," in Jon L. Wakelyn, ed., *Southern Pamphlets on Secession, November 1860-April 1861* (Chapel Hill: University of North Carolina Press, 1996), 38. Lincoln denied charges of sectionalism earlier in the year: "You say we are sectional. We deny it. That makes an issue; and the burden of proof is upon you." "Address at Cooper Institute, New York City (27 February 1860)," in *Collected Works*, 3: 536.

9. "Annual Message to Congress (8 December 1863)," in *Collected Works*, 7: 53.

10. Cited from n. 1 of "To Henry W. Beecher (27 February 1865)," in *Collected Works*, 8: 318-319.

11. Cited from n. 1 of "To Ulysses S. Grant (3 March 1865)," in *Collected Works*, 8: 331.

12. *Collected Works*, 8: 330-31.

13. John Niven, *Salmon P. Chase: A Biography* (New York: Oxford University Press, Inc., 1995), 380. The preceding verses place the text Lincoln kissed in the context of God's chastening and restoring of Israel:

> . . . they have cast away the law of the LORD of hosts, and despised the word of the Holy One of Israel. Therefore is the anger of the LORD kindled against his people, and he hath stretched forth his hand against them, and hath smitten them: . . . For all this his anger is not turned away, but his hand is stretched out still. And he will lift up an ensign to the nations from far, and will hiss unto them from the end of the earth: and behold, they shall come with speed swiftly (vv. 24-26).

14. The tentativeness of this interpretation is due to some question about the actual choosing of the verses. Historian John Niven states that a clerk had chosen the "warlike verses" randomly. *Salmon P. Chase: A Biography*, 380.

15. James M. McPherson, *Battle Cry of Freedom: The Civil War Era* (New York: Ballantine Books, 1989), 266.

16. McPherson, *Battle Cry of Freedom*, 262-67; David M. Potter, *Lincoln and His Party in the Secession Crisis* (Baton Rouge: Louisiana State University Press, 1995; orig. publ. Yale University Press, 1942), 342-45. See also Lincoln's recollection four months after his inauguration in his "Message to Congress in Special Session (4 July 1861)," in *Collected Works*, 4: 421-23.

17. Edwin C. Fishel, *The Secret War for the Union: The Untold Story of Military Intelligence in the Civil War* (Boston: Houghton Mifflin Company, 1996), 13-15.

18. For an informative discussion of Lincoln's project to promote "self-reconstruction" by southerners loyal to the federal government, see William C. Harris, *With Charity for All: Lincoln and the Restoration of the Union* (Lexington: The University Press of Kentucky, 1997), Introduction and chap. 1, "1861: An Early Start," 1-32. To wit: "However slowly the cause of the Union might advance in the South, Lincoln held firmly to the idea that the restoration of civil government in the hands of Southern Unionists should occur simultaneously with the armed suppression of the rebellion" (*With Charity for All*, 32).

19. "Speech at Peoria, Illinois (16 October 1854)," in *Collected Works*, 2: 270.

20. "To Isaac M. Schermerhorn (12 September 1864)," in *Collected Works*, 8: 1.

21. "Address at Cooper Institute, New York City (27 February 1860)," in *Collected Works*, 7: 543.

22. "Message to Congress in Special Session (4 July 1861)," in *Collected Works*, 4: 425, 426, 440.

23. "Annual Message to Congress (6 December 1864)," in *Collected Works*, 8: 152. See also his "Message to Congress (6 March 1862)," in *Collected Works*, 5: 145: "A practical re-acknowledgement of the national authority would render the war unnecessary, and it would at once cease. If, however, resistance continues, the war must also continue . . ."

24. Lincoln made the same argument in his "Fragment on Slavery [1 July 1854?]," in *Collected Works*, 2: 222-23:

> If A. can prove, however conclusively, that he may, of right, enslave B.— why may not B. snatch the same argument, and prove equally, that he may enslave A?—
>
> You say A. is white, and B. is black. It is color, then; the lighter, having the right to enslave the darker? Take care. By this rule, you are to be slave to the first man you meet, with a fairer skin than your own.

25. James Madison defined a faction as "a number of citizens, whether amounting to a majority or minority of the whole, who are united and actuated by some common impulse of passion, or of interest, adverse to the rights of other citizens, or to the permanent and aggregate interests of the community." *The Federalist*, Jacob E. Cooke, ed. (Middletown, Conn.: Wesleyan University Press, 1987), No. 10, 57.

26. "Message to Congress in Special Session (4 July 1861)," in *Collected Works*, 4: 438.

27. "Annual Message to Congress (3 December 1861)," in *Collected Works*, 5: 36.

28. "Address at Cooper Institute, New York City (27 February 1860)," in *Collected Works*, 3: 535-36.

29. "Speech at Peoria, Illinois (16 October 1854)," in *Collected Works*, 2: 255, 256.

30. "Second Inaugural Address (4 March 1865)," in *Collected Works*, 8: 332 and 333, n. 2.

31. "Message to Congress in Special Session (4 July 1861)," in *Collected Works*, 4: 428.

32. "Annual Message to Congress (1 December 1862)," in *Collected Works*, 5: 528, 529. Cf. John Jay's *Federalist* No. 2, 9: "This country and this people seem to have been made for each other, and it appears as if it was the design of Providence, that an inheritance so proper and convenient for a band of brethren, united to each other by the strongest ties, should never be split into a number of unsocial, jealous and alien sovereignties."

33. "First Inaugural Address—Final Text (4 March 1861)," in *Collected Works*, 4: 269.

34. "Second Inaugural Address (4 March 1865)," in *Collected Works*, 8: 332.

35. John C. Calhoun, "Remarks on Receiving Abolition Petitions [Revised Report] (6 February 1837)," in *The Papers of John C. Calhoun*, Clyde N. Wilson, ed., 20 vols. (Columbia: University of South Carolina Press, 1980), 13: 395 and 391-98 in general.

36. "Query XVIII: Manners," *Notes on the State of Virginia*, in *The Portable Thomas Jefferson*, Merrill D. Peterson, ed. (New York: Viking Press, 1975), 214, 215.

37. "First Debate with Stephen A. Douglas at Ottawa, Illinois (21 August 1858)," in *Collected Works*, 3: 27-30; *Dred Scott v. Sandford*, 19 How. (60 U.S.) 393 (1857).

38. U.S. Constitution, art. IV, sec. 2, cl. 3.

39. "Speech at Chicago, Illinois (10 July 1858)," in *Collected Works*, 2: 492, 501.

40. See "Address at Cooper Institute, New York City (27 February 1860)," in *Collected Works*, 3: 534-35, for Lincoln's discussion of the proper evidence and arguments needed to "supplant the opinions and policy of our Fathers."

41. "Speech at Peoria, Illinois (16 October 1854)," in *Collected Works*, 2: 255.

42. See, for example, Thomas Jefferson's letter "To Roger C. Weighton (24 June 1826)," in *The Portable Thomas Jefferson*, 585. For similar views held by other early American statesmen, see Nathan Tarcov, "Principle and Prudence in Foreign Policy: The Founders' Perspective," *The Public Interest* 76 (Summer 1984): 45-60, esp. 56-60.

43. John Quincy Adams, "An Address Delivered at the Request of a Committee of the Citizens of Washington; on the Occassion of Reading the Declaration of Independence, on the Fourth of July, 1821," cited in Greg

Russell, *John Quincy Adams and the Public Virtues of Diplomacy* (Columbia: University of Missouri Press, 1995), 3.

44. "Second Inaugural Address (4 March 1865)," in *Collected Works*, 8: 332-33.

45. U.S. Constitution, art. II, sec. 1, cl. 8.

46. "Annual Message to Congress (3 December 1861)," in *Collected Works*, 5: 49.

47. "The Prayer of Twenty Millions (19 August 1862)," in *Documents of American History*, 8th ed., Henry Steele Commager, ed., 2 vols. (Englewood Cliffs, N.J.: Prentice-Hall, Inc., 1973), 1: 415-17. For example,

[W]hat an immense majority of the loyal millions of your countrymen require of you is a frank, declared, unqualified, ungrudging execution of the laws of the land, more especially of the Confiscation Act. That act gives freedom to the slaves of rebels coming within our lines, or whom those lines may at any time inclose—we ask you to render it due obedience by publicly requiring all your subordinates to recognize and obey it. (417)

48. "To Horace Greeley (22 August 1862)," in *Collected Works*, 5: 388.

49. "First Inaugural Address—Final Text (4 March 1861)," in *Collected Works*, 4: 263.

50. "Republican Party Platform (16 May 1860)," in *Documents of American History*, 364.

51. See Phillip Shaw Paludan, *The Presidency of Abraham Lincoln* (Lawrence: University Press of Kansas, 1994), 17-20, for a cogent explanation of Lincoln as a "'process-based' egalitarian": namely, one who understood that equality could best be secured by the orderly processes of a "political-constitutional system" informed by the "self-evident truths" of the Declaration of Independence. As William Lee Miller states: "This devotion was not to the Union for its own sake but rather to the Union as the bearer of universal values. The preservation of that Union had to be his overriding commitment." *Abraham Lincoln's Second Inaugural Address: A Study in Political Ethics* (Bloomington, Ind.: The Poynter Center, 1980), 10. The best discussion of Lincoln's connection of the ideals of the Declaration of Independence with the mechanisms of the U.S. Constitution remains Harry V. Jaffa, *Crisis of the House Divided: An Interpretation of the Issues in the Lincoln-Douglas Debates* (Seattle: University of Washington Press, 1973; reprint ed., Chicago: University of Chicago Press, 1982, © 1959), esp. chap. 17, "The Meaning of Equality: Abstract and Practical," 363-86. For a recent examination of the alternatives the nation faced at the time of Lincoln's rise to national prominence, see Joseph R. Fornieri, "Biblical Republicanism: Abraham Lincoln's Civil Theology" (Ph.D. dissertation, Catholic University of America, 1996).

52. "Final Emancipation Proclamation (1 January 1863)," in *Collected Works*, 6: 30. See also his "Message to Congress (6 March 1862)," in which he first proposed that Congress "'co-operate with any state which may adopt gradual abolishment of slavery, giving to such state pecuniary aid, to be used by

such state in it's [sic] discretion, to compensate for the inconveniences public and private, produced by such change of system.'" He saw it "as one of the most efficient means of self-preservation," by which the southernmost slave states would lose hope in attracting border slave states once the process of emancipation had begun. "To deprive them of this hope," Lincoln concludes, "substantially ends the rebellion." *Collected Works*, 5: 144-45. Historians Nevins and Commager remind us that in all this, Lincoln carried out the rhetorical threat of John Quincy Adams. As a congressman in the twilight of his career, the former president "repeatedly warned the South that secession would mean war and that 'from the instant your slaveholding states become the theater of war, civil, servile, or foreign, from that moment the war powers of the Constitution extend to interference with the institution of slavery.'" Allan Nevins and Henry Steele Commager, *A Short History of the United States* (New York: Modern Library, 1942; new enlarged ed., 1956), 202.

53. "Resolution Submitting the Thirteenth Amendment to the States (1 February 1865)," in *Collected Works*, 8: 253-54 and n. 1. Basler records that the Senate passed another resolution on February 7 that declared Lincoln's approval unnecessary.

54. "To Mrs. Horace Mann (5 April 1864)," in *Collected Works*, 7: 287.

55. "To William Nast (31 October 1864)," in *Collected Works*, 8: 83. Is this providence at work, through the instrument of Lincoln's war effort "upon military necessity," or the direct interposition of a just God, as described in the letter to Mrs. Horace Mann?

56. "To Albert G. Hodges (4 April 1864)," in *Collected Works*, 7: 282.

57. "Address at Sanitary Fair, Baltimore, Maryland (18 April 1864)," in *Collected Works*, 7: 301.

58. "Second Inaugural Address (4 March 1865)," in *Collected Works*, 8: 333.

59. "Reply to Eliza P. Gurney (26 October 1862)," in *Collected Works*, 5: 478.

60. The Constitution of the Confederate States of America reads in part: "The Confederate States may acquire new territory . . . In all such territory, the institution of negro slavery, as it now exists in the Confederate States, shall be recognized and protected by Congress and by the territorial government" (Art. IV, sec. 3, cl. 3). *Documents of American History*, 1: 383.

61. "To Thurlow Weed (15 March 1865)," in *Collected Works*, 8: 356.

62. For various interpretations by southern divines of the biblical teaching regarding slavery, see Eugene D. Genovese, *A Consuming Fire: The Fall of the Confederacy in the Mind of the White Christian South* (Athens: University of Georgia Press, 1999).

63. "Reply to Emancipation Memorial by Chicago Christians of All Denominations (13 September 1862)," in *Collected Works*, 5: 420.

64. "Speech at Cincinnati, Ohio (17 September 1859)," in *Collected Works*, 3: 445.

65. Jack P. Maddox, "Proslavery Millenialism: Social Eschatology in Antebellum Southern Calvinism," *American Quarterly* 31 (Spring 1970), 49, 50.

66. "Fragment on Pro-Slavery Theology [1 October 1858?]," in *Collected Works*, 3: 204.

67. Frederick A. Ross, "Letters to Rev. A. Barnes [No. I]," in *Slavery Ordained of God* (Philadelphia: J. B. Lippincott & Co., 1857), 104, 105.

68. Ross, "Speech, Delivered in the General Assembly, New York (1856)," in *Slavery Ordained of God*, 39, 41.

69. See Mitchell Snay, *Gospel of Division: Religion and Separatism in the Antebellum South* (Chapel Hill: University of North Carolina Press, 1997; orig. publ. Cambridge University Press, 1993) and Daniel W. Stowell, *Rebuilding Zion: The Religious Reconstruction of the South, 1863-1877* (New York: Oxford University Press, 1998).

70. "Reply to Emancipation Memorial by Chicago Christians of All Denominations (13 September 1862)," in *Collected Works*, 5: 419-420, 424.

71. "Reply to Eliza P. Gurney (26 October 1862)," in *Collected Works*, 5: 478.

72. Mark Noll, "'Both . . . Pray to the Same God': The Singularity of Lincoln's Faith in the Era of the Civil War," *Journal of the Abraham Lincoln Association* 18 (Winter 1997): 18.

73. "First Inaugural Address—Final Text (4 March 1861)," in *Collected Works*, 4: 271.

74. "Speech at Worchester, Massachusetts (12 September 1848)," in *Collected Works*, 2: 3-4.

75. "To William Nast (31 October 1864)," in *Collected Works*, 8: 83.

76. "To Joshua F. Speed (24 August 1855)," in *Collected Works*, 2: 322.

77. "Fragment on Free Labor [17 September 1859?]," in *Collected Works*, 3: 462.

78. "Story Written for Noah Brooks [6 December 1864?]," in *Collected Works*, 8: 154-55.

79. "Speech at Edwardsville, Illinois (11 September 1858)," in *Collected Works*, 3: 95.

80. "Speech at Columbus, Ohio (16 September 1859)," in *Collected Works*, 3: 410.

81. "To Henry L. Pierce and Others (6 April 1859)," in *Collected Works*, 3: 376.

82. "Query XVIII: Manners," *Notes on the State of Virginia*, in *The Portable Thomas Jefferson*, 215. For direct references by Lincoln to Jefferson's "Query XVIII," see "Fifth Debate with Stephen A. Douglas, at Galesburg, Illinois (7 October 1858)," in *Collected Works*, 3: 220, and "Speech at Columbus, Ohio (16 September 1859)," in *Collected Works*, 3: 410.

83. Ross, "Speech, Delivered at Buffalo, before the General Assembly of the Presbyterian Church (27 May 1853)," in *Slavery Ordained of God*, 17.

Although Dr. Ross believed the enslavement of blacks was biblical, he had freed his own slaves by the time he published his infamous vindication of slavery.

84. "Meditation on the Divine Will [2 September 1862?]," in *Collected Works*, 5: 403-404. This battle, which occurred August 28-30, "brought Robert E. Lee and the Confederacy to the height of their power and opened the way for Lee's first invasion of the North." John Hennessy, "Second Manassas," *The Civil War Battlefield Guide*, Frances H. Kennedy, ed. (Boston: Houghton Mifflin Company for the Conservation Fund, 1990), 77.

85. "First Inaugural Address—Final Text (4 March 1861)," in *Collected Works*, 4: 270.

86. "To George Robertson (15 August 1855)," in *Collected Works*, 2: 318.

87. "Second Inaugural Address (4 March 1865)," in *Collected Works*, 8: 333.

88. Hugh Thomas, *The Slave Trade: The Story of the Atlantic Slave Trade, 1440-1870* (New York: Simon & Schuster, 1997), 571. Thomas notes that Britain's cotton imports from the United States grew from 30 percent in 1800 to 88 percent in 1860. See also McPherson, *Battle Cry of Freedom*, 39, 91-92, which explains the lucrative trade in cotton that entangled the northern "free" states as well as Great Britain.

89. "Proclamation of a National Fast-Day (12 August 1861)," in *Collected Works*, 4: 482.

90. "Proclamation Appointing a National Fast Day (30 March 1863)," in *Collected Works*, 6: 156.

91. "Proclamation of Thanksgiving (20 October 1864)," in *Collected Works*, 8: 55-56.

92. "Response to Evangelical Lutherans (13 May 1861)," in *Collected Works*, 5: 212-13.

93. "To Caleb Russell and Sallie A. Fenton (5 January 1863)," in *Collected Works*, 6: 39-40. The secretaries had closed their letter to Lincoln with the wish that at the "very late period, we can do but very little more, than bear our testimony in favor of justice and liberty and like Aaron and Him of old would gladly hold up thy hands as they did the hands of Moses." (Emphasis in original.) *Collected Works*, 6: 40 n. 1.

94. "To Joshua F. Speed (24 August 1855)," in *Collected Works*, 2: 323.

95. "Query XVIII," *Notes on the State of Virginia*, in *The Portable Thomas Jefferson*, 215.

96. Glen E. Thurow, *Abraham Lincoln and American Political Religion* (New York: State University of New York Press, 1976), 104.

97. Thurow, *Abraham Lincoln and American Political Religion*, 105-106.

98. "Revision of William H. Seward to Charles Francis Adams (21 May 1861)," in *Collected Works*, 4: 380. For the historical context, see McPherson, *Battle Cry of Freedom*, 387-89.

99. Professor James H. Nichols, Jr., of Claremont McKenna College first brought this to my attention during my research for an unpublished senior

thesis, "The Statesmanship of Abraham Lincoln in the Second Inaugural Address" (B.A. thesis, Claremont McKenna College, 1987). Glen E. Thurow makes the same observation in *Abraham Lincoln and American Political Religion*, 98-104. See also Alfred Kazin, *God and the American Writer* (New York: Alfred A. Knopf, 1997), 137-38.

100. A year before his first election to the presidency, Lincoln wrote: "But I do hope that *as there is a just and righteous God in Heaven*, our principles will and shall prevail sooner or later." "Speech at Clinton, Illinois (14 October 1859)," in *Collected Works*, 3: 488 (emphasis added).

101. See Kermit Escus White, "Abraham Lincoln and Christianity" (Ph.D. dissertation, Boston University Graduate School, 1954), 139: "The recognition of Lincoln that God 'now wills to remove' slavery does not mean that he believed God was unwilling 'to remove' slavery previous to this time. It means that he felt God was working with the enlightened conscience of men at a propitious time to effect His will."

102. See W. Harrison Daniel, "Southern Protestantism—1861 and After," *Civil War History* 5 (September 1959): 276-82, and David W. Blight, "Frederick Douglass and the American Apocalypse," *Civil War History* 31 (December 1985): 309-328.

103. Reinhold Niebuhr noted this reticence of Lincoln, as well, and attributed the third-person voice to a mixture of "both faith and skepticism concerning the concept of providence. For while the drama of history is shot through with moral meaning, the meaning is never exact. Sin and punishment, virtue and reward, are never precisely proportioned." "The Religion of Abraham Lincoln," *The Christian Century* (10 February 1965): 172.

104. As William J. Wolf states: "He could appreciate the sincerity of his foe although he believed him wrong, but because of his religious perspective he could deal magnanimously and forgivingly wthout assuming the self-righteous mantle of the victor." "Abraham Lincoln and Calvinism," *Calvinism and the Political Order*, George L. Hunt, ed. (Philadelphia: Westminster Press, 1965), 154.

105. So wrote Lincoln in reply to the committee that notified him of his reelection. "Reply to Notification Committee [1 March 1865]," in *Collected Works*, 8: 326. Congress counted the electoral votes (Lincoln's 212 to General George B. McClellan's 12) and sent word of Lincoln's reelection on Sunday, February 12th—the president's fifty-sixth birthday.

106. "To Thurlow Weed (15 March 1865)," in *Collected Works*, 8: 356.

107. "Reply to Eliza P. Gurney (26 October 1862)," in *Collected Works*, 5: 478.

108. Cf. Andrew Jackson, "Second Inaugural Address (4 March 1833)," in *A Compilation of the Messages and Papers of the Presidents: 1787-1897*, James D. Richardson, ed., 20 vols. (Washington, D.C.: Government Printing Office, 1896), 3: 3: "To do justice to all and to submit to wrong from none has been during my Administration its governing maxim, . . ."

109. "To Cuthbert Bullitt (28 July 1862)," in *Collected Works*, 5: 344-46. See also "To August Belmont (31 July 1862)," in *Collected Works*, 5: 350-51. For the context of Lincoln's overture to Bullitt and the reconstruction effort in Louisiana in general, see William C. Harris, *With Charity for All*, 72-84, and chap. 8, "Louisiana: A Tangled Skein of Reconstruction," 171-96, respectively.

110. "To Reverdy Johnson (26 July 1862)," in *Collected Works*, 5: 343. Roy P. Basler, editor of *The Collected Works of Lincoln*, mistakenly cites Brigadier General John *S*. Phelps as the offending general. *Collected Works*, 5: 343, n. 1. Lincoln's letter to Cuthbert Bullitt, which refers to a complaint that "in various ways the relation of master and slave is disturbed by the presence of" federal troops, shows that the "General Phelps" alluded to in the letter to Reverdy Johnson must be the abolitionist general (John *W*. Phelps) and not the slaveholding congressman from Missouri (John *S*. Phelps) that Lincoln appointed military governor of Arkansas. "To Cuthbert Bullitt (28 July 1862)," in *Collected Works*, 5: 345. For a brief comparison of the two generals, see entries for "John Smith Phelps" and "John Wolcott Phelps" in Ezra J. Warner, *Generals in Blue: Lives of the Union Commanders* (Baton Rouge: Louisiana State University Press, 1964), 367-69.

111. "Proclamation of Thanksgiving (20 October 1864)," in *Collected Works*, 8: 55.

112. "Annual Message to Congress (1 December 1862)," in *Collected Works*, 5: 529, 527.

113. "Response to a Serenade (10 November 1864)," in *Collected Works*, 8: 101.

114. "To Eliza P. Gurney (4 September 1864)," in *Collected Works*, 7: 535.

115. "Annual Message to Congress (3 December 1861)" *Collected Works*, 5: 53.

116. See also Job 5:17-18 and Psalms 147:2-3.

117. "To Queen Victoria (1 February 1862)," in *Collected Works*, 5: 118.

118. "Proclamation of Thanksgiving (3 October 1863)," in *Collected Works*, 6: 497.

119. "Address to the Ohio Legislature, Columbus, Ohio (13 February 1861)," in *Collected Works*, 4: 204.

120. "Proclamation for Thanksgiving (20 October 1864)," in *Collected Works*, 8: 55-56.

121. "So true is it that man proposes, and God disposes." "Address at Sanitary Fair, Baltimore, Maryland (18 April 1864)," in *Collected Works*, 7: 301.

122. "To Isaac M. Schermerhorn (12 September 1864)," in *Collected Works*, 8: 1-2.

123. "To James C. Conkling (23 August 1863)," in *Collected Works*, 6: 410.

124. "Speech at Peoria, Illinois (16 October 1854)," in *Collected Works*, 2: 276.

125. Although his name did not appear on ballots in the ten southernmost states, Lincoln still garnered 180 electoral votes—58 percent of the electoral college. Stephen A. Douglas ("Northern" Democratic Party), John C. Breckenridge ("Southern" Democratic Party), and John Bell (Constitutional Union Party) received only 123 electoral votes between them: 12, 72, and 39, respectively. Of course, Lincoln's electoral college total reflected only 39 percent of the popular vote (1,866,000), with Douglas (1,383,000), Breckenridge (848,000), and Bell (593,000). John Niven, *The Coming of the Civil War, 1837-1861* (Arlington Heights, Ill.: Harlan Davidson, Inc., 1990), 120, 129-30; Richard H. Sewell, *A House Divided: Sectionalism and Civil War, 1848-1865* (Baltimore: John Hopkins University Press, 1988), 75-76.

126. Cf. Alexander Hamilton, *The Federalist* No. 1, 3.

127. "Address before the Young Men's Lyceum of Springfield, Illinois (27 January 1838)," in *Collected Works*, 1: 115.

128. "To James C. Conkling (26 August 1863)," in *Collected Works*, 6: 410.

129. "To George B. Ide, James R. Doolittle, and A. Hubbell (30 May 1864)," in *Collected Works*, 7: 368.

130. "Speech at Peoria, Illinois (16 October 1854)," in *Collected Works*, 2: 266.

131. "To George Robertson (15 August 1855)," in *Collected Works*, 2: 318. Indiana Senator John Pettit called the equality principle of the Declaration of Independence a "self-evident lie" during the debate over the Kansas-Nebraska Act of 1854.

132. "Definition of Democracy [1 August 1858?]," in *Collected Works*, 2: 532. The Golden Rule is found in Luke 6:31 (and Matthew 7:12): "And as ye would that men should do to you, do ye also to them likewise."

133. "First Inaugural Address (4 March 1801)," in *The Portable Thomas Jefferson*, 291.

134. The seminal book on this subject in recent times is Richard John Neuhaus, *The Naked Public Square: Religion and Democracy in America*, 2nd ed. (Grand Rapids, Mich.: William B. Eerdmans Publishing Company, 1986), esp. chap. 7, "The Morality of Compromise," 114-28.

135. Thurow, *Abraham Lincoln and American Political Religion*, 117.

136. Thurow, *Abraham Lincoln and American Political Religion*, 14. "Religion is present in Lincoln's speeches because of its relevance to political problems."

137. *Life and Times of Frederick Douglass*, 801.

Bibliography

Aaron, Paul, and David Musto. "Temperance and Prohibition in America: A Historical Review." In *Alcohol and Public Policy: Beyond the Shadow of Prohibition*, edited by Mark H. Moore and Dean R. Gerstein, 121-81. Washington, D.C.: National Academy Press, 1981.

Abzug, Robert H. *Cosmos Crumbling: American Reform and the Religious Imagination.* New York: Oxford University Press, 1994.

Agresto, John. *The Supreme Court and Constitutional Democracy.* Ithaca, N.Y.: Cornell University Press, 1984.

Allen, William B. Draft of book review of James Davison Hunter and Os Guinness, *Articles of Faith, Articles of Peace: The Religious Liberty Clauses and the American Public Philosophy*, and Garry Wills, *Under God: Religion and American Politics.* Claremont, Calif.: By the Author, 1991.

Anastaplo, George. "American Constitutionalism and the Virtue of Prudence: Philadelphia, Paris, Washington, Gettysburg." In *Abraham Lincoln, The Gettysburg Address, and American Constitutionalism*, edited by Leo Paul S. de Alvarez, 77-170. Irving, Tex.: University of Dallas Press, 1976.

Andrews, James R. "Oaths Registered in Heaven: Rhetorical and Historical Legitimacy in the Inaugural Addresses of Jefferson Davis and Abraham Lincoln." In *Doing Rhetorical History: Concepts and Cases*, edited by Kathleen J. Turner, 95-117. Tuscaloosa: University of Alabama Press, 1998.

Angle, Paul M. *"Here I Have Lived": The Story of Lincoln's Springfield, 1821-1865.* New Brunswick, N.J.: Rutgers University Press, 1935.

Aristotle, *The Politics.* Translated by Carnes Lord. Chicago: University of Chicago Press, 1984.

———. *The Rhetoric.* Translated by W. Rhys Roberts. New York: Random House, Inc., 1954.

Barnes, Gilbert Hobbs. *The Antislavery Impulse, 1830-1844.* New York: D. Appleton-Century Company, Inc., 1933.

Barton, William E. *The Soul of Abraham Lincoln.* New York: George H. Doran Company, 1920.

Bateman, Newton, and Paul Selby, eds. *Historical Encyclopedia of Illinois and History of Sangamon County*, 2 vols. Chicago: Munsell Publishing Company, 1912.

Bellah, Robert N. *The Broken Covenant: American Civil Religion in Time of*

Trial. New York: Seabury Press, 1975.

―――. "Civil Religion in America." *Daedalus* 96 (Winter 1967): 1-21.

Bellah, Robert N., and Phillip E. Hammond. *Varieties of Civil Religion.* San Francisco: Harper & Row, Publishers, 1980.

Berger, Max. *The British Traveller in America, 1836-1860.* New York: Columbia University Press, 1943.

Berwanger, Eugene H. *The Frontier against Slavery: Western Anti-Negro Prejudice and the Slavery Extension System.* Urbana: University of Illinois Press, 1967.

Beveridge, Albert J. *Abraham Lincoln, 1809-1858,* 2 vols. Cambridge, Mass.: Riverside Press, 1928.

Blight, David W. "Frederick Douglass and the American Apocalypse." *Civil War History* 31 (December 1985): 309-328.

Blocker, Jack S., Jr. *American Temperance Movements: Cycles of Reform.* Boston: Twayne Publishers, 1989.

Blumberg, Leonard U., with William L. Pittman. *Beware the First Drink: The Washington Temperance Movement and Alcoholics Anonymous.* Seattle: Glen Abbey Books, 1991.

Bode, Carl. *The American Lyceum: Town Meeting of the Mind.* New York: Oxford University Press, 1956.

Brann, Eva. "A Reading of the Gettysburg Address." In *Abraham Lincoln, The Gettysburg Address, and American Constitutionalism,* edited by Leo Paul S. de Alvarez, 15-53. Irving, Tex.: University of Dallas Press, 1976.

Brooks, Noah. *Washington in Lincoln's Time.* New York: The Century Co., 1896.

Burlingame, Michael. *The Inner World of Abraham Lincoln.* Urbana: University of Illinois Press, 1994.

―――. "New Light on the Bixby Letter." *Journal of the Abraham Lincoln Association* 16 (Winter 1995): 59-71.

Cain, William E., ed. *William Lloyd Garrison and the Fight against Slavery.* Boston: Bedford Books of St. Martin's Press, 1995.

Calhoun, John C. "Remarks on Receiving Abolition Petitions [Revised Report] (6 February 1837)." *The Papers of John C. Calhoun,* 20 vols. Edited by Clyde N. Wilson. Vol. 13: 391-98. Columbia: University of South Carolina Press, 1980.

Carpenter, F. B. *The Inner Life of Abraham Lincoln.* Lincoln: University of Nebraska Press, 1995; originally published as *Six Months at the White House with Abraham Lincoln* by Hurd and Houghton, New York, 1866.

Charnwood, Lord. *Abraham Lincoln: A Biography.* Introduction by Peter W. Schramm. Lanham, Md.: Madison Books, 1996; Garden City, N.Y.: Henry Holt and Company, 1917.

Cicero, Marcus Tullius. *De Legibus.* Translated by Clinton Walker Keyes. Cambridge: Harvard University Press, 1988.

Commager, Henry Steele, ed. *Documents of American History,* 8th ed., 2 vols.

New York: Meredith Corporation, 1968.

Corlett, William S., Jr. "The Availability of Lincoln's Political Religion." *Political Theory* 10 (November 1982): 520-40.

Cousins, Norman, ed. *In God We Trust: The Religious Beliefs and Ideas of the American Founding Fathers.* New York: Harper & Brothers, 1958.

Crowley, John W. "Slaves to the Bottle: Gough's *Autobiography* and Douglass's *Narrative.*" In *The Serpent in the Cup: Temperance in American Literature,* edited by David S. Reynolds and Debra J. Rosenthal, 115-35. Amherst: University of Massachusetts Press, 1997.

Current, Richard N. *The Lincoln Nobody Knows.* New York: McGraw-Hill Book Company, Inc., 1958.

Daniel, W. Harrison. "Southern Protestantism—1861 and After." *Civil War History* 5 (September 1959): 276-282.

Dawson, Christopher. *Religion and the Modern State.* London: Sheed and Ward, 1935.

de Alvarez, Leo Paul S., ed. *Abraham Lincoln, the Gettysburg Address, and American Constitutionalism.* Irving, Tex.: University of Dallas Press, 1976.

Delbanco, Andrew. *The Death of Satan: How Americans Have Lost the Sense of Evil.* New York: Farrar, Straus & Giroux, 1995.

Donald, David Herbert. *Lincoln.* New York: Simon & Schuster, 1995.

Dos Passos, John. "Lincoln and His Almost Chosen People." In *Lincoln and the Gettysburg Address: Commemorative Papers,* edited by Allan Nevins, 15-37. Urbana: University of Illinois Press, 1964.

Douglass, Frederick. *Life and Times of Frederick Douglass.* In *Frederick Douglass: Autobiographies.* New York: Library of America, 1994.

———. *The Life and Writings of Frederick Douglass,* 5 vols. Edited by Philip S. Foner. New York: International Publishers, Co., Inc., 1955.

Fehrenbacher, Don E. *The Dred Scott Case: Its Significance in American Law and Politics.* New York: Oxford University Press, 1978.

———. *Lincoln in Text and Context: Collected Essays.* Stanford, Calif.: Stanford University Press, 1987.

———. *Prelude to Greatness: Lincoln in the 1850's.* Stanford, Calif.: Stanford University Press, 1962.

Fehrenbacher, Don E., and Virgina Fehrenbacher, eds. *Recollected Words of Abraham Lincoln.* Stanford, Calif.: Stanford University Press, 1996.

Fishel, Edwin C. *The Secret War for the Union: The Untold Story of Military Intelligence in the Civil War.* Boston: Houghton Mifflin Company, 1996.

Fornieri, Joseph R. "Biblical Republicanism: Abraham Lincoln's Civil Theology." Ph.D. dissertation, Catholic University of America, 1996.

Fustel de Coulanges, Numa Denis. *The Ancient City: A Study on the Religion, Laws, and Institutions of Greece and Rome.* Baltimore: Johns Hopkins University Press, 1980.

Garrison, William Lloyd. *William Lloyd Garrison, 1805-1879: The Story of His Life Told by His Children,* 4 vols. Edited by Wendell Phillips Garrison and Francis Jackson Garrison. Boston: Houghton, Mifflin and Company, 1889.

Vol. 3: *The Beginning of the End, 1841-1860.*

Gaustad, Edwin S., ed. *A Documentary History of Religion in America: To the Civil War.* Grand Rapids, Mich.: William B. Eerdmans Publishing Company, 1982.

Genovese, Eugene D. *A Consuming Fire: The Fall of the Confederacy in the Mind of the White Christian South.* Athens: University of Georgia Press, 1999.

Grimsted, David. *American Mobbing, 1828-1861: Toward Civil War.* New York: Oxford University Press, 1998.

———. "Rioting in Its Jacksonian Setting." *American Historical Review* 77 (April 1972): 361-97.

Grow, Galusha A. 37th Cong., 1st sess. *Congressional Globe* (4 July 1861), 4-5.

Guelzo, Allen C. "Abraham Lincoln and the Doctrine of Necessity." *Journal of the Abraham Lincoln Association* 18 (Winter 1997): 57-81.

Gusfield, Joseph R. *Symbolic Crusade: Status Politics and the American Temperance Movement.* Urbana: University of Illinois Press, 1972.

Hamilton, Alexander, James Madison, and John Jay. *The Federalist.* Edited by Jacob E. Cooke. Middletown, Conn.: Wesleyan University Press, 1961.

Hanley, Mark Y. *Beyond a Christian Commonwealth: The Protestant Quarrel with the American Republic, 1830-1860.* Chapel Hill: University of North Carolina Press, 1994.

Harris, William C. *With Charity for All: Lincoln and the Restoration of the Union.* Lexington: University Press of Kentucky, 1997.

Hedrick, Joan D. *Harriet Beecher Stowe: A Life.* New York: Oxford University Press, 1994.

Hein, David. "Lincoln's Theology and Political Ethics." In *Essays on Lincoln's Faith and Politics,* edited by Kenneth W. Thompson, 103-179. Lanham, Md.: University Press of America, 1983.

Hennessy, John. "Second Manassas." In *The Civil War Battlefield Guide,* edited by Frances H. Kennedy. Boston: Houghton Mifflin Company for the Conservation Fund, 1990.

Herndon, William H., and Jesse W. Weik. *Herndon's Life of Lincoln: The History and Personal Recollections of Abraham Lincoln.* Introduction and notes by Paul M. Angle and new introduction by Henry Steele Commager. Cleveland: World Pub. Co., 1942; reprint edition, New York: Da Capo Press, Inc., 1983.

Hobson, J. T. *Footprints of Abraham Lincoln.* Dayton, Ohio: Otterbein Press, 1909.

Hofstadter, Richard. *The American Political Tradition and the Men Who Made It.* New York: Alfred A. Knopf, Inc., 1948.

Holzer, Harold, ed. *Dear Mr. Lincoln: Letters to the President.* Reading, Mass.: Addison-Wesley Publishing Company, 1995.

Jackson, Andrew. "Farewell Address (4 March 1837)." In *A Compilation of the Messages and Papers of the Presidents: 1789-1897,* 20 vols. Edited by

James D. Richardson. Vol. 3: 292-308. Washington, D.C.: Government Printing Office, 1896.

———. "Second Inaugural Address (4 March 1833)." In *A Compilation of the Messages and Papers of the Presidents: 1789-1897*, 20 vols. Edited by James D. Richardson. Vol. 3: 3-5. Washington, D.C.: Government Printing Office, 1896.

Jaffa, Harry V. "The American Founding as the Best Regime: The Bonding of Civil and Religious Liberty." Claremont, Calif.: Claremont Institute for the Study of Statesmanship and Political Philosophy, 1990.

———. *Crisis of the House Divided: An Interpretation of the Issues in the Lincoln-Douglas Debates*. Seattle: University of Washington Press, 1973; reprint ed., Chicago: University of Chicago Press, 1982, © 1959.

Jefferson, Thomas. *The Portable Thomas Jefferson*. Edited by Merrill D. Peterson. New York: Viking Press, 1975.

Johnson, William J. *Abraham Lincoln: The Christian*. New York: Eaton & Mains, 1913.

Jones, Edgar DeWitt. *Lincoln and the Preachers*. New York: Harper & Brothers, Publishers, 1948.

Kazin, Alfred. *God and the American Writer*. New York: Alfred A. Knopf, 1997.

Korn, Bertram W. *American Jewry and the Civil War*. Philadelphia: Meridian Books for the Jewish Publication Society of America, 1961.

Kramnick, Isaac, and R. Laurence Moore. *The Godless Constitution: The Case Against Religious Correctness*. New York: W. W. Norton & Company, 1996.

LaFantasie, Glenn. "Lincoln and the Gettysburg Awakening." *Journal of the Abraham Lincoln Association* 16 (Winter 1995): 73-89.

Lamon, Ward Hill. *Recollections of Abraham Lincoln, 1847-1865*. Edited by Dorothy Lamon Teillard. Lincoln: University of Nebraska Press, 1994; orig. publ. A. C. McClurg & Co., 1895, 2nd ed. expanded in 1911, Washington, D.C.

Lincoln, Abraham. *Abraham Lincoln: Speeches and Writings*, 2 vols. Edited by Don E. Fehrenbacher. New York: Library of America, 1989.

———. *The Collected Works of Abraham Lincoln*, 9 vols. Edited by Roy P. Basler. New Brunswick, N.J.: Rutgers University Press, 1955.

Machiavelli, Niccolò. *The Prince*. Translated by Harvey C. Mansfield, Jr. Chicago: University of Chicago Press, 1985.

Maddox, Jack P. "Proslavery Millenialism: Social Eschatology in Antebellum Southern Calvinism." *American Quarterly* 31 (Spring 1970): 46-62.

Madison, James. "Memorial and Remonstrance against Religious Assessments (October 1785)." In *The Mind of the Founder: Sources of the Political Thought of James Madison*, edited by Marvin Meyers. Indianapolis: Bobbs-Merrill Company, Inc., 1973; revised ed., Hanover: University Press of New England, 1981.

Maier, Pauline. *American Scripture: Making the Declaration of Independence*.

New York: Alfred A. Knopf, 1997.

Marszalek, John F. *Sherman: A Soldier's Passion for Order*. New York: Vintage Civil War Library—Random House, Inc., 1993.

Mayer, Henry. *All on Fire: William Lloyd Garrison and the Abolition of Slavery*. New York: St. Martin's Press, 1998.

McPherson, James M. *Battle Cry of Freedom: The Civil War Era*. New York: Ballantine Books, 1989.

Mead, Frank S., ed., and Samuel S. Hill, rev. ed. *Handbook of Denominations in the United States*, 9th ed. Nashville: Abingdon Press, 1985.

Mead, Sidney E. "Abraham Lincoln's 'Last, Best Hope of Earth': The American Dream of Destiny and Democracy." *Church History* 23 (March 1954): 3-16.

Miers, Earl Schenck, ed. *Lincoln Day by Day: A Chronology, 1809-1865*, 2 vols. Washington: Lincoln Sesquicentennial Commission, 1960.

Miller, William Lee. *Abraham Lincoln's Second Inaugural Address: A Study in Political Ethics*. Bloomington, Ind.: The Poynter Center, 1980.

Morel, Lucas. "The Statesmanship of Abraham Lincoln in the Second Inaugural Address." B.A. thesis, Claremont McKenna College, 1987.

Morgenthau, Hans J. "The Mind of Abraham Lincoln: A Study in Detachment and Practicality." In *Essays on Lincoln's Faith and Politics*, edited by Kenneth W. Thompson, 1-101. Lanham, Md.: University Press of America, 1983.

Murray, John Courtney. *We Hold These Truths: Catholic Reflections on the American Proposition*. New York: Sheed and Ward, Inc., 1960.

Neuhaus, Richard John. *The Naked Public Square: Religion and Democracy in America*, 2nd ed. Grand Rapids, Mich.: William B. Eerdmans Publishing Company, 1986.

Nevins, Allan, and Henry Steele Commager. *A Short History of the United States*. New York: Modern Library, 1942; new enlarged ed., 1956.

Niebuhr, Reinhold. "The Religion of Abraham Lincoln." *The Christian Century* (10 February 1965): 172-75.

Niven, John. *Salmon P. Chase: A Biography*. New York: Oxford University Press, Inc., 1995.

———. *The Coming of the Civil War, 1837-1861*. Arlington Heights, Ill.: Harlan Davidson, Inc., 1990.

Noll, Mark A. "'Both . . . Pray to the Same God': The Singularity of Lincoln's Faith in the Era of the Civil War." *Journal of the Abraham Lincoln Association* 18 (Winter 1997): 1-26.

———. *One Nation under God? Christian Faith and Political Action in America*. San Francisco: Harper & Row, Publishers, 1988.

———. "The Perplexing Faith of Abraham Lincoln," *Christianity Today* 29 (15 February 1985): 12-14.

———. "The Struggle for Lincoln's Soul." *Books & Culture: A Christian Review* 1 (September/October 1995): 3, 5-7.

Olmstead, Clifton E. *History of Religion in the United States.* Englewood Cliffs, N.J.: Prentice-Hall, Inc., 1960.

Owen, G. Frederick. *Abraham Lincoln: The Man & His Faith.* Wheaton, Ill.: Tyndale House Publishers, Inc., 1976; originally published under the title *A Heart That Yearned for God* by Third Century Publishers, Inc.

Palm, Daniel C. "'Where Locke Stopped Short We May Go On': Religious Toleration and Religious Liberty at the Founding." In *On Faith and Free Government,* edited by Daniel C. Palm, 29-42. Lanham, Md.: Rowman & Littlefield Publishers, Inc., 1997.

Paludan, Phillip Shaw. *The Presidency of Abraham Lincoln.* Lawrence: University Press of Kansas, 1994.

Peterson, Merrill D. *Lincoln in American Memory.* New York: Oxford University Press, 1994.

Pierard, Richard V., and Robert D. Linder, *Civil Religion and the Presidency.* Grand Rapids, Mich.: Academie Books-Zondervan Publishing House, 1988.

Potter, David M. *Lincoln and His Party in the Secession Crisis.* Baton Rouge: Louisiana State University Press, 1995; orig. publ. Yale University Press, 1942.

Randall, J. G. *Lincoln: The Liberal Statesman.* New York: Dodd, Mead, & Company, Inc., 1947.

Randall, J. G., and Richard N. Current. *Lincoln the President: Last Full Measure.* New York: Dodd, Mead & Company, Inc., 1955.

Reid, Daniel G., with Robert D. Linder, Bruce L. Shelley, and Harry S. Stout, eds. *Dictionary of Christianity in America.* Downers Grove, Ill.: InterVarsity Press, 1990.

Reynolds, David S. "Black Cats and Delirium Tremens: Temperance and the American Renaissance." In *The Serpent in the Cup: Temperance in American Literature,* edited by Davis S. Reynolds and Debra J. Rosenthal, 22-59. Amherst: University of Massachusetts Press, 1997.

Ross, Frederick A. *Slavery Ordained of God.* Philadelphia: J. B. Lippincott & Co., 1857.

Rousseau, Jean-Jacques. *Social Contract.* Translated by Maurice Cranston. New York: Viking Penguin, Inc., 1986.

Russell, Greg. *John Quincy Adams and the Public Virtues of Diplomacy.* Columbia: University of Missouri Press, 1995.

Sandburg, Carl. *Abraham Lincoln,* Sangamon Edition, 6 vols. New York: Charles Scribner's Sons, 1950. Vol. 1: *The Prairie Years* and Vol. 5: *The War Years—III.*

Schmitz, Neil. "Murdered McIntosh, Murdered Lovejoy: Abraham Lincoln and the Problem of Jacksonian Address." *Arizona Republic* 44, no. 3 (Autumn 1988): 15-39.

Schönborn, Christoph. "The Hope of Heaven, the Hope of Earth." *First Things* (April 1995): 32-38.

Schwartz, Thomas F. "The Springfield Lyceums and Lincoln's 1838 Speech."

Illinois Historical Journal 83 (Spring 1990): 45-49.

Sewell, Richard H. *A House Divided: Sectionalism and Civil War, 1848-1865.* Baltimore: Johns Hopkins University Press, 1988.

Smith, James. "A Discourse on the Bottle—Its Evils, and the Remedy; or, A Vindication of the Liquor-Seller, and the Liquor Drinker, from Certain Aspersions Cast upon Them by Many." Springfield, Ill.: 1892; orig. publ. 1853.

Snay, Mitchell. *Gospel of Division: Religion and Separatism in the Antebellum South.* Chapel Hill: University of North Carolina Press, 1997; orig. publ. Cambridge University Press, 1993.

Spalding, Matthew, and Patrick J. Garrity. *A Sacred Union of Citizens: George Washington's Farewell Address and the American Character.* Lanham, Md.: Rowman & Littlefield Publishers, Inc., 1996.

Speed, Joshua F. *Reminiscences of Abraham Lincoln and Notes of a Visit to California.* Louisville, Ky.: John P. Morton and Company, 1884.

Staiger, C. Bruce. "Abolitionism and the Presbyterian Schism of 1837-1838." *Mississippi Valley Historical Review* 36 (December 1949): 391-414.

Stokes, Anson Phelps, ed. *Church and State in the United States: Historical Development and Contemporary Problems of Religious Freedom under the Constitution*, 3 vols. New York: Harper & Brothers, 1950. Vols. 1-2.

Stowe, Harriet Beecher. *Uncle Tom's Cabin.* New York: Signet Classic— Penguin USA Inc., 1966.

Stowell, Daniel W. *Rebuilding Zion: The Religious Reconstruction of the South, 1863-1877.* New York: Oxford University Press, 1998.

Strunk, William, Jr., and E. B. White. *The Elements of Style*, 3rd ed. New York: Macmillan Publishing Company, Inc., 1979.

Tarcov, Nathan. "Principle and Prudence in Foreign Policy: The Founders' Perspective." *The Public Interest* 76 (Summer 1984): 45-60.

Taylor, John M. *William Henry Seward: Lincoln's Right Hand.* Washington, D.C.: Brassey's, 1991.

Temple, Wayne C. *Abraham Lincoln: From Skeptic to Prophet.* Mahomet, Ill.: Mayhaven Publishing, 1995.

Thomas, Benjamin P. *Abraham Lincoln: A Biography.* New York: First Modern Library Edition—Random House, Inc., 1968.

Thomas, Clarence. "The Virtue of Practical Wisdom." Remarks delivered at the Third Annual Claremont Institute Lincoln Day Colloquium and Dinner in Washington, D.C. on February 9, 1999. Claremont, Calif.: Claremont Institute for the Study of Statesmanship and Political Philosophy, 1999.

Thomas, Hugh. *The Slave Trade: The Story of the Atlantic Slave Trade, 1440-1870.* New York: Simon & Schuster, 1997.

Thomas, John L., ed. *Slavery Attacked: The Abolitionist Crusade.* Englewood Cliffs, N.J.: Prentice-Hall, Inc., 1965.

Thurow, Glen E. *Abraham Lincoln and American Political Religion.* Albany: State University of New York Press, 1976.

———. "Abraham Lincoln and American Political Religion." In *The Historian's Lincoln: Pseudohistory, Psychohistory, and History*, edited by Gabor S. Boritt, 125-43. Urbana: University of Illinois Press, 1988.

Townsend, William H. *Lincoln and Liquor*. New York: Press of the Pioneers, Inc., 1934.

Trueblood, Elton. *Abraham Lincoln: Theologian of American Anguish*. New York: Harper & Row, Publishers, 1973.

Tyrrell, Ian R. *Sobering Up: From Temperance to Prohibition in Antebellum America, 1800-1860*. Westport, Conn.: Greenwood Press, 1979.

Van Buren, Martin. "Inaugural Address (4 March 1837)." *A Compilation of the Messages and Papers of the Presidents: 1789-1897*, 20 vols. Edited by James D. Richardson. Vol. 3: 313-20. Washington, D.C.: Government Printing Office, 1896.

Van Deusen, Glyndon G. *William Henry Seward*. New York: Oxford University Press, 1967.

Wakelyn, Jon L., ed. *Southern Pamphlets on Secession, November 1860-April 1861*. Chapel Hill: University of North Carolina Press, 1996.

Ward, Geoffrey C., with Ric Burns and Ken Burns. *The Civil War: An Illustrated History*. New York: Alfred A. Knopf, Inc., 1991.

Warner, Ezra J. *Generals in Blue: Lives of the Union Commanders*. Baton Rouge: Louisiana State University Press, 1964.

Washington, George. *George Washington: A Collection*. Edited by W. B. Allen. Indianapolis: Liberty Fund, Inc., 1988.

"The Washington Society." *Illinois State Register*, 11 March 1842, 2.

Weeks, Louis. "Presbyterianism." *Encyclopedia of the American Religious Experience: Studies of Traditions and Movements*, 3 vols. Edited by Charles H. Lippy and Peter W. Williams. Vol. 1: 502-503. New York: Charles Scribner's Sons, 1988.

Weigel, George. "The Church's Political Hopes for the World; or, Diognetus Revisited." In *The Two Cities of God: The Church's Responsibility for the Earthly City*, edited by Carl E. Braaten and Robert W. Jenson, 59-77. Grand Rapids, Mich.: Wm. B. Eerdmans Publishing Company, 1997.

Welter, Rush. *The Mind of America, 1820-1860*. New York: Columbia University Press, 1975.

West, John G., Jr. *The Politics of Revelation and Reason: Religion and Civic Life in the New Nation*. Lawrence: University of Kansas Press, 1996.

White, Kermit Escus. "Abraham Lincoln and Christianity." Ph.D. dissertation, Boston University Graduate School, 1954.

White, Ronald C., Jr. "Lincoln's Sermon on the Mount: The Second Inaugural Address." In *Religion and the American Civil War*, edited by Randall M. Miller, Harry S. Stout, and Charles Reagan Wilson, 208-23. New York: Oxford University Press, 1998.

Williamson, G. I. *The Westminster Confession of Faith for Study Classes*. Philadelphia: Presbyterian and Reformed Publishing Co., 1964.

Wills, Garry. *Under God: Religion and American Politics*. New York: Simon and Schuster, 1990.

————. *Lincoln at Gettysburg: The Words That Remade America.* New York: Simon and Schuster, 1992.

Wilson, Douglas L., and Rodney O. Davis, eds. *Herndon's Informants: Letters, Interviews, and Statements about Abraham Lincoln.* Urbana: University of Illinois Press, 1998.

Wilson, Edmund. *Patriotic Gore: Studies in the Literature of the American Civil War.* New York: Oxford University Press, 1962.

Wilson, Major L. "Lincoln and Van Buren in the Steps of the Fathers: Another Look at the Lyceum Address." *Civil War History* 29 (September 1983): 197-211.

————. "Lincoln on the Perpetuation of Republican Institutions: Whig and Republican Strategies." *Journal of the Abraham Lincoln Association* 18 (Winter 1997): 15-25.

————. *The Presidency of Martin Van Buren.* Lawrence: University Press of Kansas, 1984.

Wolf, William J. "Abraham Lincoln and Calvinism." In *Calvinism and the Political Order*, edited by George L. Hunt, 140-56. Philadelphia: Westminster Press, 1965.

————. *The Religion of Abraham Lincoln.* New York: Seabury Press, 1963; originally published as *The Almost Chosen People: A Study of the Religion of Abraham Lincoln* by Doubleday & Company, Inc., 1959.

Zarefsky, David. "'Public Sentiment Is Everything': Lincoln's View of Political Persuasion." *Journal of the Abraham Lincoln Association* 15, no. 2 (1994): 23-40.

Zuckert, Michael P. "Lincoln and the Problem of Civil Religion." In *Law and Philosophy: The Practice of Theory—Essays in Honor of George Anastaplo*, 2 vols. Edited by John A. Murley, Robert L. Stone, and William T. Braithwaite. Vol. 2: 720-743. Athens: Ohio University Press, 1992.

————. "Locke and the Problem of Civil Religion: Bicentennial Essay No. 6." Claremont, Calif.: Claremont Institute for the Study of Statesmanship and Political Philosophy, 1984.

Index to Lincoln's Speeches and Writings

General Index

abolitionism: anti-abolitionist
violence, 25-26; anti-slavery
resolutions, 99; churches
denounced, 10, 18n10;
condemned, 152n3;
constitutional rights,
enforcement, 5n6; duty of
rebuke, 131, 155n38; Lincoln
on, 125-26; mob violence,
growth of, 25-26, 71n11; New
School Presbyterians, 140,
158n70; passions versus
reason, 26; religious aspect of,
125-26; self-government issue,
9-10; of slavery as unexpected
outcome, 180-82; southern
defense of slavery, 176; *Uncle
Tom's Cabin*, 125; Weld, 136
Abram, the chosen one, 60
absolutism, political, 10
abstinence. *See* temperance
movement
Acts 17:24-31, 205
Acts 17:28, 108
Adams, Charles Francis, 197
Adams, John Quincy, 178, 216n52
alcohol use: addiction described,
139; Lincoln's teetotalism,
150; liquor-sellers and,
147-51; nationally, 127. *See
also* temperance movement
all men are created equal:
self-government vis-à-vis, 52;
significance of July 4th, 47
Allen, William B., 93

ambitions, Lincoln's, 42, 75n56
American Baptist Home Mission
Society, 98-99
American Founders:
accomplishments, 41; equality
issue, 51-52; Lincoln on
improving work of, 70n4;
public profession of religious
convictions, 89; slavery issue,
177
American Founding: Jeffersonian
premise, 52; Lincoln as
finisher, 43; "men of ambition
and talents," 35-36, 37;
motives of Founders, 35;
passions of the people, 36-38;
temperance "revolution"
compared, 144-46; Thurow's
critique, 16
American Temperance Society,
130
American Temperance Union, 150
Ames, Reverend Bishop, 106
Anastaplo, George, 20n28, 94,
117n35
Annual Message to Congress
(1862), 67-68, 82n137, 175,
178
anti-Catholic sentiment, 128
anti-slavery. *See* abolitionism
apocalypse, four horsemen of,
133-34
approachability, 129
Aristotle, 14, 27, 112
armed neutrality, 174

About the Author

Lucas E. Morel (Ph.D., Claremont Graduate School) is assistant professor of politics at Washington and Lee University in Lexington, Virginia, and an adjunct fellow of the John M. Ashbrook Center for Public Affairs at Ashland University and the Claremont Institute for the Study of Statesmanship and Political Philosophy.

He is a contributing editor to *Books & Culture: A Christian Review* and has written for the *Journal of the Abraham Lincoln Association*, *Perspectives on Political Science*, and *First Things*. He was a contributing editor to *American Virtues, Values and Triumphs* (Publications International, 1996) and is currently working on a book about the political thought of Ralph Ellison.

Breinigsville, PA USA
16 August 2010
243719BV00004B/1/P